THE
ASSASSINS

The Story of Medieval Islam's
Secret Sect

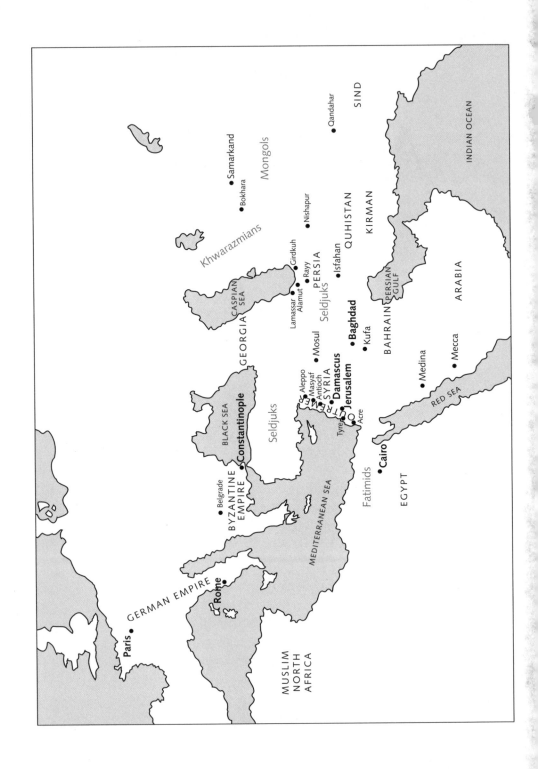

Paris •

GERMAN EMPIRE

Rome

MUSLIM
NORTH
AFRICA

MEDITERRANEAN SEA

BYZANTINE
EMPIRE

Belgrade •

Constantinople

BLACK SEA

Seldjuks

GEORGIA

CASPIAN
SEA

Khwarazmians

Samarkand •

Bokhara •

Mongols

Qandahar •

SIND

INDIAN OCEAN

Tyre •
Acre •

Jerusalem
Antioch
Masyaf
Aleppo

Damascus

SYRIA

TRIPOLI

Cairo

EGYPT

Fatimids

RED SEA

Medina •

Mecca •

ARABIA

BAHRAIN

PERSIAN
GULF

KIRMAN

QUHISTAN

Isfahan •

Mosul •

Baghdad •
Kufa •

Seldjuks

PERSIA

Rayy •
Alamut •
Lamassar •

Girdkuh •

Nishapur •

THE ASSASSINS

The Story of Medieval Islam's Secret Sect

W.B. Bartlett

SUTTON PUBLISHING

First published in the United Kingdom in 2001 by
Sutton Publishing Limited · Phoenix Mill
Thrupp · Stroud · Gloucestershire · GL5 2BU

British Library Cataloguing in Publication Data
A catalogue record for this book is available from the British Library

ISBN 0-7509-2527-2

Typeset in 11/14.5 pt Sabon.
Typesetting and origination by Sutton Publishing Limited.
Printed and bound in Great Britain by
J.H. Haynes & Co. Ltd, Sparkford.

Contents

Acknowledgements

A book of this nature does not come together without the support of a great number of people. I would first like to thank those academics whose work has been an inspiration to me. Without their research and dedication this book would not have been written. To the long list of such historians, whom I shall not name as I would not wish to inadvertently miss anyone out, my sincere thanks as well as my apologies for any errors that I might have made, which are my responsibility alone. To those who have given direct help, my especial thanks. I would also like to thank staff at the British Library and Southampton University Library for the help they have given during the course of my research.

As always, the team at Suttons have performed a tremendously professional job. I would like to offer my gratitude to the readers of the original manuscript for their suggestions for improvement. My thanks to the whole team at Suttons but especially to Jane Crompton, Christopher Feeney and Paul Ingrams who have pointed me in the right direction when I have wandered from the straight and narrow. For Jane, who has moved on to new challenges, my admiration will remain undiminished – your help has been greatly appreciated.

Last but not least, my eternal gratitude to my family, Angela and Deyna first and foremost, whose love and support were the most important element in writing this book. Without you, none of this would have been possible.

List of Illustrations

Black and white, between pages 78 and 79

Inside the Dome of the Rock, Jerusalem.
Exterior, Dome of the Rock.
Louis IX receives a Nizari deputation.
Aleppo, seen from the walls of its castle.
The Great Mosque, Aleppo.
The castle of Masyaf.
The medieval walls of Cairo.
The Omayyad Mosque, Damascus.
Mausoleum of Sultan Baibars.
Carved stone inscription of Sultan Khwarazm.
Mameluke incense burner.
The mausoleum of Aga Khan III.

Colour plates, between pages 174 and 175

French troops attacking a citadel.
A knight and a Saracen do battle.
Map of the Middle East, 1573.
King Louis IX lands at Tunis.
The sacking of Isfahan by Mongol troops.
'The battle of Ghengis Khan and Prester John'.

The Qu'ran of Sultan Baibars.
Deathbed of Godfrey de Bouillon.
'The Archangel Gabriel'.
Destruction of the Holy Sepulchre by Al-Hakim.
Saracens attack a Christian camp.
The capture of Acre, 1191.
Mongol cavalry doing battle.

Note:
All colour plates, except where indicated, appear by permission of The British Library (BL) or The British Museum (BM)/Heritage-Images. Heritage Image Partnership is a digital archive accessing the UK's major art collections. Contact info@heritage-images.com or visit website www.heritage-images.com for details.

DEDICATED TO MY GRANDMOTHER, EMMA HECKFORD, WHO HAS ALWAYS BEEN A SOURCE OF SUPPORT AND ENCOURAGEMENT TO ME.

Prologue

In the middle of the thirteenth century, a French army set out on Crusade, travelling far across the Mediterranean to the distant shores of Egypt. The expedition proved to be a disaster. The army, led by King Louis IX of France, was surrounded and trapped. Thousands of Crusaders were taken prisoner; many of them were killed in cold blood. The pitiful remnant that survived made the short sea crossing to Palestine, where at the time a small Crusader kingdom, known as Outremer – 'The Land Beyond The Sea' – clung precariously to a tenuous existence, surrounded by hostile Muslim states. The army remained here for several years. In its ranks was a chronicler, Jean de Joinville, a close confidant of the King. He subsequently wrote an account of his time in the region.

In it, he told how, in about 1250 AD, a priest named Yves the Breton was sent by the King on a mission to the court of a mysterious man who led an equally mysterious group. There were a number of things that fascinated the Western envoy during his visit, for example the unorthodox religious beliefs of the group which suggested (a hopelessly optimistic prospect as it transpired) that they were ripe for conversion to Christianity. But of all the things that the priest discovered, there was one above all others which caught his imagination, and sent a shiver down his spine. According to him, these men were dealers in death.

De Joinville told his readers how the leader of this group, 'The Old Man of the Mountain' as he entitled him, processed through his territories:

'Whenever the Old Man of the Mountain went out riding, a crier would go before him bearing a Danish axe with a long haft encased in silver, to which many knives were affixed. As he went the man would continually cry out: "Turn out of the way of him who bears in his hands the death of kings"'.[1]

De Joinville's story added to an already established legend, of a sinister group living in the mountain fastnesses of Syria, from where they launched murderous attacks on any who they perceived to be enemies. None were safe from their suicidal assassins; even Kings and Emperors trembled at the thought of falling victim to the knives of these killers. What made them especially frightening was that the assassins had no fear of death; in fact, if they were to die in the execution of their mission, then they were hailed as martyrs who would receive the eternal blessings of Paradise as a result of their sacrifice. They were adept at ingratiating themselves almost unnoticed into the good graces of their would-be victim. They would wait for months before attempting to carry out their mission, during which time they would show themselves to be good friends so that they could subsequently catch him off his guard. In such an atmosphere, no one could be trusted. A century later, the Western writer Brocardus offered this piece of advice to a later French king who was planning a Crusade:

'I therefore know only one single remedy for the safeguarding and protection of the King, that in all the royal household, for whatever service, however small or brief or mean, none should be admitted, save those whose country, place, lineage, condition and person are certainly, fully and clearly known'.[2]

But this group were also well known to Muslims in the region, who could have told Brocardus – if he could speak their language – that knowing the antecedents of servants and guards was no guarantee of safety. Many stories concerning the group related a number of incidents where previously highly trusted servants showed themselves to have fallen victim to the spell of the movement's beliefs. Without any warning, respected confidants of many years standing showed themselves as would-be murderers. Virtually the last thing that many victims of the group must have felt was a sense of horror and betrayal as they looked into the face of a respected servant coming at them, dagger in hand.

The group struck terror into the hearts and minds of their near neighbours. In one contemporary Muslim account, a warrior returned to his castle where the garrison had beaten off one of their attacks. He found his mother sitting with his sister on a balcony. He asked her why she was there, to which she replied that 'I have given [your sister] a seat at the balcony and sat behind her so that in case I found that [the enemy] had reached us, I could push her and throw her into the valley, preferring to see her dead rather than fall into the hands of the peasants and ravishers'.[3] Great rulers whose armies outnumbered the group many times over were always on their guard, watching the shadows for a sudden, murderous assault. Their enemies gave members of the movement a particular name. They called them *hashishiyyun*. It was a derogatory term that meant 'hashish taker'. It was not meant to be taken literally; it was a term applied by Muslims to those that they regarded as moral reprobates. The Western knights who populated the Crusader kingdom of Outremer heard the name applied, and they started to use it themselves. But they would pronounce the term with their own dialect. It would, within a couple of hundred years of their arrival in the region, pass into their own language, as a noun that still survives into modern, everyday use. They would call members of the group 'Assassins'.

It would be far more accurate to describe them as Nizaris. At least one modern writer has pointed out with a hint of polite correction that even his eminent and very well informed contemporary colleagues incorrectly use the term Assassins.[4] But the same writer acknowledges why this is the case when he admits that 'the term Assassins, with its aura of mystery and sensation, has acquired an independent currency'.[5] He is undoubtedly right and it is for this reason that this book carries the title it does. Hopefully at its conclusion the reader will understand why the term 'Assassin' is wrong, while at the same time realizing how members of the group came to be so-called.

Certainly, members of the group would be surprised to hear themselves described in this way. The term *hashishiyyun* or 'Assassin' would not be recognized by them. They traced their roots back to a time, towards the close of the eleventh century, when there was a great division within the Islamic world. Such divisions were a not uncommon occurrence during the formative centuries of Islam. Not long after Muhammad, the great Prophet who founded Islam, died in 632, a bitter civil war erupted which split the Muslim world into a number of factions. Several centuries later, one of these, the Shiites, would itself fragment and a group known as the Ismailis formed. Later still, the Ismailis would also divide. One element would call themselves after the last leader they recognized as being the legitimate head of the movement. His name was Nizar and his followers called themselves 'Nizari'. After he was murdered in Egypt in 1095, this was the name by which most of the so-called Assassins would recognize themselves. But, over time, the name would be lost, and later generations in the West would know them exclusively by the bastardized version of that derogatory term, *hashishiyyun*.

The Nizaris were to have a psychological impact on those who came into contact with them out of all proportion to the numbers of members that they had. Powers many times greater than the Nizaris – who were never numerous – would develop an interest in and a fear of the movement which would ultimately prove fatal for it. The first great enemy of the movement was the powerful but fragmented Seldjuk Empire that established itself in Persia and the lands surrounding it during the eleventh century. But, although the group would outlive the Seldjuks, it would later be overwhelmed by one of the mightiest and most destructive regimes that the Middle East, or indeed the world, has ever seen, that of the Mongols.

Yet, even then, when faced by the unstoppable Mongol tide, one of the Nizari castles (a number of which were held by the movement in parts of Persia and Syria during its heyday) would resist the inevitable for seventeen years before it finally fell in or around 1270. The fact that this siege lasted for such a lengthy period testifies amply to the fear that the movement generated among its enemies, who persisted for so long to ensure that the castle eventually fell. And the fate of the garrison after its ultimate capture equally supports this contention. The extended length of time for which the garrison, whose position had for most of the time been hopeless, had held out, might have been considered by its enemies as an especially gallant defence; and when the castle finally fell, the garrison (who eventually surrendered because of – among other things – the fact that they had run out of clothes) might have hoped to have been treated as valiant adversaries who deserved to live. But no such kindness would be meted out to these men; they were all summarily killed.

An appreciation of the fear that the Nizaris generated is crucial if the history of the movement is to be understood. Because they themselves left few written records,[6] and the documents relating to them which survive were largely written by their enemies, there is a great danger that the view subsequently formed of the movement is inevitably coloured against them. The greatest contemporary influences on the development of the story of the movement – judging by the chronicles that have survived to modern times – were Persian writers: Alā-Malik Juwayni, Rashid al-Din Fadl Allah and Abu'l-Qasim 'Abd Allah Kashani. All were vehemently inimical on religious grounds towards the Nizaris. All of them based their accounts on original Nizari sources but none of them were friendly towards them, giving them both opportunity and motive to amend their accounts as they saw fit.[7]

A twentieth century historian, Marshall Hodgson, notes that although Rashid al-Din and Juwayni probably prepared their accounts from the same basic sources their approaches are different: 'Rashid al-Din has more facts than Juwayni, where Juwayni has more opinions than Rashid al-Din'.[8] And it is certainly true that Juwayni provides an especially strong example of anti-Nizari bias, making it particularly important that due caution is exercised in interpreting his account. He was in the employ of the Mongols when they finally subdued the Nizaris in Persia and, before they destroyed the greatest of all their strongholds, the castle at Alamut in 1256, they let him sift through the books in the magnificent library there. What he wished to keep, he could take; the rest – mostly religious literature – was consigned to oblivion in a great funeral pyre, the flames of which marked the end of an independent Nizari state in Persia. Rarely can there have been a more extreme opportunity for a historian to shape history in the image that he desired.

Given Juwayni's affiliations, such bias is unsurprising; not long after the capture of Alamut he would be rewarded when the Mongols gave him the governorship of Baghdad; a significant prize indeed. As one modern historian noted, 'Juwayni wrote with a distinctly anti-Ismaili perspective, often manifesting itself in outright condemnation of the sectarians, a position not incomprehensible for a Sunni historian aiming to please a master who had almost exterminated the Nizari Ismailis of Persia'.[9]

There is a wealth of evidence in the style and content of Juwayni's writing to support the contention that he is far from being an objective witness to history in the making. As one example of many, Juwayni's comments after the fall of Alamut serve as comprehensive support of this analysis:

> So was the world cleansed which had been polluted by their evil. Wayfarers now ply to and fro without fear or dread or the inconvenience of paying a toll and pray for the [continued] fortune of the happy King who uprooted their foundations and left no trace of any one of them. And in truth that act was the balm of Muslim wounds and the cure to the disorders of the Faith. Let those who shall come after this age and era know the extent of the mischief they wrought and the confusion they cast into the hearts of men. Such as were on terms of agreement with them, whether kings of former times or contemporary rulers, went in fear and trembling and [those who were] hostile to them were day and night in the straits of prison for dread of their scoundrelly minions. It is a cup that had been filled to overflowing; it seemed as if a wind had died.[10]

But, for all Juwayni's hyperbole, it is the accounts of Western chroniclers that have, perhaps understandably, done the most to shape the subsequent perceptions of Western minds. The movement made a great impression on those Western writers who came to know of them. The general perception was one of a sinister, shadowy group of assassins who struck at their victims with impunity. The fact that the assassins (the killers were known to the Nizaris as *fida'is* or 'devotees') did not fear their own death, and indeed actively seemed to welcome it, did nothing to lessen the impact of the movement on contemporary Western consciousness. In this environment, all kinds of fantastical embellishments were added to the core of truth that underlay tales of the movement.

It was a trend that continued beyond Medieval times. When eighteenth and nineteenth century Western historians began to show an interest in them, if anything the myths that had by this time developed became more, rather than less, rigid. It is only a good deal of work carried out by twentieth century historians, such as Bernard Lewis, Farhad Daftary, Wilferd Madelung and Hodgson, as well as a number of historians from India (where the Nizaris were later to form a significant presence) that has started to redress the balance, and which has begun to swing the pendulum back away from myth and towards history. These historians have brought a new objectivity, a new scientific approach, to their subject. As such, the clouds of obscurity that obstruct our view of the Nizaris have begun to lift. However, the veil of mythology that obscures the history of the Nizaris is so firmly established, and the sources of evidence for the historical realities of the movement are so limited, that there is in reality little chance of conclusively reconstructing every detail of the Nizaris in their historical perspective.

As one example, the reader will note a certain vagueness in some of the dates quoted in this book. This is a reflection of a lack of clarity sometimes apparent in the historical record that has survived. But an examination of what evidence is available, and a comparison of the accounts that do exist about the movement, can at least help to reconstruct a credible picture in overview of the Nizaris' historical position. It can also help to show how the historical fact of the Nizaris became the spectacular legend of the Assassins.

Because they left few historical records of their own, legends attached themselves almost inevitably to the movement from a very early stage. The virtual destruction of the Nizaris by the Mongols left the movement with no way of defending itself against the more extreme allegations of their enemies. Although they lived on for centuries after the disaster that befell them at the hands of the Mongols, the independent states that they had set up were overrun. Effectively, they only remained as relatively small and isolated communities. Their enemies had carte blanche to say what they wished about them with little fear of any recourse against their more excessive and wild accusations. In this environment, the Assassin myth took root and flourished.

At the heart of it all was their employment of murder as a weapon of state. The use of assassins was effectively a defensive mechanism employed by a group who were at a hopeless disadvantage, in terms of both size and power, when matched with the resources of their enemies. It was one strand in a strategy that also included the use of out-of-the-way, easily defensible castles in remote mountain retreats and an extraordinary – and sometimes very confusing – ability to change their allegiances, their political alliances and even their religious affiliations with bewildering frequency. One tactic in particular creates great difficulties for the historian, and (one suspects) also generated uncertainty in the minds of the movement's affiliates at the time. This was a tactic known as *taqiyya* (the word literally means 'caution' or 'prudence'). It was a concept that allowed the Nizaris to conceal their true affiliations as a way of surviving the traumatic upheavals that frequently threatened to overwhelm them. Essentially, a man could deny his faith if he wished so that his survival could be ensured.

At times, the whole group adopted the approach. Employing this tactic, the leader of the movement could declare that all previous protestations of religious belief were now invalid. Diametrically opposed policies were adopted instead so that new political alliances could be formed. This led to some confusing variations in policy that subsequent Nizari historians and theologians would claim were only introduced as a ruse to manipulate political opponents.

The concept of '*taqiyya*' perhaps lacks glamour, and on occasion must surely have confused adherents to the Nizari cause. It may also have helped subsequent Nizari supporters to be wise after the event and claim that previous leaders had never really changed their policy at all – they had only pretended to in order to dupe their enemies. *Taqiyya* added another layer to the myth of Assassin duplicity, and the overall blanket of sinister overtones. That said, it was a spectacularly successful tactic in helping to ensure the survival of the movement as an independent power for far longer than could have been expected given the resources at its disposal. And it led to a characteristic that was to be the key to the viability of the Nizaris; adaptability. For, as one writer recently stated, 'Ismailism has always survived because of its flexibility and its ability to adapt to the process of historical evolution'.[11]

These factors helped to mould the myth around the historical fact of the Nizaris. In the account of the movement and its history that follows, I have tried to separate fact from legend. This is a difficult objective at the best of times but it becomes a more challenging task than usual when the accounts of the movement that remain are so one-sided. However, modern advances in understanding have helped considerably in dismantling some of the more exaggerated 'Assassin' legends that have grown up. The efforts of the modern scholars already mentioned have partially succeeded in putting the movement into some kind of historical context, and because of them there has been something of a re-evaluation of the true place of the Nizaris in history.

Nevertheless, the legend continues to exercise a fascination to the present day, partly because it is undeniably rooted in fact. There is no doubt that a number of the acts of assassination ascribed to the Nizaris were committed by them, although in individual cases there may be some room for debate as every political killing was conveniently ascribed to them regardless of their actual involvement or not. But the whole picture became so exaggerated that what was created in terms of perceptions of the movement was a distorted and grotesque caricature of the historical reality.

Even some great historians have been misled by this image. When Sir Steven Runciman wrote of the hardships facing Western colonists in Outremer, one of them was the fact that 'no one knew when he might not receive a knife thrust from a devotee of the Assassins'.[12] Yet despite the impression that the group made on the imagination of the West, one modern writer estimates that maybe fewer than five Westerners fell victim to them.[13]

The perpetrators of these acts became, in popular imagination, drug-crazed fanatics, despite the fact that they acted in such a calculated fashion that it is inconceivable that they were really out of their minds because of drugs when they carried them out. In the imagination, the Assassins also threw themselves from the tops of the lofty towers of their castles at the click of their master's fingers just to prove their contempt for life and their loyalty to their lord. They even became phantoms and made their way unseen through the serried ranks of heavily armed bodyguards in order to carry out their mission. Few exaggerations were spared in the attempt to embellish the myth.

The reality was somewhat different. The Nizaris were a political and religious movement whose history is every bit as interesting as their legend. During the Medieval period, politics and religion were hopelessly enmeshed in the Islamic (and for that matter, the Christian) world, and one could not exist without the other. The Nizaris used assassination as just one of many tools for ensuring their survival and advancing their cause. Throughout their history, the movement were more likely to use missionaries (known as '*daïs*') than they were assassins. The permanent effects of the former were much greater than those of the latter. As a result of the efforts of the *daïs*, the Nizari creed spread beyond its point of origin in Persia into Syria, Central Asia and India, where significant Nizari communities remain to this day. Such men made great sacrifices and took enormous risks in the cause that they espoused. In the conduct of their mission, known as the '*daʿwa*', they risked discovery and death every day. A number of them paid the ultimate price for their faith. Their supporters viewed them as martyrs. To them, self-sacrifice and devotion to their cause hold a much greater place in the story of the Nizaris than either murder or intrigue.

It is largely because of the wealth of recent research that this book has been written. It attempts to sift through the many layers of legend that have attached themselves to the Nizaris, and place the movement in its historical context. Due to the durability of the legends themselves this is no easy task. Nevertheless, given the remarkable story of the Nizaris it is well worth the effort.

I have aimed this book at the general reader. I have tried to assume no prior knowledge, and I hope the specialist will forgive me for examining some areas in greater depth than they might think necessary. I have therefore attempted to explain some of the subsidiary events that were relevant to the growth of the Nizaris, such as the evolution of Islam and Western European Crusades, so that the general reader can comprehend better the events that led to the foundation of the movement and its subsequent development. Otherwise, they will not fully understand the environment in which the Nizaris existed and what effect they had on events, or indeed what effect events had on them.

It is my objective that, by examining the history of the Nizaris, from the evolution of Islam itself in the early seventh century, through the founding of the Nizaris in the eleventh century, and completing the story by continuing on into the modern age, I will place the movement in some form of perspective. In my opinion, this is only truly possible if the reader understands something of the great changes that took place within Islam as it developed, as well as the wider events that shaped the world in which the Nizaris lived.

The legends surrounding the Nizaris will, to many readers, have their own fascination. But they are in many ways unhelpful, as they have moulded erroneous perceptions of the movement, especially in the West. In the process, they have distorted perceptions of the Nizaris. The real achievement of the Nizaris lies in the very fact of their survival against what at many times appeared to be impossible odds. For that reason, if for no other, the history of the movement deserves to be re-told.

ONE

The Early Years of Islam

In the middle of the first millennium following the birth of Christ, a great storm came out of the Arabian desert. Irresistible, unstoppable, it overwhelmed the lands of the Middle East and then spread outwards across the world, consuming all who dared to stand in its path. It seemed that no one could resist its power, which inexorably overcame all resistance. Those obstinate, or misguided, enough to resist were broken like saplings in the path of a whirlwind. Its advance was unprecedented and hard to credit, given the longevity of the regimes that perished in the storm. Yet for all its force, all the fear it inspired in the hearts and minds of those exposed to its effects, in the remains of the cultures that were subsumed by it, new civilization took root. A new world order was born, one in which art and science would hold an exalted place. The storm had conquered old beliefs and ways of life so that they could be replaced with something far better.[1]

But this new and vibrant force was, from early on, hampered by its own internal difficulties. The storm, which was Islam, unleashed powers that it itself found difficult to control. In common with many great religions, it was soon divided by internal dissent as men argued that theirs alone was the one way to religious truth. In the dissent fomented by these disputes, new factions would gestate, groups with, in their opponents' eyes, strange and heretical codes of belief.

No study of the so-called 'Assassins' can be complete without first of all attempting to explain the religious and political environment in which the movement was born, for the early years of Islam shaped and moulded its

1

beliefs. Those early years were momentous in terms of their future effects. The Middle East is a region that has known more than its fair share of turbulence in its time, but there can have been few more uncertain periods in its history than the centuries that immediately preceded the creation of the group most properly known as the Nizaris. The new forces unleashed by the birth of Islam dramatically amended the structure of the Middle East, and indeed the regions beyond. They would be re-shaped by a series of invasions and political and religious re-alignments. It was in a much-changed Middle Eastern region that the Nizaris would ultimately establish themselves.

The new religion evolved in Mecca, in the early years of the seventh century AD. Before the arrival of Islam in the region, the city was already a sacred place. Within its walls was to be found the *Ka'ba*, literally 'The Cube', the site where Ismail, the eldest son of Abraham, had set up his first home after being sent away by his father.[2] It was here that a merchant named Muhammad, husband to a rich wife, received a revelation in the year 610. As a consequence of this divine inspiration, he developed a new creed. It owed much to other religions, namely Judaism and Christianity. Muhammad believed that there was much that was right in the Christian creed. He accepted that Christ was not only a prophet, but was in fact one of the foremost of all holy men. He had no difficulty even in accepting the principle of the miraculous Virgin birth. What, however, he would not countenance was the concept of the Trinity: Father, Son and Holy Ghost. To him, it implied that there was more than one God and this he would not accept. Primarily, his new religion was based on what he regarded as pure, monotheistic principles and in his pantheon there was only room for one deity.

Inevitably, as these doctrines developed during the formative years of his new creed, they began to impinge on political and social issues. That Islam was first and foremost a religious force need not be doubted; but, as it matured, it inevitably impacted in other spheres. This meant that a clash with those of the established order who held opposing views was more or less inevitable. It was merely a question of when such tensions would lead to outright confrontation.

Naturally enough, at the outset there was not a huge groundswell of support for Muhammad's beliefs. His first followers were his wife Khadija, and his cousin and son-in-law Ali, a man who would assume an important role in the development of Islam. But, in a small way at first, his creed took root. His immediate neighbours came to accept his doctrines, and by the year 619 he had gathered around him in Mecca a small but loyal group of followers.

However, in that year his life was to veer off in a new direction, as Muhammad began a literal and spiritual journey that would not only transform his own being but also that of millions of others subsequently. He had been fortunate to have at the outset a powerful patron in Mecca, his uncle Abu Talib, who acted as his protector. However, when Abu Talib died Muhammad felt himself to be dangerously exposed, surrounded by strong and determined enemies. The threat seemed so great that he fled to Medina.

During his subsequent time in Medina, the green shoots of Muhammad's creed blossomed to full fruition. There was a large and influential Jewish community in the city, and Muhammad experimented with many of their beliefs. For a while, his personal creed appeared to be moving ever closer to Judaism. But something happened to alter his course. Muhammad's house in Medina became the first mosque of the new religion. Symbolically, the main entrance of this building had been placed to face towards Jerusalem. But after a time the direction of the entrance was changed so that it faced Mecca. It was a symbolic assertion that the focus of the new faith had shifted towards the latter city. In 625, the relationship between the Jewish community in Medina and the supporters of Muhammad tangibly disintegrated. Some of the Jews were expelled from the city, others were slain.

Muhammad's new religion was not merely a passive, contemplative creed. The development of Islam was accompanied by an increasing militarization of the community around the Prophet. For this was an approach to religion that judged that, if persuasion would not work as a means of converting the heathen to the one true way, then force would do just as well. This was not to say that warfare was the sole policy available to, or used by, Muhammad. The sagacious use of peace treaties with potential opponents proved an invaluable tactic. But Muhammad also frequently employed military options.

From Medina, in 624 Muhammad began to attack Mecca. Raids were launched by Muhammad's supporters, focussing particularly on the trade caravans that criss-crossed the desert lands of Arabia towards Mecca, with great frequency. Relying on the income from such trading, the inhabitants of the city felt the resultant losses very keenly. No doubt disconcerted by this loss of income, by 628 the inhabitants of Mecca had reached a peace agreement with Muhammad, under the terms of which the pilgrimage route to the Ka'ba in Mecca was re-opened. In 630, an army of 10,000 of his supporters made the pilgrimage to Mecca.

The influence of the new religion quickly spread both north and south from its birthplace. By this period in history, many of the existing religions were becoming increasingly complicated. As one example, Christianity had long been involved in an ongoing dispute concerning the nature of Christ, and whether He was wholly human, wholly divine or a combination of the two. That these differences were keenly felt by those who held one view or another is not seriously in doubt; the Monophysite controversy that scarred the late fifth century and the period beyond is evidence enough of that. But although such doctrinal niceties gave the intelligentsia great intellectual satisfaction, to other elements of society they seemed little more than sophistry. To these it appeared that the spiritual imperatives of religion were being subsumed by an excessive concentration on a debate that appeared to have become increasingly academic. In contrast to the tortuous, endless arguments that marked the development of Christianity in the first half of the first millennium, Islam offered a return to older, simpler beliefs. The attraction of this so-called 'new' religion was that it was based on traditional and conservative values.

In contrast to the complications that came to characterize parts of Christianity, the early doctrines of Islam were not complex. There were five basic precepts, 'The Five Pillars' as they came to be known, that formed the bedrock on which the creed was based.

The first of these 'Pillars' was that the religion was monotheistic. It was expressed early on in the development of the religion in the phrase 'There is no God but God: and Muhammad is the messenger of God'.[3] Thus was the ultimate and unchallenged position of Allah stated, along with an assertion of the importance of Muhammad, His Prophet, to the religion. On this basis alone, the legitimacy of Christianity was challenged and rebutted: the confusing status of the Trinity, as the followers of Muhammad saw it, in itself made Christianity a distortion of the true way to God.

Giving support to this primary precept, the other 'Pillars' exemplified how the true believer should behave. The importance of prayer was especially emphasized, and the necessity of setting aside certain times of the day as moments when prayer to Allah was to be engaged in was developed. Such moments were times of great ritual, when the community would join together and offer their prayers both corporately and individually. These occasions fostered a bond of community, which welded the people of Islam together, giving them a powerful impetus that other, more divided communities found difficult to resist.

Fasting was also important in Islamic doctrine. It was already a part of the other religions that pre-dated Islam in the region.[4] Muhammad would have been particularly aware of the emphasis placed on the Feast of the Passover by the Jewish inhabitants of Medina. He built on the importance of this festival but expanded it significantly. The followers of Islam would fast for a month, during the period that would become known as Ramadan.

It would also be important for the true believer to give overt expression to his beliefs by undertaking pilgrimages to the places that were held important by the faith. Such pilgrimages, known as the *hajj*, were not only acts that gave the participants a sense of vicarious connection with individuals such as Abraham – and eventually Muhammad himself – who were important to their faith, they were again corporate undertakings which fostered the community spirit of the religion. Finally, Islam also emphasised the importance of almsgiving. As Allah had honoured individuals with the wealth that they held, then in return those individuals should honour Him by offering back a proportion of what they had been blessed with materially. Thus, a fixed proportion of income was to be offered back to Him, equating to one tenth of the wealth of individuals.

These Five Pillars, that is monotheism, the emphasis on prayer, the importance of fasting, the requirement for believers to participate in acts of pilgrimage and the necessity for almsgiving, were supported by a sub-stratum of other beliefs, known as 'good practices'. One of these was to become very important in its own right. This was the concept of *jihad*, the armed struggle undertaken by believers to conquer those who did not share their beliefs.

This is not to say that all other religions were treated with disrespect; the reverse was in fact often the case. Although Islam preached that both Judaism and Christianity were flawed distortions of the true faith, there was nevertheless an acceptance that some elements of both religions were doctrinally sound. Christians and Jews were described as 'People of the Book', referring to the fact that many of their writings, the Jewish Torah and the Christian Bible for example, found echoes in the Islamic holy book, the Qur'an. Both religions would therefore be treated with a degree of tolerance (though over the course of the centuries the tide of such understanding would ebb and flow on occasion) and were normally allowed to practice their religions unmolested, albeit with certain curbs on their freedom. For those people who did not belong to either of these faiths however there was a much greater degree of intolerance exhibited.

Despite the use on many occasions of peaceful tactics in the formative years of Islam, more aggressive measures were also employed. The consequences of the forces unleashed by the development of Islam, both military and idealistic, particularly evidenced in the strong sense of unity that it inspired among its believers, were profound and rarely rivalled for their effects at any other point in the course of human history. When the faith of Muhammad made its way up through the desert wastes of Arabia and into the Middle East, then the centre of civilization, its progress was astounding.

Islam was fortunate in that it timed its appearance to perfection. The West, traditional repository of the balance of power in Rome for the past 700 years, was at the time in a state of constant, bewildering flux. Much of Europe had been overrun as Rome lost its dominance and retreated into a state of irrevocable decline. New cultures were even now taking its place but they were as yet only in their formative years and had much maturation to go through before their promise reached fruition.

Despite the decline of Rome itself, the city's former Empire lived on, though in a much changed and Hellenistic form, in Constantinople, where the Emperor of Byzantium had inherited the title of Imperator from the Caesars of old. The balance of power shifted markedly to the east. The sixth century had seen some remarkable periods of reconquest by

Byzantium. Parts of the Italian peninsula itself were occupied once more (they had been lost to a series of barbarian invasions in the previous century) although in the long run it would be shown that they could not be held. A vibrant successor to Rome appeared to have been established.

In the far east of its empire however Byzantium did not have things all its own way. Here it came into contact with the other great power in the region at that time, the Persian Empire. Although, arguably, the golden age of Persia had come and gone a thousand years before, it was still a force to be reckoned with. Given the close proximity of the two empires, the one Byzantine, the other Persian, it was inevitable that there would often be friction. Ironically, at the same time that Byzantium was winning great victories in Italy and North Africa, the Persians themselves were resurgent.

During the opening years of the seventh century, Persia and Byzantium were constantly at each other's throats. As far as Islam is concerned, the real importance of this extended period of warfare between Byzantium and Persia revolves around a coincidence of timing. For, at the same time that the Muslim faith was being established in the Arabian Peninsula, which had up until now generally been on the periphery of world affairs, the two traditional great powers in the immediate area were exhausted by the long campaigns that each had been waging against the other. When the forces of Islam moved northwards up the Arabian Peninsula soon after the death of Muhammad from a fever in 632, the nations bordering the Arabs were much weakened by the exertions of the decades immediately past. Their emaciation heralded in a period of extraordinary success for the emergent Islamic religion. The forces of this new creed burst forth from the desert and advanced on Syria. Caught off guard, the Byzantine defences in the region were overrun.

It must have come as an enormous shock when Damascus, at that time held by Byzantium, fell to these Muslim warriors. Certainly, the city's loss prompted a huge counter-attack. A force of some 80,000 men marched out of Constantinople and across Asia Minor to drive away the forces of Islam. The two armies eventually met near the River Yarmuk in Palestine in 636. At a critical moment in the battle a sandstorm blew up in the faces of the Byzantine troops. Taking advantage of the chaos that ensued, the Islamic forces charged ferociously at the Byzantines. Overwhelmed by the vigour of their attack, the Byzantines started to crack and then broke completely. In a defeat of cataclysmic proportions, their army was overrun. It was a reverse of enormous magnitude.

Jerusalem itself fell soon after and for a time the Muslim tide seemed unstoppable. Having conquered Palestine and Syria, the Islamic forces then turned their attention to Persia. The Sassanid dynasty in Persia proved no more capable of resisting the Muslims than the Byzantines had. The Persians suffered two massive defeats at the Battles of Qadisaya (637) and Nihavand (642). The ruling dynasty was overthrown. Persia was then incorporated into the rapidly expanding Islamic Empire.

This was not the end of this procession of conquest. Egypt fell into Islamic hands. The Muslim armies then advanced across Asia Minor and in 673 they threatened Constantinople itself, though the great walls of the mighty city were too powerful for them to breach, as they were still inexperienced in siege warfare. The Muslim tidal wave then swept across North Africa, engulfing the frail Byzantine territories in the region. From here, they made the short crossing from Africa to Europe across the Straits of Gibraltar. The ruling Visigoth dynasty in Spain was overwhelmed. It was not until the Islamic forces were within two hundred miles of the English Channel that their progress was finally halted by the Franks in 732 under their warrior-king, Charles Martel.

It was an astonishing sequence of successes, which dramatically changed the course of history. Nothing, it appeared, could halt the progress of Islam. The vision of Muhammad had achieved unprecedented results in the world. It took Christianity three hundred years to become the official religion of the Roman Empire. In three quarters of a century the Muslims established an Empire that stretched from the borders of India in the East to France in the West. But from the outset there was one fatal flaw that threatened the very bedrock on which the religion was founded. It is self-evident that Muhammad was an extraordinary man. Who then was to succeed him?

The uncertain answer to this very basic question was to cause schisms within Islam that would divide it violently, inflicting wounds that are still unhealed in modern times. The bitter succession disputes that followed the death of Muhammad would create a fundamental difference of view which in turn would lead to the creation of movements who saw their role as being warriors for what they believed was the true faith, the 'correct' form of Islam. Not least among these groups would be that of the Nizaris, whose foundation stemmed ultimately from the chain of events that followed.

Muhammad was first succeeded as caliph by his father-in-law, Abu Bakr.[5] He was elected at Medina and died soon after, to be replaced by the Caliph 'Umar, who started the spectacular period of Islamic conquest. 'Umar instituted a body of electors who were to choose his successor. However, he made enemies. In the year 644, in a scene which presaged the actions of the Nizaris some centuries into the future, he was leading prayers in a mosque when an assassin ran forward and stabbed him six times.

The body of electors chose in his place 'Uthmān, one of the first converts to Islam, who was married to two of Muhammad's daughters. Even now the differences within Islam began to come to a head. 'Uthmān sought to change certain elements of the Qur'an, the holy book of the new religion, and in the process antagonized others who formed a party to oppose him. At their head was Ali, son-in-law of Muhammad through his marriage to the Prophet's daughter, Fatima. Opposition to 'Uthmān grew to such an extent that in 656 he too fell victim to a murderer's knife. Assassination had an early effect on the development of Islam, it was clearly not a later Nizari innovation.

Ali subsequently laid claim to be caliph, but in the aftermath of 'Uthmān's death, dangerous tensions were all too tangible. The supporters of 'Uthmān not unnaturally thirsted for vengeance. Inevitably, many of them saw the hand of Ali behind the death of their late leader. Resistance to Ali centred around the Governor of Syria, Mu'awiya. In an act which was calculated to further increase the thirst for revenge among 'Uthmān's supporters, the dead caliph's bloodied robes were displayed prominently in Damascus.

Falteringly, Ali sought to achieve compromise; but civil war was inevitable. In the subsequent conflict, an indecisive battle was fought at Siffin in Iraq, but the balance turned in Mu'awiya's favour when Egypt fell to him. Soon after, in 661, Ali himself was assassinated. He was succeeded by his son, Hassan, who resigned soon afterwards. Shortly after his resignation, Hassan was reportedly poisoned by one of his wives.[6] Inevitably, some blamed Mu'awiya for his death, seeing his hand behind all the adverse events suffered by Ali and his family.

In the wake of the deaths of Ali and Hassan, Mu'awiya assumed sole control. Not unreasonably, given the tensions of the past few years, he felt that his line of succession was insecure. He therefore resolved that, rather than rely on a system of election by which his successor would be agreed upon after his death, he would nominate a man to succeed him while he was alive. He consequently declared that his son Yezid was to take his place when he died.

Both Iraq and Syria confirmed his choice. However, the spiritual heartland of Islam was in Arabia. Mu'awiya therefore decided to travel to Medina and Mecca to have his nominated successor, Yezid, recognized by the inhabitants of these cities. There was a great deal of friction at Medina. Hussein, the son of Ali, and Abud al Rahman, son of Abu Bakr, both refused to recognize the legitimacy of Yezid's proposed adoption. However, they were not strong enough to resist the might of Mu'awiya so they fled to Mecca. Mu'awiya then turned his attentions to the inhabitants of Mecca, attempting to convince them that it would be best for everyone if Yezid were confirmed as heir to his position. When it became clear that his attempts at subtle coercion were not going to succeed, he dropped all pretence. Virtually at swordpoint, the citizens of Mecca were forced to confirm that Yezid would succeed to Mu'awiya's position on his death. With the holiest city in Islam having thus declared its support for Yezid, the rest of the Islamic Empire duly followed suit.

That, it appeared, was the end of the matter. The capitulation of Mecca was a crucial act of recognition from the most symbolically important city in the Empire. However, the violent threats accompanying Mu'awiya's coup left a bitter aftertaste. Although he had set a precedent, and from his time onwards the caliph in power nominated his successor – who was usually his oldest son – the way that he had achieved his success antagonized many. It was no real surprise then when, after his father's death in 680, Yezid did not achieve universal support. Hussein still rested safe in Mecca, protected by the vast desert sands which separated him from the heart of Yezid's support in Syria. Although he had refused to recognize the legitimacy of Yezid's claims, he was unlikely to alter the situation while he was in Mecca which, although it was the spiritual home of Islam, was somewhat on the periphery of the main political events in the Islamic Empire (by this time, Damascus was the political capital of the Muslim world). He might, in other words, be safe enough in Mecca, but he was not in a position to significantly influence events.

Consequently, when in 680 Hussein received offers of support from the city of Kufa in Iraq, he resolved to show his hand and make his way to the city. His friends around him in Mecca cautioned him against making the journey, unconvinced of the sincerity of the offer. Hussein however would have none of it. Reasoning that, if he did not throw caution to the winds, he could never hope to ascend to the highest position in Islam, he made his way across the desert, accompanied by a small band of followers. Ominously, his cousin, who had been sent on ahead to drum up support for him, was intercepted by one of Yezid's lieutenants and killed. However, although Hussein heard of his fate, he pushed on regardless. En route, he was met by a famous poet named Farazdak, who told him plainly that 'the heart of the city [Kufa] is on your side but its sword is against you'.

Dismayed at the lack of tangible support for Hussein as he advanced, the Bedouins with him abandoned him in droves. With so few men left, those remaining urged him to return to the safe haven of Mecca. However, he was accompanied by a large number of women and children and he feared that they would not survive the journey home, so he pressed onwards. When he neared Kufa, a large force of men loyal to Yezid rode forth to meet him. They demanded that he should give himself over into their custody. He refused, but instead moved north about 25 miles to a place called Karbala on the Euphrates. Yezid sent out a force to subdue him. It surrounded Hussein's army and cut off its water supplies. Something of the esteem in which Hussein was held can be gauged by the fact that, although all the non-combatants with him were given the chance to leave freely, none availed themselves of it.

On 10 October 680, Hussein held a parley with Amr, the commander of Yezid's force. Hussein asked for a personal audience with Yezid but he was refused. Soon after these abortive attempts to negotiate a peaceful solution to the impasse, matters took a violent turn for the worse. Amr had decided to attack Hussein and overcome him by force. The die was cast. He was about to launch an assault, the results of which would have repercussions far into the future. Hussein was massively outnumbered, and the only possible outcome to a battle would be a massacre. Within minutes the forces of Amr were in Hussein's camp, striking out violently at Hussein and his supporters. Many of his men fell at his side. At the end Hussein himself, racked with thirst in the baking heat, tried to make his way to a nearby river. As he did so, he was run down by the horses of his enemies who trampled over him, leaving only his bloodied, still corpse in their wake.

The massacre of the men with Hussein's party was absolute. Muhammad's last surviving grandson was reputedly the last to die. With his comrades lying dead around him he charged into the ranks of his enemies. The resultant struggle was fierce but brief. A violent blow decapitated him. Some of those gathered around him in his enemies' army expressed their horror when they saw his head, with its lips that had been kissed by the Prophet Himself, lying there in the dust.

The effects of this one-sided battle were enormous. Since the death of Muhammad, a bitter succession dispute had raged over who should rule over Islam. But although this battle appeared to decide the outcome of the argument once and for all, in fact the opposite was the case. Amr's actions made a martyr of Hussein and his family. The sense of injustice that the subsequently formed Shiite strand of Islam came to feel as a result of his martyrdom was profound, and was responsible for generating intense and radical reactions as a result. In the short-term, rather than killing off resistance to the rule of Yezid, it in fact stoked up opposition to him. In the longer term, the outcome of the battle carved a fissure in the midst of Islam, which would unlock deeply held tensions and feed a long-lasting desire for revenge on the part of the sub-division of Islam known as the Shiites.

At first, it appeared that the massacre of Hussein and his supporters had irrevocably secured the leadership of Islam for Yezid and his successors. Based first of all on the city of Damascus, an outstanding civilization began to flourish. The Arab conquerors, who barely a century before had largely lived a nomadic desert life (although of course the existence of places such as Mecca meant that they were not wholly unfamiliar with town life), adapted to an urbanized existence with remarkable adroitness. It would be wrong to think though that transformation in the conquered territories was in any way immediate. Many of the existing structures of the newly won territories were retained. Byzantine and Persian taxation policies were at first continued, but in the longer term, naturally enough, some changes became apparent. Land taxes were introduced, known as the *kharaj*, and in an attempt to avoid them ever more residents of the countryside moved to the cities, increasing the urbanization of Muslim civilization.

Despite these impressive achievements, divisions within Islam were there for all to see. Even as the eighth century began, and Islam seemed to be a power that was unstoppable, the tensions within the religion were intensifying. A number of distinct modes of belief called into question any notion of Islamic unity. The frictions that existed between these different modes and their supporters were about to increase in intensity.

Yezid's supporters formed a dynasty in Damascus – the Umayyad – which for a time appeared to hold a position of unrivalled and unassailable power. However, a new Islamic dynasty eventually established itself in a new city in the East. In 762, this group – known to history as the Abbasid dynasty – established a settlement that would eventually become the great city of Baghdad. However much it may have appeared that the ultimate triumph of Yezid and his successors was assured, such was in fact far from the case. Opposition to them grew. Rejecting the legitimacy of Umayyad rule, another branch of Islam, whose supporters were known as Shiites, also grew ever stronger. In 685 – five years after Hussein's death – a revolt in Kufa led by al-Mukhtar, who supported Hussein's half-brother, Muhammad (the third son of the Caliph Ali), presaged the rise of an aggressive and vibrant Shiite reaction against the Umayyads. Significantly, al-Mukhtar declared Muhammad the Mahdi – 'the divinely guided one' – a term that would develop very important connotations in the theology of the Shiites.

Shiites held that to be a legitimate successor to Muhammad, the leader of Islam should be able to prove direct descent from Ali, the son-in-law and cousin of the Prophet. The name Shiite in fact derives from 'Shi'at Ali', which means 'of the party of Ali'. An essential part of their doctrine was that a great prophet, known as the Mahdi, would come to earth to presage the end of the world and the destruction of all that is evil. Opponents of the Shiites, who always formed the majority, did not accept this. But the Shiites believed that the Umayyad dynasty was guilty of shedding holy blood by their treatment of Hussein.

In token of their grief at Hussein's death, the Shiites dressed in black and carried banners of the same hue, unmistakable signs of their dismay at what they saw as the usurpation of power by the Umayyads. Thus when the Abbasids, representing a rival branch of the Prophet's family, attacked the Umayyads, some Shiites were quick to offer their support. There had been increasingly frequent revolts against the Umayyads – significantly, in view of the birthplace of the Nizaris, many of them from Persia – and when the Abbasids launched their great assault on the Umayyads in the middle of the eighth century, the latter – their society rent by economic difficulties, their

Empire grossly over-extended, their claim seeming to some illegitimate, and with large numbers of militants opposed to them on religious grounds – were powerless to resist. The ruling Umayyad caste was overthrown, although one of their leaders managed to flee far to the west, to Spain, where the Umayyads would give impetus to a magnificent late flowering of the dynasty based on Cordoba.

But those Shiites who expected to benefit from the resultant change of regime were largely disappointed. Closer examination of the structure of the Shiite element within Islam gives a very clear signal why this was the case: they themselves were not united. Although they were agreed that the only legitimate leader of Islam must come from Ali's branch of the Prophet's family, they could not agreed on which one. Thus, although they were largely united in their hatred of rival forms of Islam, the Shiites were a very diverse and disparate group. Those Shiites who supported the Abbasids, for example, believed that one of Ali's family, Abu Hashim, had bequeathed his claim to the Abbasid Ibrahim, which enabled this group to support the Abbasids' successful attempts to overthrow the status quo. But the installation of the first Abbasid caliph, one Abu'l Abbas, did not presage the beginnings of a new period of Shiite supremacy. Shiite hopes of a dramatic upsurge in fortunes were to prove very over-optimistic. This in itself led to the evolution of a very strong militant tendency within the movement, and fissures within its ideology.

Eventually, the Shiites further divided into a number of sub-groups. These held some beliefs in common. All accepted that the head of state, the 'Imam', should be a man who was descended from Ali. This Imam would be an infallible interpreter of God's will. Various interpretations of his powers were offered, with the more extreme attributing something approaching the status of divinity to him. There were however disputes over his identity. A number of Shiites believed in the legitimacy of the first twelve Imams descended from the Prophet in what they regarded as the legitimate line following the foundation of the religion by Muhammad. They believed that the last of these Imams had disappeared – described as 'going into occultation' in the doctrine of the Shiites – but that, when the time was right, the Hidden Imam as he was known would ultimately reappear and restore righteousness to the world. But there was a division as other Shiites disagreed with this interpretation.

The division revolved around the legitimacy of Ismail, the son of the 6th Imam, Ja'far Sadiq. Ja'far died in 765, and his death would lead to a debate over the legitimate line of succession, which would in turn mark a serious schism within the Shiite movement. Ismail had originally been named Ja'far's successor, but it was claimed that his succession was ultimately cancelled.[7] Thus 'Twelver' Shiites would not recognize the claims of Ismail to become Imam and traced the line of succession through to their last, the twelfth Imam, ignoring him.

But the supporters of Ismail refused to recognize the validity of this cancellation. The sons of Ismail fled from Medina to safety elsewhere. What became of Ismail himself is disputed. Some accounts say that he died, and was buried by Ja'far, after the latter had shown the governor of Medina his son's corpse to prove his death. But some of Ismail's adherents rebutted these stories, saying that he was not dead. They indeed went so far as to say that, five years after Ja'far's death Ismail could be seen in Basra, where he had assumed miraculous powers, giving sight to the blind and curing the lame. Those that supported the claims of Ismail and his descendants became known as 'Isma'ilis'. Given the importance of the Imam to their creed, this dispute over who the legitimate Imam might be inevitably led to bitter divisions among the Shiites themselves.

These disputes cumulatively demonstrate that, within just over a century of Muhammad's death in 632, there were very serious divisions within the religion that he had founded. These had already manifested themselves in bloodshed and confrontation. The succeeding centuries would see little resolution of these differences. On the contrary, they would frequently be exacerbated. Islam had already started to fragment, exposing a series of deep wounds that would fester with dramatic effect. It was these divisions that would act as the catalyst for a chain of events that would lead directly to the formation of the movement known as the Nizaris.

TWO

The Rise of the Isma'ilis

Despite the fact that the Abbasids came to power partly with the support of some of the Shiites, their assumption of authority in the Muslim world did little to further the cause of the latter group. The Abbasids subsequently made it clear that they did not agree with the Shiites' particular interpretation of Islam. Instead, on a number of occasions the Shiites would be persecuted (a notable example would be when the Abbasid Mutawakkil destroyed the shrine to the martyred Hussein at Karbala in 851, which was guaranteed to inflame the emotions of the Shiites).[1]

The Abbasids themselves were very interested in religious matters. Their caliphs sought to prove their religious credentials by adopting religious names when they came to power (for example, the most famous of the early caliphs, Harun, adopted the name 'al Rashid', which means the 'right guided'). However, there was discontent from some quarters against their rule. There would be a number of religious revolts against the Abbasids, such as one in Medina in 762 and another in Mecca in 786. Generally speaking however the disunity of the Abbasids' opponents at this particular time ensured that there was not enough co-ordination in their efforts to seriously threaten to displace them, at least in the short term.

It would be wrong to think that these threats to Abbasid hegemony came merely from Shiite sources. A number of revolts against their rule came from other Islamic groups. These challenges revealed themselves not only in outbreaks of violence; intellectual wars fought between the spiritual academics of the Islamic world contributed to an ongoing and evolving debate which developed ever more complicated strands of theological argument. The combined effect of the armed revolts against Abbasid authority and the increasingly bold intellectual questioning of religious doctrines adopted by them was decisive. There was no massive outbreak against the Abbasids which sent their dynasty tumbling into rubble, rather a subversive chipping away at the fabric of the society that they had created. Nevertheless, the end result would be the same in either case, though much less immediate and spectacular in the latter form. Ultimately, these factors would conspire together to bring down the Abbasids.

On the surface, it may have appeared that all was well. Arts and sciences thrived under the patronage of the Abbasids. But they were constantly beset with political difficulties. They were not well blessed with strong leadership, with the occasional exception to the general rule, and their control over the widely dispersed Islamic world was transient and chimerical. The territory that they attempted to govern was vast. It contained many diverse cultural elements, and the pressures that this created perhaps made it inevitable that the Abbasid Empire would not remain one coherent entity for long.

The early successes of Islam had been built on a process of Arabisation in the lands that their armies (which were mainly Bedouin) had conquered. However, this process of cultural conquest was never successfully completed. There were some very strong and resistant counter-cultures present, which proved eventually to present an insurmountable barrier to this quest for cultural dominance. One of the strongest such counter-cultures was that found in Persia. This is little surprise given the wonderful heritage of the Persian empires of old. Unable to subdue Persian culture, the Abbasids would eventually find themselves overwhelmed by it. By the close of the ninth century, the court of the caliphs would be heavily populated with Persian advisers, and even the dress code adopted by the caliphs would be Persian in nature. Similarly, the composition of the army changed; the influence of the Bedouins decreased and others, especially Persian and ultimately Turkish mercenaries, took their place. These factors were not just of academic interest; they exemplified the increasing breakdown in cohesion in the Islamic world.

Over time, the Abbasid empire would become much more decentralized. As a result, local rulers would frequently avail themselves of the opportunity to throw off the yoke of rule from Baghdad. This generated further problems for the Abbasids. The consequent social unrest would lead to an increase in militancy at many levels of Islamic society and would create great social tensions. The dynasty would be consistently threatened by plots against its hegemony, and its grip on power would eventually become so tenuous that it had to be propped up by imported tribesmen.[2] To compound its woes, it would also lose its grip on the economy. The loss of many lands from effective control inevitably reduced taxation receipts and the dynasty, with its burgeoning and sometimes suffocating bureaucracy, would find it increasingly difficult to support the necessary trappings of a modern and advanced state. This would be evidenced above all else in constant debasements of the currency as matters progressively worsened, the last resort of impecunious and desperate sovereign states throughout history.

The lesser Shiite threat to the Abbasids would come from the 'Twelvers', those who believed that the 12th Imam in the line of succession from Muhammad (through, of course, the Alid branch of the family) had disappeared and would return to restore the world to the rule of righteousness at some destined point in the future. They certainly believed in the future emergence of the redeemer known as the Mahdi, and they also developed a martyrology around some of the Imams who had been murdered for their faith in the past. But their attitude to the concept of the Mahdi was essentially a passive one. He would return to rule the world when the time was right, regardless of the intervention of men. They were therefore, generally speaking, happy to leave the status quo well alone, and they consequently entered into a form of accommodation with the Abbasids, although the ruling dynasty in actuality did little to advance the 'Twelver' cause.

In contrast to this passive acceptance of fate, the Isma'ilis, also known as 'Seveners' because a majority of early Isma'ilis recognized only seven Imans, ending with Muhammad ibn Ismail, adopted a far more vigorous and evangelical role than the more orthodox, reserved 'Twelvers'. They believed that they should prepare for the return of the Mahdi by their active intervention. They therefore proved far less willing to meekly accept Abbasid rule, and quickly became a focus for social discontent (of which there was a good deal) in many diverse parts of the Islamic world, such as

Persia, North Africa and especially Yemen. Their zeal and radicalism when compared to the less assertive 'Twelvers' inevitably led to a growth in factionalism within the Muslim world. It was from such a tradition that militant groups like the Nizaris would emerge.

The claims of the Isma'ilis were widely rebutted by their enemies. Eventually, the threat posed by those who refused to accept the claims of Ismail and his line became too great, and Muhammad ibn Ismail, the 7th Imam of the Isma'ilis, was forced to go into hiding. He therefore became known as al-Maktum – 'The Hidden One'. So the Imamate was concealed, although during the subsequent century or so that it remained obscured, the Imamate was, according to the Isma'ilis, passed down through Muhammad's successors, albeit in secret.

The Isma'ilis were subsequently forced to adopt an attitude of strict secrecy in their approach both to their religion and their evangelism. With respect to the first of these factors, their faith, their very doctrines were shrouded in mystery. They argued for example that the Qu'ran, the Holy Book of Islam, was not to be read as a series of literal statements. Rather, they believed that they were veiled in allegory, and they should be interpreted in a non-literal manner after deep interrogation of its words had revealed its hidden inner meanings. To many orthodox Sunni Muslims this was anathema, leaving as it did great scope for interpretation.[3] This on its own was enough to guarantee the persecution of the Isma'ilis.

The Shiites generally regarded the Sunnis as representing a strand of Islam that did not reflect the legitimate order. The Shiites, as we have seen, believed that only a descendant of Ali could legitimately be the spiritual leader of the Islamic world. Therefore, in their eyes, those who were not of this branch of Muhammad's family, such as the first caliphs following the Prophet's death, or indeed the Umayyad and Abbasid dynasties, were nothing but interlopers who had overturned the natural order of succession. This inexorably led to serious and often violent disagreements between Sunnism and Shiism, especially in the Isma'ili form of the latter.

These disagreements arose as a result of fundamentally different paradigms on the part of the Sunnis and Shiites. The Sunnis believed that legitimacy arose from representing the wishes of 'the majority of the community'. This could lead to lengthy debates in an attempt to reach consensus on certain key issues. Muhammad himself was said to have encouraged such intellectualizing – one analysis notes that 'a putative tradition of the Prophet that says "differences of opinion among my community are a blessing" was given wide currency'. Such consensus ('*ijma*') was at direct odds with the Shiites' approach to religious matters, which was that 'knowledge derived from fallible sources is useless and that sure and true knowledge can only come through a contact with the infallible Imam', who therefore assumed a predominant position within the Shiite community.

Given the different stances of the two strands of Islam, there was never any doubt that there would be problems between them. It has been noted that 'the concept of the community so vigorously pronounced by the earliest doctrine of the Qur'an gained both a new emphasis and a fresh context with the rise of Sunnism. Whereas the Qur'an had marked out the Muslim community from other communities, Sunnism now emphasized the views and customs of the majority of the community in contradistinction to peripheral [sic] groups. An abundance of tradition came to be attributed to the Prophet to the effect that Muslims must follow the majority's way, that minority groups are all doomed to hell, and that God's protective hand is always on the majority of the community, which can never be in error'.[4]

The Sunnis, and indeed some of the 'Twelver' Shiites, were bitterly opposed to the Isma'ilis, who developed doctrines that were, in their eyes, unconventional. Some strident propaganda was therefore directed at the Isma'ilis. The more extreme of the accusations levelled at them claimed that they were plotting to destroy Islam from within. It was the start of the development of what became known as 'the black legend' and an early intimation of just how deep the feelings generated by the Isma'ilis would run.[5]

These differences were exaggerated by the way that the Isma'ilis interpreted the hidden meanings of the Qur'an. Before a new Isma'ili convert could have these hidden meanings (known as the '*batin*') explained they had to go through an initiation ceremony.[6] Only after a secret series of rituals would they be accepted into the Isma'ili brotherhood and the batin revealed to them. The key point about secret rituals is that they are of course intended to remain secret, a cause that is hardly helped if they are committed to writing. Thus it seems that from the start, as a general rule, the Isma'ilis committed little to writing. This is not universally true and there are exceptions to this general statement. Some documents were indeed prepared by the Isma'ilis. But those that remain generally concern theological rather than historical issues – meaning that we have more clues about the beliefs of the Isma'ilis than we do about their early historical development.[7]

Given these qualifications, we still catch an occasional glimpse of the movement during the latter part of the eighth century and throughout the ninth century – decades when the hold of the Isma'ilis on any kind of continuing existence was frail indeed. The fragility of their existence meant that the movement was effectively forced underground, and had no option but to operate in a clandestine manner. However, it appears that a network of *da'is* (missionaries) was set up across many parts of the Middle East during these difficult years. Persia and Syria appear to have been particularly fertile soil for the religious beliefs of the Isma'ilis.

These *da'is* were specially trained before they set out on their appointed mission. When they arrived in the area that had been allocated to them for their proselytising efforts, they first of all attempted to integrate themselves into the local community as surreptitiously as possible, often disguising themselves as merchants or artisans. Once established, they would remain on the lookout for potential converts whom they could bring into the true path through their secret initiation ceremonies. The operation was undoubtedly clandestine but this was as much through pragmatism as duplicity. So insecure was their place in the world that a doctrine was developed (that of *taqiyya* or 'caution') which allowed Isma'ilis to deny their faith when faced with danger or death. Perhaps such attitudes appear unusual to Western philosophies that have evolved around stories of Christian martyrs refusing to deny their faith in the face of torture and execution, but what cannot be denied is that the concept appears to have been mightily successful in prolonging the longevity of the Isma'ilis.

At the heart of the Isma'ilis' beliefs was the Hidden Imam, the successor of Muhammad ibn Ismail, who was the religious leader of the Isma'ilis until the Mahdi, 'the divinely guided one', returned to herald in the age of righteousness. So well disguised was this Hidden Imam, however, that few had any provable knowledge of who he actually was. While in the short term this perhaps prevented his extermination – which was absolutely crucial to the Isma'ilis as their faith demanded that the Imam should be in the bloodline of Ismail – in the longer term it meant that his identity was so well protected that, when he made himself a public figure at the start of the tenth century when the Fatimid dynasty was born, it was easy for his enemies to aver that he was an impostor and practically impossible for him to prove his case to the contrary.

It was only in the second half of the ninth century that the Isma'ilis began to emerge from their concealed hiding places into the full light of day. What appears to have encouraged them to do so were increasing social tensions within the Abbasid empire. Within the towns, there was simmering discontent from the underprivileged classes of the community. This led to a greater willingness on the part of such people to identify themselves with the more radical elements of the Isma'ilis. But it was on the coasts of Iraq, around Basra, that the most obvious manifestation of unrest was to show itself.

Islamic traders had opened up previously little known areas of the African hinterland to trade, as well as other far distant parts of the globe.[8] But the goods traded were not merely inanimate objects. Slave labour was widely employed. In the area around Basra, there was a heavy top layer of nitrous soil which had to be broken through before the cultivatable and fertile soil underneath could be exposed and made usable for the purposes of agriculture. The work was backbreaking and extremely unhealthy, the risks of illness being greatly increased by the widespread presence of salt marshes in the area. Black African slaves were employed in this work in what must have been quite unbearable conditions. Eventually the slaves (known as the Zanj) could take no more of this hardship. They resolved to no longer offer the sweat of their brow to their hard taskmasters and their fury exploded in a full-scale revolt.

The Zanj revolt hit the Abbasid empire in the Middle East at a time when it seemed ill-prepared to cope with it. There had been revolutions within the Abbasid domains before but this one seems to have proved beyond the capabilities of the dynasty to control. Eventually, a Zanj enclave was set up in Southern Iraq which would survive for fourteen years in what seems to have been some kind of early communistic state. But the importance of the revolt for our story is that it appears to have been one of the many illustrations of social unrest which collectively encouraged Isma'ilism to emerge from its cocoon. It was indeed in Iraq that we find the most obvious sign of Isma'ili radicalism emerging.

The Isma'ili mission to spread the movement's beliefs (the '*dáwa*') was controlled during its 'hidden' years from Syria, with the town of Salamiya becoming its epicentre. As the ninth century progressed, the Isma'ilis' cause developed significant momentum. But its success in the latter part of the century would initiate events which would eventually lead to the loss of Syrian control over the missionary activities of the *dáis*.

One of the *dáis* was a man named al-Husayn al-Ahwazi. He preached in the region of Kufa, and one of his recruits was named Hamdan Qarmat. The latter, fired up with the zeal of a new convert, quickly starting preaching on his own behalf, winning large numbers to his side. So successful was his preaching that his followers were soon called Qarmatis after him. Their success was founded on militant exploitation of the social discontent then existing in the region, and was helped immensely by the Zanj revolt (by 880, the Qarmatis had tried to form an alliance with the Zanj). Many of the exploited classes in the area were, at the time, unhappy at the generally passive tone towards the ruling caste adopted by many of the Shiite leaders. The more radical social revolution expounded by the Qarmatis touched a chord with their supporters. The Qarmatis took advantage of the discontent by imposing heavy levels of tax (at a fifth of income) in the regions that they controlled so that they could better finance their revolution. Their chances of success were greatly enhanced by the disintegration of Abbasid power in southern Iraq as a result of the Zanj revolt and other social tensions – the Qarmatis had existed for several decades before the Abbasids were even aware of the threat that they posed, so great had been the breakdown in communications. It was not until the last decade of the ninth century that the Abbasids took active steps to repress the Qarmatis, and by that stage the genie had been irreversibly released from the bottle.

It was not only in Iraq however that the *dáis* found success. Southern Persia and Yemen were also targeted by these Isma'ili evangelists. Yemen particularly proved to be a profitable recruiting ground for the Isma'ilis. The *dái* Ali ibn al-Fadl was especially successful in the region. He had converted to the Isma'ili cause while on a visit to Karbala. He and his supporters and colleagues set themselves up in mountain fastnesses, wild, remote and inaccessible regions, from which they launched their evangelism in the area. From these protected parts of the Yemeni mountains, they could

23

shield themselves from the power of local enemies (an interesting precursor of the approach subsequently to be adopted by the Nizaris).

They met with strong tribal support and, by 906, effectively controlled most of Yemen. Although some of Yemen was subsequently lost, from this time on the country was an important Isma'ili base (the Isma'ilis survived in the country into modern times). From here, new missionary expeditions were launched, eastwards into the Indian sub-continent through Sind and westward into the Maghrib in north-west Africa, whence one of the greatest moments in Isma'ili history would arrive through the founding of the Fatimid dynasty. There were other areas in the Arabian Peninsula which were also affected by the Isma'ili resurgence, particularly in Bahrain and Oman. Further north, Khurasan and Transoxiana, in the distant lands of Central Asia, were also visited with some success by the *da'is*. This latter drive was subsequently inherited by the *da'i* Abu Hatim ibn al-Razi who carried the mission into Azerbaijan. In summary, the Isma'ilis were energetic and widely successful in furthering their cause at this time.

This sudden emergence of the Isma'ilis from a century of hidden development led to unforeseen consequences. At the outset, the *da'is* – even the very successful Hamdan Qarmat – accepted a degree of centralized control from Syria. But the secret and esoteric development of Isma'ili doctrine, and the concept of the Hidden Imam, led to problems of its own. The mystery surrounding the evolution of Isma'ilism led to uncertainty. From such uncertainty it was a very small step to misunderstanding, even – perhaps especially – within the movement itself. Thus the process of Islamic fragmentation was about to accelerate once again.

Islam had, as we have seen, already divided itself into Orthodox Sunni and Shiite tendencies but, by the middle of the eighth century, the Shiites had themselves broadly divided into 'Twelvers', Isma'ilis and a third group, not as yet considered, known as the Zaydis. This latter group took their name from their founder, Zayd ibn Ali, who led a revolt against the Umayyad dynasty in 740, which ended in defeat. The actions of this latter group in many ways appear contradictory. The Zaydis would develop a reputation for being religiously restrained, in that they did not condemn the early caliphs before Ali and were subdued in their criticism of those Muslims who did not acknowledge the rights of Ali's descendants to succeed him. At the same time, they were politically revolutionary, frequently advocating armed rebellion against the ruling caste. There would be a number of occasions when these different segments of Shiism would fall out among themselves in the succeeding centuries.[9]

Now the Isma'ilis themselves were about to experience division. As the ninth century neared its close, the Islamic world was about to witness a further disagreement, this time striking at the heart of the Isma'ili movement. Ironically, these divisions would act as a catalyst for a chain reaction of events that was to lead to a massive advance in Isma'ili fortunes. These events were precipitated by a clash between the Qarmatis and other Shiite Muslims. Hamdan Qarmat lost control of the movement that he had set up. The radical tendencies exposed by his movement were eventually to prove too strong for him to restrain, and effective leadership of the militant wing of the Qarmatis passed to a man named Zakruya. Under his direction, they armed themselves and launched a series of bitter raids on Iraq and Syria.

An army sent to destroy them by the Abbasids was itself routed and the Qarmati forces, largely composed of fierce Bedouin warriors, experienced a great deal of success. In 903, they attacked and ransacked Salamiya, headquarters of the Isma'ili movement. They had clearly fallen out with the Isma'ili leadership in a serious way but if they planned to eliminate the leader himself, they missed their prize. Perhaps aware that he was their target, the Imam who was then at the head of the Isma'ili movement, Ubaid Allah al-Mahdi, had already fled before the Qarmatis arrived in Salamiya. The Abbasids, alerted to his departure, launched a desperate but futile attempt to intercept and capture him. He made his way far to the west, through Egypt and into the Maghrib (approximately in the region of modern day Tunisia).

Al-Mahdi was a remarkable man. He was far from a fanatical zealot. On the contrary, he appears to have possessed an extraordinary capacity for acting with great political sagacity, capable of ingratiating himself with a wide range of potentially unlikely allies. Perhaps the authorities in the Maghrib – who were not naturally well disposed towards him – sensed that this made him a potentially dangerous focal point for any disaffected subjects within their realm, for they quickly threw al-Mahdi into prison. But he clearly had some powerful allies. The strongest of these was an influential man named Abu Abdallah. He had been espousing Isma'ili teachings in the region since 893, and by the time that al-Mahdi arrived in the first decade of the ninth century, he had already attracted a deal of support to the Isma'ili cause. It is possible that he had been negotiating with al-Mahdi for some time, and it may have been at his instigation that the Imam had made his way to the Maghrib.

When al-Mahdi was flung into prison, Abu Abdallah felt that the moment was ripe for active revolution. Accordingly, he assembled his forces together and proclaimed the incarcerated al-Mahdi to be the Imam whose re-appearance had been long awaited by the Isma'ilis. Caught up in a wave of millenarian emotions, many flocked to support him. This led to open conflict; the ruling class was overthrown and al-Mahdi was released from his prison. In 909, the Isma'ili Imamate, hidden since the days of Muhammad ibn Ismail over a century before, was restored to the full light of day.

It was a great moment of triumph for both al-Mahdi and Abu Abdallah, but little good would it do the latter. Within a year, the Imam who had been given his freedom and his power by Abu Abdallah felt so threatened by him that he had arranged for him to be executed. It is unclear why this happened, although one of the most plausible explanations that has been offered is that Abu Abdallah, who appeared to be something of a hard-line Isma'ili in his attitudes, was too extreme for Al-Mahdi's tastes.[10] For the Imam proved to be something of a diplomat in his relationships with many of his new subjects, which indeed was as well as they were in the main Berbers, renowned for their ferocity and independent spirit. Such a flexibility of philosophy and attitudes would be characteristic of some later Nizari leaders.

Although al-Mahdi succeeded in establishing himself in the Maghrib, and in the process founded a new and powerful dynasty in the north of Africa, it was at a cost. For he found himself on the horns of a seemingly unresolvable dilemma. On the one hand, he needed to ensure that he retained the loyalty of the peoples of the Maghrib. This was no easy task. There were two major Berber tribes in the region, the Zanata and the Sanhaja, and given their reputation for independence it is perhaps little surprise to find that they were constantly at each other's throats. This made for a highly volatile environment. Aware perhaps that he himself had effectively come to power through a coup that overthrew the existing establishment, it would not be unnatural for Al-Mahdi to be extremely cautious in his dealings with his subjects so that he could avoid a similar fate. Further, he was surrounded by enemies; a regime in Egypt that was hostile to him, the Abbasids further afield and, not far away on the other side of the Mediterranean, the remains of the Umayyad dynasty in Spain.

But on the other hand, the Isma'ilis included among their number many radical elements. These were inevitably disappointed that the Fatimid dynasty,[11] as Al-Mahdi and his descendants became known, failed to deliver the changes that they were expecting as part of the period leading up to the introduction of an Islamic paradise on earth. Until recent years, it was widely assumed that the Fatimids and the Qarmatis acted hand in hand but modern research suggests that this was not in fact the case.[12] The former assumption was held to be true because, by and large, the two parties were widely distrusted by many other powerful Islamic groups, many of whom incorrectly regarded the Qarmatis as being synonymous with the Isma'ili movement as a whole. As such it was assumed that, because the Abbasids were naturally a common enemy, then Fatimid and Qarmati policy must have worked hand in glove.

But this in fact over-simplifies the situation. The Qarmatis' vigour was eventually exhausted but when they were finally defeated in Syria, it only served to usher in an increase in the ferocity of their actions. They shocked the Muslim world with their regular attacks on pilgrim caravans on their way to Mecca, on one occasion reputedly killing 20,000 people. Several major cities, such as Kufa and Basra, were also pillaged by the Qarmatis. Then in 930 came the most shocking event of all. In that year, the Qarmatis fell on the unsuspecting city of Mecca itself while it was thronged with pilgrims. Mecca was completely unprepared and fell quickly to the Qarmatis. It was then subjected to a horrific sack. The streets ran with blood as pilgrims were slaughtered by the score. But most shockingly of all, the revered black stone that was encased in the Ka'ba was torn down and carried away.

This act illustrates that there were a number of theological tensions within Islam. There were clearly some elements who were dissatisfied with the state of affairs within the Islamic world, and wished to re-define them. Undoubtedly, the sacking of Mecca – Islam's birthplace – must have come as a shock to many other Muslims. It gave anti-Isma'ili propagandists a tremendous opportunity to accuse the Isma'ilis generally of plotting to destroy Islam: the fact that the Qarmatis had now diverged from many other Isma'ilis would have meant little to such commentators. But the most radical act of the Qarmatis was yet to come.

In 931, they were led by a man named Abu Tahir, who had been responsible for the attack on Mecca. He claimed to have recognized the true Mahdi in the person of a young Persian who had arrived in Bahrain (which was ultimately the principal base of the Qarmatis) a short time previously. The fact that such a claim could be made at all demonstrates well enough that the Qarmatis were not at one with the Fatimids. For the latter claimed that their Imams were descended directly from Muhammad, and had been hidden away during the decades of persecution against the Isma'ilis; as such, the Fatimids were the only true spiritual leaders of Islam and the Qarmatis' claim to have discovered the Mahdi was a direct challenge to their authority.

In the event, the proclaiming of the Mahdi proved an unmitigated disaster for the Qarmatis. That they had made a serious error of judgement quickly became apparent. For a start, he proved to have some strange religious tendencies. He was not alone in this – the Qarmatis themselves were fascinated by cosmology and one of the main reasons they identified the Mahdi when they did was because the planets Jupiter and Saturn were in conjunction, which was deemed to be a sign that a major event was imminent. The Mahdi though, was, it appears, extremely interested in fire worship. This suggested that he had a Zoroastrian pedigree.[13] As such, it was a strange qualification for an Islamic prophet. To make matters worse, the Mahdi was either extremely over-confident or lacking in any degree of political skill. He soon started to assert his dominance over the same group who had given him power. Leading figures within the Qarmati leadership were accused of a series of crimes and executed. Even close relatives of Abu Tahir were not immune. Realizing that he had made a grave mistake, Abu Tahir undid his folly before it was too late, removing the Mahdi from power after 80 terrifying days and having him killed shortly afterwards.

The Qarmati aberration showed that the Isma'ili movement could give birth to some very radical groups, but the heyday of the Qarmatis had passed. Although they would live on in Bahrain into the next century, they would become more and more isolated and irrelevant. Their militancy would in fact increase; travellers to Bahrain in the eleventh century would notice that there seemed to be no mosques in the country, and their enemies would aver that they shared both their goods and their women as a community. It was also rumoured that the Qarmatis, who were experts at raiding and plundering, were so adept at it that they did not pay taxes because of the huge amounts of booty that were brought into the country. The extreme views attributed to the Qarmatis in terms of both their religious beliefs and their unbridled promiscuity are resonant of later accusations made against the Nizaris.

As the Qarmatis' star sank lower in the sky, so that of the Fatimids rose higher. They were helped enormously in this by the ongoing demise of the Abbasid dynasty. By the middle of the tenth century, the Abbasids were on their knees. Cursed with a succession of weak caliphs and assaulted internally both by bitter social divisions and economic woes, the dynasty was in its last days of real power. A Shiite dynasty from Persia established itself in Baghdad, known as the Buyid. It was effectively the end of Abbasid rule. Although the caliph remained, he was in fact no more than a powerless figurehead; worse, he was a Sunni figurehead supported by a Shiite faction. It must have been a terrible humiliation for the caliph to endure.

But it was equally a disappointment for the radical Shiites. The fact that the Buyids chose to support a Sunni caliph, even if his power was broken, must have been a great blow for those who wished to see militant Shiism triumphant. For these radicals who wished to see what they believed to be the only true way to spiritual fulfilment, a holy, pure, Shiite regime, established, or indeed for those who were dissatisfied with their lot for social reasons, it was a bitter pill to swallow. Radical Isma'ilism became the only alternative to the Sunnis. As one commentator has noted, by their actions the Buyids 'further discredited the already tarnished Sunni caliphate; at the same time, they finally eliminated moderate Shiism as a serious alternative to it'.[14]

In Africa, the strength of the Fatimids waxed ever stronger. Several times in the opening decades of the tenth century they had launched an assault on Egypt, although these were rebuffed. They adopted direct assault as a weapon in their attempts on the country, but also set up a network of agents within the country, secreted away both to foment discontent and supply information to the Fatimid leadership in the Maghrib. Again, it is important to note that clandestine operations were not the exclusive preserve of later Nizaris.

The eventual triumph of the Fatimids was brought about with the accession of the Caliph Mu'izz. His greatest general was a man of foreign (probably Sicilian) descent, Jawhar al-Rumi. In 969, Jawhar marched across the desert to Egypt at the head of a huge army supposedly 100,000 men strong. The Turkish dynasty then ruling Egypt was routed near the old city of Fustat and the country was captured for the Fatimids. Jawhar had brought with him a plan for a new city, which he mapped out near Fustat by the Nile. Amidst a sandy wasteland the great city was laid out and built. It was named al-Qahira – 'The Victorious' – but it would be better known to the West as Cairo.

The triumph of the Fatimids was apparently complete in 973, when Mu'izz entered his new capital to claim his crown. He brought with him a vast array of treasures to ingratiate himself with his new subjects, as well as the coffins of his ancestors whom he planned to re-inter in Egypt. He founded many prestigious establishments, such as a religious college named the al-Azhar which some claim to be the first university in the world. The Fatimids had long asserted that they were destined to be the unrivalled leaders of the Islamic world. Nothing or nobody, it seemed, was now powerful enough to prevent them from making good their boasts.

But in fact their timing was slightly awry. Many of the Shiite ruling class moved with the dynasty from the Maghrib to Egypt. Many of their subjects in the Maghrib still retained their independent spirits, and they quickly began to lose their grip on the region now that their attention had been diverted eastwards. Further east still there were also problems for the Fatimids. The Qarmatis, though past their prime, were still a powerful force and had little in common with the more moderate Fatimids. They came to blows with the Fatimids, helping to debar them from moving into the heartlands of Islam in Iraq and Persia.

Naturally enough, the Buyids were hardly keen to give up their hard-won gains in Iraq either. They were Shiites of the more moderate 'Twelver' persuasion, as opposed to the Fatimids, who were Isma'ilis. They were certainly powerful and ambitious men who had no intention of handing over their territories meekly to this rival dynasty. And to the north, the Byzantine Empire was in a period of resurgence after many years of decline, effectively blocking the Fatimids from progressing too far in that direction. Thus the Fatimids, although sending *da'is* far to the east and having some success in setting up isolated groups in a number of areas, were hemmed in by these opponents, their further progress blocked by a number of potential enemies whose collective power was significant.

The Fatimids reached the zenith of their powers at the close of the tenth century under the leadership of al-Aziz. As caliph, he practised a great deal of tolerance towards the Christians within his domains. This was possibly because his wife was a Christian princess. Under his rule, Christians were even raised to the highest offices of state. This must have caused concerns for some of his Islamic subjects. But, on the other hand, Egypt had become a wealthy state, reaching levels of prosperity not seen in the region since the days of antiquity. Alexandria became a great seaport once more. There was also a trend of traffic away from the land route across Iraq and towards the Red Sea and Egypt, which did little to lend the Fatimid cause towards the Sunni rulers who lost out as a result. Egyptian prosperity was significantly enhanced by the development of a strong and powerful fleet – something that had been a key objective of the Fatimid dynasty since its early days – and its possession of the island of Sicily. From here and other isolated enclaves, for example on the Mediterranean coast of what is now France, Muslim pirates had long created havoc with their neighbours, who had been subject to constant raids and harassment.

It therefore appeared that the Fatimids' fortunes were continuing to rise. But there were several aspects of al-Aziz's rule which collectively left a dangerous legacy when he died. He introduced Turks into his armies, quarrelsome, independent-spirited men who soon fell out with the Berbers who had previously made up the bulk of the caliph's forces. Armed conflict soon broke out between the two groups and the army began to disintegrate. And al-Aziz's liberal attitude, although it ingratiated him with his Christian subjects, became an increasing source of resentment to those who were Muslim. When his son, who took the reign name of al-Hakim, became caliph on his death, he was to herald in an era of uncertainty to the Fatimid world, largely fuelled by a bitter counter-reaction against the liberalism of the late caliph.

Al-Hakim was too young to become caliph when his father died in 996, being then a boy of 11 years of age. The eunuch Barjawan therefore assumed power until the boy should be of an age when he could rule in his own right. Barjawan was a cruel and overbearing man who treated both the caliph and his people with disdain. He delighted in calling al-Hakim 'lizard' and seized every opportunity that presented itself to humiliate him. In so doing, he effectively signed his own death warrant, for the caliph would prove to be a very dangerous man to make an enemy of.

When he was in his mid-teens, al-Hakim led a coup to assert his right to rule: one of the first victims of this was Barjawan. The subsequent reign of al-Hakim is something of a mystery, though he would become an important figure within the development of the Isma'ilis. Al-Hakim appears as a dark and sinister character. He made many enemies, and his dynasty would eventually fall. When it was overthrown, many of the records of the Fatimids were suppressed. Therefore, most of the accounts that remain were written by men hostile to the Isma'ilis. Much of what we know of al-Hakim is written by representatives of a religious group who detested him and all that he stood for. As such, we should be cautious in analysing what they wrote about him.[15]

Given all these caveats, it appears that al-Hakim was nevertheless an extraordinary character. In an attempt to compensate for what he saw as the excessive liberalism of his late father, al-Hakim swung far in the opposite direction. On a number of occasions, Christians and other non-Islamic groups were persecuted (although one of the confusing aspects of his reign is that such periods of oppression were often followed by times of relative toleration). Strict moral codes were laid down, and some asserted that al-Hakim wandered the streets of his capital at night in disguise trying to catch his people being non-compliant with them. If they were caught, then dreadful punishments would ensue. Leading members of society were frequently arrested and executed. A cloud of terror hung over Egypt.

Then, in 1009, al-Hakim turned on the Christians. In that year, he committed an act that was the most sacrilegious possible in the eyes of all Christians. The Church of the Holy Sepulchre in Jerusalem supposedly stood on the spot where Jesus died. As such, it was revered by Christians everywhere. Determined to demonstrate the supremacy of Islam, al-Hakim razed it to the ground.[16] The Christian world was outraged. In recent years, the Byzantines had been on good terms with the Fatimids but the desecration of the Holy Sepulchre changed all that. Relationships between the two powers became decidedly frosty. Al-Hakim was forced to moderate his stance as a result. But other events in al-Hakim's reign were to cause further divisions within the Isma'ili movement. In 1017, a group of holy men made their way to Egypt from the Lebanon. They began to declaim that al-Hakim was not only a holy man, he was in fact divine. Such assertions seemed blasphemous to many of al-Hakim's subjects and although the caliph never actually publicly accepted the teachings of these men, particularly those concerning his divinity, the fact that they were made at all must have had some impact on at least some of his people.

Eventually, rioting broke out in the streets of Cairo and the man who had now assumed control of this revolutionary movement, Darazi, was forced to flee back to Lebanon. Al-Hakim was a marked man though. He frequently went out at night on his own, walking the city and the surrounding countryside. One night in 1021 he went out into the hills near Cairo and was never seen again. He was probably murdered but his body was never found and nothing was ever heard of what had become of him. Darazi and his followers established themselves in the mountains of Lebanon. They averred that al-Hakim had in fact gone into occultation, that is he had not died but would return at some point in the future to herald in the last days of the world. Darazi's sect, known as the Druze, would become a very secretive group (in this respect at least they were not dissimilar to the Nizaris), whose teachings and beliefs were a mystery to the outside world. The importance of the Druze though was that they provide another example of the schisms that rent both the Muslim world and the Isma'ilis more specifically in the early centuries of Islam. It also sowed confusion; some later historians on occasion even confused the Druze with the Nizaris.

Al-Hakim's reign exposed further fault lines in the Isma'ili movement. There was little sign of unity among the Isma'ilis and, as time went on, divisions were becoming increasingly marked. There was perhaps an air of inevitability about this: the esoteric nature of the Isma'ilis' creed, its *'batin'* (the hidden meanings of the Qur'an) and the fact that the Imamate had been hidden for so long during the latter part of the eighth and all of the ninth century meant that universal agreement on everything to do with matters spiritual was unlikely, perhaps even impossible. Many Muslims refused to accept point-blank that the Fatimids were in truth descended from Ali at all, casting doubts on their legitimacy. And the Fatimids were never widely accepted within the heartlands of the Muslim world inside

Iraq and Persia, even by the Isma'ili groups that were present there. Therefore, Fatimid supremacy never became absolute or all-embracing.

Yet in the reign of al-Hakim's immediate successors it appeared that the great dream of the Fatimids was about to be fulfilled. In 1058 Baghdad itself was taken by a Turkish warrior who was sympathetic to the Isma'ili cause and for the best part of a year the city nominally belonged to the Isma'ilis. But this success was a temporary one. Baghdad had always been primarily Sunni (it did have a Shiite community within its walls, which on occasion managed to live in relative harmony with the Sunnis, although such periods were interspersed with frequent outbreaks of persecution directed against them) and the fact that a small ruling caste adopted Shiite ways meant little to the mass of the people.

A new force was about to enter the equation within the Islamic world. More accurately, a force that had been present for centuries was about to assume a degree of prominence that it had hitherto lacked. The Turks were first noticed by historians in the sixth century. It is a great over-simplification to talk of the Turks as if they were one people. They were composed of many different tribes, sharing some basic characteristics but differentiated in other respects. But there were certain aspects that most held in common. The tribes were nomadic. Further, they were usually headstrong and independently minded peoples. A number of them sold their services as mercenaries to foreign potentates, and this had already involved them in Islamic politics. The presence of the Turks in Egypt has already been noted very briefly, and they were also heavily involved in other parts of the Islamic world such as Iraq and Persia. Indeed, their influence extended as far as the borders of India.

One of the Turkish groups that was to rise to prominence was known as the Seldjuks. In the middle of the tenth century, many of them converted to Islam, having previously largely been shamanistic nature worshippers. In common with many other new converts, they were passionate about their new faith (although they still retained a number of their headstrong characteristics from times past). They were Sunni Muslims and consequently they violently opposed the Fatimids. They had previously occupied Baghdad before its capture by the Isma'ilis but their subsequent actions had alienated many of the local population from their cause. Now, in 1060, they fought their way back in. Their leader, Tughril Bey, declared himself Sultan, which denoted that he regarded himself as the secular ruler of the region. The Abbasid caliphate was restored but it was now more powerless than ever, being completely at the mercy of the Turks and as such nothing more than a figurehead.

Inevitably, the Turks and the Fatimids soon clashed. But the Turks also had other targets for their expansionism. Asia Minor was the most critical part of the Byzantine Empire, providing vast stores of provisions and manpower which were critical to the wellbeing of the Greeks. The Turks now started to push their way into the region. The Greek Emperor, Romanus Diogenes, could not let this pass without a vigorous response. Accordingly, he made his way from Constantinople at the head of a large army. He met the Turks at Manzikert in the far east of Asia Minor. The result of the battle, fought in August 1071, was a catastrophic defeat for Byzantium, probably unsurpassed in its history, which left the whole of Asia Minor at the mercy of the Turks. The latter were quick to exploit the opportunity and poured into the region.

But the Turks could not take full advantage of the situation. They were not a unified people and quickly fell out among themselves. A myriad of different Turkish leaders set up their own regional chiefdoms and it was not long before they were as aggressive towards each other as they were to the Byzantines or the Fatimids. As a result, much of the Middle East fragmented. Syria, Asia Minor and the Mediterranean coastal belt were governed by a number of regional rulers, who in many cases owed nominal allegiance to other men but in practice were virtually independent because of the chaotic state of the region. Further east, there were enclaves of resistance to the Turks, who were resented by many of the Isma'ilis in the area (particularly in Persia) as unwanted interlopers.

The Fatimid dynasty proved incapable of driving back the Turks. A frequent battleground of the two sides was in Palestine where Jerusalem, which had been part of the Fatimid empire for some time, changed hands on several occasions. But under the Caliph al-Mustansir, who ruled for over half a century, the Fatimids lost their energy and direction, and were increasingly forced on to the back foot at the end of the eleventh century and onwards into the twelfth. To many of the more radical Isma'ili groups, it seemed clear that the Fatimid dynasty was not the answer to Islam's problems, and was not destined to usher in a new age of holiness.

The one overriding characteristic that epitomized the region in its fragmented state as the eleventh century came to a close was decentralization. Centralized control declined markedly. This left significant weaknesses in the structure of the area which determined enemies could exploit. In the western parts of the region, on the shores of the Mediterranean, Christian warriors from Western Europe launched a great crusade which succeeded in 1099 in attaining its ultimate objective by capturing Jerusalem, a great insult to Muslims who valued the city as sacred to their own religion as well as being revered by Christians and the Jews alike.

Further east, other groups would also take advantage of the opportunities offered by the divisions within Islam. More radical Isma'ilis were disheartened by the demise of the Fatimids and their willingness to temporize with the enemies of what the militants saw as the true path of Islam. This created something of a vacuum, which other Isma'ili groups sought to fill. Radical elements were present throughout the history of the Isma'ilis, of which the Qarmatis and the Druzes were just two examples. Now, a new group was about to be launched, one which would leave the greatest mark of all on future historians – particularly those of the West – and, more especially, on their vivid imaginations.

THREE

The Visionary

In the middle of the eleventh century (the exact date is not known) a boy was born in the city of Qumm in Persia. It had been one of the first cities in the country to be populated by the Arabs when they had burst forth from the desert a few centuries earlier. By the time that this child, who was named Hasan-i Sabbah, was born, it was an established centre of the 'Twelver' Shiite community in Persia. Hasan-i Sabbah's family's original roots lay far to the south. His father 'Ali ibn Muhammad al-Sabbah al-Himyanhad come from the city of Kufa (which, it may be remembered, was the place to which the ill-fated Hussein had made his way immediately prior to his martyrdom), but his family had originated, it was claimed, in Yemen. If what we know of his early life is true then he was an unusual child.[1] His biographer claimed that when he was seven he already knew that he wished to become a religious scholar, as well as showing an active interest in other branches of learning.

His early religious leanings however were conventional in terms of his family history. He accepted that the teachings of the 'Twelver' Shiites were the legitimate doctrines to live by. But late in his teens he started to come into the company of other, more radical, theological scholars. He was introduced to a man by the name of Amira Zarrab, who was an Isma'ili. Perhaps seeing a potential convert in the young, impressionable youth before him, he started to argue with Hasan-i Sabbah, trying to convince him that his 'Twelver' beliefs were misguided.

But the youth would at first have none of this. Brought up as a devout and fervent 'Twelver', Hasan told him to desist from his blasphemies, for he would have none of them. But despite his protestations of outrage it seems that Amira Zarrab's arguments started to sow seeds of doubt in Hasan's mind because he later admitted to his biographer that when he reflected in solitude on what had been told to him, he started to question the validity of his own beliefs, though he did not admit as much to the man who was attempting to convert him. Hasan's biographer reports him as saying: 'There were controversies and debates between us, and he disproved and destroyed my belief. I did not admit this to him, but in my heart these words had great effect'. Amira Zarib told him bluntly that 'when you think in your bed at night you know that what I say convinces you'.

Perhaps nothing would have come of these musings if Hasan had not gone through a period of great personal crisis. Not for the first, nor the last, time in history the thought of imminent death was to radically alter an individual's religious beliefs. Hasan fell ill, and it was thought that nothing more could be done for him. When the end appeared near, Hasan was convinced that he was doomed to die in a state of sin or, as his biographer put it, that 'I shall have perished without attaining the truth'.[2] But, miraculously as it seemed, he did not die. When he recovered from his illness, he espoused the Isma'ili cause passionately. He was, in his religious affections, a man transformed, a man with a mission. That mission was to be fulfilled by the setting up of an Isma'ili state within Persia that would dramatically impact on the politics of the region, and on the imaginations of future generations.

This story is virtually all we know of Hasan's early days apart from one other anecdote. This is worth quoting because it illustrates graphically how stories about him, and the group he was to lead, siezed the minds of so many people possessed of a romantic disposition. The story is told that Hasan was at school with two other pupils destined for greatness. One of them was a man named Nizam al-Mulk who was to become an extremely important political figure in the Seldjuk Empire, while the other was the famous poet and astronomer, Omar Khayyam. The three youths became close friends and, believing that at least one of them would achieve great things, they all swore a solemn pact. By the terms of this, whoever became great first of all would advance the career of the other two. It transpired that Nizam al-Mulk would achieve his ambitions first, and he rose to become vizier (Chief Minister) of the Seldjuk Sultanate. Remembering his oath of earlier years, he offered provincial governorships to his old school friends. Omar did not want the post but happily accepted an income from Nizam instead. Hasan however felt that the post was beneath him and, aspiring for a more important position, also refused. Nizam graciously therefore offered him another, more prominent, post.

In this position, Hasan showed himself to be a very able politician and soon began to be perceived as a threat to Nizam himself. The latter was therefore consumed with jealousy and turned on Hasan, who was forced to flee for his life. Hasan however did not forget his actions. When he founded the movement known to the West as the Assassins, its first important victim was Nizam al-Mulk.

It is a wonderful story, and establishes very early on in Hasan's life a motive for his fanatical tendencies, the desire to gain revenge, to right a wrong. It has only one inherent problem and that is that it is almost certainly untrue. All the evidence we have suggests that the three men lived nowhere near each other in their youth, residing in different parts of Persia. Even more decisively, there is an enormous disparity in their ages. When Omar Khayyam was born, Nizam was nearly thirty years old, and unless he was over 100 years old when he died (we know that he died in 1124) Hasan was also not of the same age as Nizam. Therefore, it appears highly unlikely that the men ever shared a schoolroom together. Yet the inherent implausibility of the story has not stopped it being widely believed in the past.[3]

Following his dramatic conversion, Hasan made to his way to Rayy (which is near to modern Tehran), a traditional centre of Isma'ili radicalism. Here, in 1072, he met a holy man named Abd al-Malik ibn Attash. The Fatimids had continued to send their missionaries (or *da'is*) on missions abroad to attempt to encourage more followers to support their cause (the Isma'ilis did not as a rule force anybody to convert to their creed), indeed the much reviled al-Hakim had set up several schools in Egypt especially for this purpose. Ibn Attash was the chief of these *da'is* in Persia. He was a man of some ability, who recognized early on that this new recruit had outstanding potential. He told the young Hasan that he should journey to Egypt to complete his education, as this was still the centre of the Isma'ili world.

Although this may have seemed like an excellent idea to Hasan it would in fact be a number of years before he made the journey. He first spent some time in the central Persian city of Isfahan. Significantly, this was the centre of the Isma'ili mission (the '*da'wa*') in Persia. Eventually however it was decided that he should visit Egypt and he set out for the country, with the support of Ibn Attash who acted as his benefactor, in around 1076–77. He took a surprisingly roundabout route to get there, however, journeying first of all to the north into Azerbaijan and then into Syria and the town of Mayyafariqin. On the way, he entered into regular religious arguments with those who espoused the Sunni cause, so much so that on one occasion he was forcibly ejected from a town. Then he travelled on to Mosul and Damascus. Finding that further progress was blocked by the constant warfare between the Fatimids and the Seldjuks in Palestine, he travelled to the coast and caught a ship from Caesarea to Egypt.

Although he was to spend several years in the country, little is known of Hasan's time in Egypt. He was evidently greeted by leading officials when he arrived, presumably in deference to his esteemed sponsor in Persia, but he was never to meet the Fatimid caliph, the long-lived al-Mustansir, who reigned from 1036 to 1094. All that is known of his stay is an anecdotal tale that he fell out with the caliph's vizier, one Badr al-Jamali, who seems to have been the major power broker in the country. The truth of the story has been questioned; it is suggested that it was written into the tale retrospectively as a way of explaining the ultimate division between Egypt and Hasan some years into the future. The story ends by relating that Hasan was eventually forced to flee the country but the ship that he was in, which was a Frankish vessel ('Franks' was the name given collectively to West Europeans by the Muslim world), was shipwrecked. Eventually, he made his way by land across Syria and back to Isfahan, arriving back in 1081.[4]

Given the paucity of evidence it is difficult to read too much into this visit. However, Hasan was a man of great wisdom and insight. He would already have been aware that the Fatimid star was in the decline; the successes of the Seldjuks were evidence enough of that. It is unlikely that his time in Egypt did anything to disabuse him of the idea that the Isma'ilis in Persia should not rely on the Fatimids for ongoing support when they clearly had so many problems of their own. The Persians would have to look after their own interests.

Hasan's moment of greatness had not yet come. When he arrived back in Persia, he spent the best part of a decade travelling around the country, preaching the Isma'ili cause with passion and vigour. But in his journeys he would have seen how powerful the Seldjuks were. They were great in number, and they were ferocious warriors. Further, they were committed to the Sunni cause. This combination meant that they posed a great threat to the future of the Isma'ilis in the region. But they were far too powerful a foe for the Isma'ilis to take on in open battle. In such a contest there could only be one winner. Devout man though he might appear, Hasan was also a practical one. As he roamed around Persia attempting to convert new recruits to the Isma'ili cause, he agonised over the way to overcome the Seldjuk threat.

It is clear that, among his other qualities, Hasan was a strategist of the highest order. Realizing that might was not on his side, Hasan looked around for other weapons that he could usefully employ. His travels around the country had taught him much of its geography. Within Persia there are areas of wide-open plains. These were tailor-made for the massed attacks of Seldjuk cavalry. To fight the Seldjuks there at a numerical disadvantage would be tantamount to suicide.

But there were also many mountainous regions in the country. Here, strategically placed forts and villages could remain virtually impervious to Seldjuk assault, the difficulty of access to the regions presenting a very serious barrier to their much larger forces. In such an environment numerical superiority counted for nothing; indeed, it might cause active harm, as a large number of mouths to feed could create some major logistical problems. Hasan resolved to launch a revolt against the Seldjuks. He certainly had reason to be optimistic of a good deal of support. The Turks were Sunnis and there were many Shiites in Persia, but religious dissent was not the only reason that many Persians were opposed to the Seldjuks. Persia had a proud heritage, leading to sentiments in the region that were almost 'nationalistic'. There was also a good deal of economic and social discontent and the Persian Isma'ilis, who under Hasan-i Sabbah were virtually classless, attracted many Persians to their cause, including a number who were not Isma'ilis.

Hasan decided that he would launch his revolt deep in the mountains of Persia, where the Seldjuks would find it hardest to fight back. If conquest of the whole country was not, at this stage, an option, then control of a part of it would do for the time being. This did not mean, as we shall see, that the towns would be ignored; but it was in remoter, outlying areas that his movement would become most powerful. Ibn Attash was still alive and remained the chief *da'i* in the region. We do not know if he approved of open rebellion or not, but Hasan anyway went ahead with his plans. The first decision to be made concerned where he should start his revolt. He then had to decide how he would launch it. The way he went about it demonstrates categorically that, in Hasan, there was a wonderfully ordered character, capable of assessing the strengths and weaknesses of his position and adopting the course of action which best utilized the former and underplayed the latter.

Away in the northern regions of Persia, not far from the southern shores of the Caspian Sea, was a range of mountains, rising so steeply that they seemed to touch the clouds. There were numerous rocky peaks framing the skyline, but there was one in particular that caught the eye, standing sheer above the surrounding countryside and seemingly inaccessible to all but the eagles. Even today it catches the eye, as it 'stands out like a ship, broadside on, from a concave mountainside that guards it in the north'.[5] Another writer was moved to say of it that it resembles 'a kneeling camel with its neck resting on the ground'.[6] This peak, in the shadow of the Elburz Mountains, was already encased in legend. The land round about, the region of Daylam, had long been sympathetic to the Shiite cause. It was renowned as an area with strong independent tendencies and many Shiites, especially those who were Zaydis, had found refuge there. The peak, and the castle on it, were known as Alamut.

Traditionally, the first fortress on the site at Alamut had been built by an ancient king of the region. Seeing an eagle land on the rock, he was struck immediately by the strategic strength of the site. A fortification was constructed there, which had been rebuilt in 860. Because of the guidance of the eagle, the place was named 'Aluh Amut', which means 'the eagle's teaching'. More romantic mistranslations would later convert this to 'the eagle's nest'. As the castle of Alamut, it would etch itself permanently into the legend of the Assassins.

Hasan too saw the strength of the site, and realized that this could be the base of his Persian revolt, a haven from which the followers of the one true way, the Isma'ili path, could launch their revolution, knowing that they would be safe from any enemy, however powerful, behind those unconquerable walls. Many fortresses over the centuries have been called impregnable, and yet many of them have fallen. But Alamut rebuffed repeated attacks while the Nizaris held it. It would eventually fall only when the Nizaris were faced by overwhelming and hopeless odds.

It stood on a narrow ridge, some 6,000 feet above sea level and several hundred feet above the base of the rock from which it rose. There was only one way in, a steep, narrow, serpentine track which could only be reached after travelling through a gorge surrounded by vertical cliffs which often overhung the path below. A small party of defenders could resist an army a hundred times stronger given the advantages of its situation. But, to cap it all, the castle was at the far end of a fertile valley which could be farmed to produce large volumes of food to supply the garrison in peacetime, thus offering the best of both worlds to its owner.

Hasan was no fool. Given the resources at his disposal, capture of the castle was impossible through armed assault. But the greatest walls can be powerless to resist an attack based on subtler tactics. Hasan's scheme to capture Alamut was a masterpiece of strategy. In 1090, he put his plan to take Alamut into effect. His first step was to flood the area around the castle with his *da'is* so that the local population could be converted to the Isma'ili cause. The Seldjuk vizier, that same Nizam al-Mulk who the storytellers would have us believe shared a classroom with Hasan, was by now thoroughly alerted to the danger posed by him, and sent out orders for his arrest. But Hasan just disappeared from the scene, as if he had melted away, and journeyed to the neighbourhood of Alamut unseen, evading all attempts to capture him.

The castle of Alamut was held by a man named Mahdi, who had received his appointment from the Seldjuk Sultan of the time, Malikshah. He, it could be assumed, would prove impervious to any attempt by Hasan to persuade him to meekly hand it over. However, one man cannot hold a castle, even Alamut, and Hasan's *da'is* had been busy recruiting members of the garrison to their party. Mahdi realized this but was powerless to do much about it; so, unsure of what his next move should be, he pretended to have come over to the Isma'ilis' side. Hasan's response was to send yet more *da'is* to the area to convert even more of the local population. For their part, the locals were very sympathetic to his cause, both because of the success it appeared to be having and also because they saw it as an attempt to assert the rights of the Persians against what they saw as the invading Turkish forces that were occupying much of their country. Allied to the strong regional affiliation with the Shiite Muslim party generally, a powerful groundswell of popular support for Hasan was started which generated a momentum of its own.

Hasan imported Isma'ilis from other parts of Persia into the area, tipping the balance yet more in his favour. Then, on 4 September 1090, a stranger was escorted secretly into the castle of Alamut and assumed a life within its walls, attracting little attention from most of the people living alongside him. He called himself Dihkhuda. Eventually, one day, an awful realization dawned upon Mahdi. Suddenly, it became clear to him who this stranger was. It was Hasan-i Sabbah.

Seeing that a man who was potentially a very dangerous enemy was now inside the castle, Mahdi looked around to his garrison for help, but it was a vain hope. So many of them had surreptitiously become Isma'ilis that there were hardly any left to defend the castle who were not sympathetic to Hasan's cause. Seeing that there was little more he could do, Mahdi gave up any attempt at resistance and handed Alamut over to Hasan. Thus the impregnable rock had fallen without a blow being struck. The picture painted of Hasan's movement by later historians would suggest that Mahdi might expect to suffer the most dreadful of deaths, but this was not in fact the case. Mahdi was allowed to leave in peace. He took with him a signed warrant declaring that Hasan guaranteed to pay him the sizeable sum of 3,000 gold dinars in return for the castle. Mahdi was presumably shaken to the core when the money was subsequently paid over as promised.[7]

It was an amazing start to Hasan's campaign of resistance towards the Seldjuks, and it heralded a change in Isma'ili policy in Persia. Up until now, this had been underground and clandestine but the spectacular capture of Alamut gave the Isma'ilis in the region the self-belief to indulge in open warfare with the Seldjuks. But Hasan realized well enough that a strong reaction from the Turks was to be expected. He quickly threw his energies into the task of strengthening the castle, building up the walls (which had suffered much from an extended period of neglect) and, most importantly, reviewing its water supply. Aware that he needed to live off the land in the immediate vicinity he also introduced advanced irrigation systems into the valley to maximize its yield, as well as planting many trees.[8] He then sought to create a protective outer ring around Alamut. He captured other castles on some of the high peaks in the region around the castle and built new ones on other virtually inaccessible summits. There was a pattern in his choice of sites; always high, imposing, remote, each capable of resisting for a significant length of time even when faced with a much stronger foe. He also at the same time continued his mission to convert new recruits to the Isma'ili cause with some success, adding further strength to his position.

His enemies accused him of adopting a variety of tactics, saying that 'he won them [the people] over by the tricks of his propaganda while such places as were unaffected by his blandishments he seized with slaughter, ravishment, bloodshed and war'.[9] They, especially the Seldjuks, were clearly perturbed at his initial successes. When the inevitable backlash arrived, it was to be a forceful one. The Seldjuk lord who had been given the region as his fief, a man named Yurun Tash, gathered together a large force to attack Alamut. He raided the area round the castle right up to the base of the rock on which it stood, massacring large numbers of Isma'ilis indiscriminately in the process. Hasan's efforts to provide adequate supplies for the castle had not yet had time to bear fruit and the garrison very quickly found itself faced with starvation. Many of them wanted to surrender and throw themselves on the dubious mercy of Yurun Tash. However, Hasan inspired them to greater efforts. He told them that the Fatimid caliph, al-Mustansir, had told them to be in good heart as Alamut was a place of good fortune. They were moved by his oratory, and the castle held out. From that day forward, Alamut was often called '*baldat al-iqbal*' – 'the place of good fortune'.

The revolt spread. It was particularly successful in the region of Quhistan, on the borders of modern day Iran and Afghanistan. The population here was remote, centred around a series of oases in the middle of a great salt desert. Its bleak position had always made it an independent land, populated by a proud and fierce-spirited people. It was ruled at this time by a domineering and aggressive Seldjuk lord. Inspired by Hasan's *da'i*, a very capable individual by the name of Husayn Qa-ini, the whole region, goaded by the severity of Seldjuk rule, erupted. Always susceptible to esoteric religions (the area had been steeped in Zoroastrianism before it had proved a successful recruiting ground for Shiite missionaries), Quhistan exploded in an outpouring of rage directed at the Turks occupying the land.

It met with astounding success. Completely thrown off guard by this turn of events, in some areas of Persia the Seldjuk yoke was thrown off. A new Isma'ili state had been born.

Hasan had tapped into deeply-rooted feelings among the people of Persia against the Turks. Some of these animosities were religious but others were social and nationalistic. Nizari policy matched the aspirations of the disadvantaged classes splendidly. Some of the approaches adopted seem almost modern in their egalitarianism. There were to be no social ranks within the Nizari hierarchy: members of the community were simply to refer to themselves as comrades ('*rafiq*'). Leaders would be appointed on merit rather than social status – Hasan's eventual successor Kiya Buzurg-Ummid was just one example of an eminent Nizari who came from a relatively humble background. The movement took great pride in communal projects, which reflected well on the collective and co-operative efforts of the wider community rather than the gloriifcation of individuals. It was also an openly Persian movement, which appealed to proud nationalistic emotions in the region. Hasan used Persian rather than Arabic as the religious language of the movement, a significant departure from previous precedent. As a result, there was a great deal of support for the Nizaris as a wide cross-section of people, burdened by onerous Seldjuk taxation and angered by the oppression of alien and loosely-disciplined overlords, threw in their lot with Hasan and his movement – including, it must be emphasised, a number who were not actually Shiites.

It remained to be seen whether these first successes could be sustained, however. Significant though the early results had been, the Seldjuks were still a powerful enemy, temporarily bested certainly but possessed of large resources of manpower with which to fight back. When the sultan Malikshah heard of the setbacks that had been suffered by his followers, he despatched a sizeable army to Alamut itself. Arriving there in 1092, he found Hasan's garrison in a parlous state. Hasan had only seventy men available to him, and he was still desperately short of provisions. The cause seemed hopeless and frantic messages were despatched to *dā'is* in the surrounding areas begging them to send help as a matter of urgency. A small party of 300 reinforcements eventually broke through the Seldjuk lines and made their way into the castle. Co-ordinating its attacks with supporters from the local population around Alamut, a sortie was launched from the castle in October 1092. Caught off guard, the vastly superior Turkish army was over run and had to withdraw. The Nizaris were in no doubt of the reason for their success, believing that 'by divine preparation the [Seldjuk] army was put to flight and, leaving Alamut, returned to Malikshah'.[10]

These defensive actions were heroic efforts on the part of the Isma'ilis but they were fought in desperate circumstances. Heavily outnumbered and unable to use their unorthodox tactics in the lowland regions of Persia, a different approach was needed if the Isma'ilis were to advance their cause still further. They were helped by the fact that the Turkish hold on the region was still extremely insecure. The Turks were far from united among their own ranks. Individual warlords held little more than nominal allegiance to Malikshah and routinely acted independently in their own best interests. And many areas were still seething with discontent, sometimes manifesting itself in open revolt. These factors combined made for a region that was deeply fragmented, with power essentially decentralized. Local lords were very powerful, and great disruption would ensue if some of these influential individuals were to be eliminated.

As a result of this inherent weakness in the Seldjuk situation, a dramatic new policy was about to be adopted. There was a small town near Rayy called Sava. An Isma'ili community was present there. A group of them held a prayer meeting, which was broken up by the Seldjuk authorities. This group then attempted to convert a local muezzin, who however refused to listen to their arguments. Afraid that he would tell the authorities of their actions, they turned on him and murdered him. The murderer, a man named Tahir, was brutally executed and his body dragged through the marketplace at Sava. It was the first act of a drama, characterized by intrigue and murder, that would be played out for another 200 years.

The timing of this act is unclear; it perhaps happened even before Hasan captured Alamut and reflects more of a panicked response to a situation than a planned assassination. However, there is much greater certainty about the dramatic act that was soon to follow. Nizam al-Mulk was an avowed enemy of Hasan and, in many ways, was the real power behind the Seldjuks. He was also a fierce critic of the Isma'ilis, seeing them as little more than heretics and saying of them that: 'never has there been a more sinister, more perverted or iniquitous crowd than these people, who behind walls are plotting harm to this country and seeking to destroy the religion . . .'[11]

He was, in Hasan's eyes, a marked man. Rashid al-Din, in a statement eerily reminiscent of King Henry II of England's outburst against Thomas à Beckett a century later, says that: 'with the jugglery of deceit and the trickery of untruth, with guileful preparations and specious obfuscations, he laid the foundations of the *fida'is* ['devotees'] and he [Hasan] said; 'who of you will rid this state of the evil of Nizam al-Mulk Tusi?'.[12]

Nizam al-Mulk accompanied Malikshah on a progress through western Persia. While he was there, on 16 October 1092, a stranger, a man named Bu Tahir Arrani, approached his litter as it was being carried from his audience chamber to his harem. Without warning and oblivious to the guards at Nizam's side, Bu Tahir Arrani jumped on him and plunged a sharp dagger deep into his body, striking him dead. The assassin had been specially chosen for the mission, the first *fida'i* to risk his life in the cause of Hasan and his movement. Many more would follow.[13]

It was indeed the actions of these *fida'is* in the future ('Assassins' as they would eventually become known to the West) for which Hasan's supporters were to become notorious. Assassination was not a new tactic, indeed the murder of one's enemies to obtain a political advantage is a crime almost as old as man himself. It had indeed been present in Islam right from its very beginnings.[14] But what differentiated Hasan's followers from many of those who went before was the way that the tactic became one of their core policies.

This derived largely from their relative weakness vis-à-vis the Seldjuk 'occupation forces', as the Isma'ilis would have seen them. It was not a unique tactic for a vastly outnumbered movement to employ but it was fraught with dangers as time would amply demonstrate. Although the elimination of political leaders could indeed sow seeds of confusion and doubt in the minds of the enemy, other passions would also be released as a result of their deaths. Not least of these was a sense of outrage, usually manifesting itself as a blind thirst for revenge. When such emotions were released, then any Isma'ili supporter, however humble or passive, would become a valid target for vengeance. Because of the policy of assassination, many Isma'ilis would lose their lives in violent reprisals. As one modern commentator noted, 'the ruthlessness of the policy [of assassination] was reflected in the ruthlessness of the Sunni response – the Nizaris were feared and detested as few other heretics have been'.[15]

Heretics to their enemies, these *fida'is* were martyrs to their comrades. Many of the assassinations that took place over the next two centuries were carried out in a very public manner. This meant that there was often little chance that the assassins themselves would escape with their lives, and they were therefore effectively undertaking suicide missions. But they undertook this risk gladly. Such devotion was incomprehensible to many of their enemies. Men, particularly from the West, would speculate in all kinds of strange ways about the motivations of the killers, suggesting that they were either literally out of their minds because of the use of hallucinogenic drugs or that they had been duped by their master by some kind of fabricated vision of paradise.

We will consider these fantastic tales at length at a later point,[16] but for now it is perhaps best simply to say that the killers did think that they were undertaking an act which would increase their chances of spiritual benefits in the world that was to come. They therefore went gladly to their fate (although they did on occasion escape, suggesting that a few at least were not necessarily just content to die without a fight after they had completed their mission) and were in their turn greatly respected by their fellow Isma'ilis. Indeed, there would be a roll of honour maintained at Alamut listing the names of those who had taken part in missions as well as their victims.

After the death of Nizam al-Mulk, which was a significant blow against the stability of the Seldjuk territories in the Middle East, the situation deteriorated still more for the Turks with the death of the Sultan Malikshah in that same year, 1092. This led to a complete abandonment of all immediate plans to assault Alamut. Still worse for the Seldjuks, a bitter civil war broke out among the Turks. The succession to Malikshah was disputed, and all efforts to win back the lost territories in Quhistan was given up for the time being. One of the major difficulties for the Turks was that tribesmen usually owed their loyalties to the person of their Sultan and, as a result, if he should die, then their ties of allegiance would die with him. Such was the case now. Malikshah's oldest son, a man named Barkiyaruq, claimed the succession but the right to rule had already been granted to a much younger son, a four-year-old named Mahmud.

Not unnaturally, Barkiyaruq resisted Mahmud's coup, and it perhaps had been a very dangerous move to award the Sultanate to one so young, who would clearly be dominated by advisers who would virtually rule the country in his stead. The party of the murdered Nizam al-Mulk threw in their lot with Barkiyaruq, who was marched to Rayy and placed on the throne. As it happened, Mahmud died in 1094, but this did not end the troubles. New claimants to the throne emerged, and open hostility broke out between the various factions of the Turks. The war that followed was to last for a decade.

It appeared to be a golden opportunity for the Isma'ilis. They had already made great progress in their revolt against the Turks, and many gains had been made. Already a form of Isma'ili state had been established, which, although still vulnerable, had resisted concerted initial attempts by the Seldjuks to recover all their lost territories. Encouraged by this, new converts were continuing to join their cause. And now the Seldjuks were at each other's throats, a condition that could not but reduce the effectiveness of their counter-attacks against the Isma'ilis. Indeed, the next few years were to see yet more successes for the nascent Isma'ili state.

These encouraging developments however would be overshadowed by an event of the greatest significance. The Isma'ilis in Persia still recognized al-Mustansir in Egypt as their rightful Imam, the spiritual leader of their faith. But the caliph was old, and had not long to live. Following his death in 1094, there would be developments within Egypt which would split the Isma'ili movement again. Ever since its birth, Islam had been riven with fragmentation as one movement after another declared their independence from other branches of the faith. Another division was about to occur which would threaten to stop the Isma'ili advances in Persia dead in their tracks. None of this however could overshadow the achievement of Hasan-i Sabbah, who had delivered the most incredible of results and shown himself to be a strong warrior, a master strategist and, above all, a leader of outstanding vision. All these skills would be needed in abundance in the difficult times that lay ahead.

FOUR

The Division

The latter part of the eleventh century had amply demonstrated that the Fatimid Empire had lost much of its earlier vitality. The avowed objective of the Fatimids to rule the entire Muslim world had been fatally compromised by the incursions of the Sunni Turks. It was not only externally that Egypt was weak however. There were many internal pressures within the country itself which threatened to further hamper the Fatimids in their bid to be the dominant power in Islam. The Caliph al-Mustansir was the longest reigning Fatimid caliph, holding power for nearly sixty years from his accession in 1036. Throughout this time he was the figurehead of the Isma'ili movement, recognized by both Egypt and the Isma'ili communities further east as the Imam of the party. But, the longer his reign went on, the more it lost its vitality, with very damaging effects on the viability of the Fatimid dynasty in the longer term.

The status of the Imam was vital to the Isma'ilis. Following the death of Muhammad, the Imams were, to the Shiites, responsible for spiritual leadership of the movement. When the Imam arbitrated on matters spiritual, he was infallible. Since the foundation of the Fatimid dynasty, he had been both religious and secular head of state. However, just as the Abbasid caliphs in Baghdad had lost much of their power in the Sunni portion of the Islamic world, first ruling by the sufferance of the Buyids and latterly completely reliant on the Seldjuks, so the pre-eminence of the Fatimid caliph in the secular sector of the Shiite territories would come into question.

As al-Mustansir grew older, many believed that the real power in Egypt was increasingly wielded by an Armenian soldier, Badr al-Jamali, the same man whom chroniclers asserted had fallen out with Hasan-i Sabbah when he had visited Egypt. He had started life as a slave but his military talents were noticed, and he eventually rose to be governor of Damascus and then the port of Acre on the Mediterranean coast. By 1073, Seldjuk incursions were already alarming al-Mustansir. To make matters worse, he had many Turkish mercenaries within his own kingdom who effectively held the balance of power in Egypt. Wanting to assert his independence, al-Mustansir secretly sent word to al-Jamali, asking him to journey to Egypt and lead his armies. Al-Jamali agreed to do so, provided that he could bring his own Armenian soldiery with him. Being in no position to argue, the caliph agreed to the request. Al-Jamali arrived unannounced in Cairo, seized and killed many of the Turks who had previously been controlling the country and effectively rescued the Fatimids from ostensibly becoming a mere puppet regime. But soon it became clear that control of the strings had merely been transferred to a new puppet-master.

From that day on until the end of his reign, al-Mustansir was heavily in the debt of al-Jamali, who was clearly the power behind the throne. Matters came to a head in 1094 when both al-Jamali and al-Mustansir died. Al-Jamali was the first to expire, but it made little practical difference to affairs in Egypt as his son, al-Afdal, succeeded him as vizier (a position that al-Jamali had previously held, under the auspices of which he was effectively commander of the army, as well as being head of many secular institutions and even some religious ones).

When al-Mustansir died towards the end of that year, al-Afdal quickly moved to ensure that his chosen candidate as successor was installed. The title of caliph had been expected to be handed down to al-Mustansir's eldest son, Nizar, who was an experienced man of about fifty years of age. However, the youngest son of the late caliph, one Abu'l-Qasim Ahmad, was already married to al-Afdal's sister. Further, being only twenty years old, he would be a much more pliable figure that the vastly more experienced Nizar. Al-Afdal was quick to stage a coup that placed Ahmad on the caliph's throne. The day after al-Mustansir died, Ahmad was proclaimed caliph. The members of the court at Cairo were by and large persuaded to fall in with the coup, and Ahmad was duly made caliph, taking the title of al-Mustali billah. His supporters subsequently became known as Mustalian Isma'ilis.

Naturally Nizar was not prepared to stand meekly by and let his inheritance slip away unchallenged. There was little doubt that he had at one time been the legitimate successor to the late caliph; even later opponents of the Nizaris would admit that Nizar was originally designated to succeed by al-Mustansir himself. When he received news that he had been robbed of the prize for which he had worked and hoped for so long he sprung into action. Despite some half-hearted attempts at propaganda on the part of the Mustalians who stated that al-Mustansir had named al-Mustali his successor on his deathbed, few were in fact convinced that he had had such a change of heart.

Such a story was altogether too convenient. Nizar fled as fast as he could to the great port of Alexandria accompanied by a few supporters. Here he declared that al-Mustali's claim was lacking in any legal or moral substance, and declared open rebellion against the new regime. Within the city, many had suffered at the hands of al-Jamali, and the late vizier's son and successor, al-Afdal, consequently had many enemies within its walls. There was therefore a good deal of support for Nizar. Nizar was delighted at this turn of events, and his joy was further increased when an army sent from Cairo to crush his rebellion was easily repulsed. He then launched an attack of his own, managing to lead an army right up to the edge of Cairo. But this was the high-water mark of his efforts and a counter-attack was initiated by al-Mustali and al-Afdal. Eventually, holed up in Alexandria and with no hope of escape, Nizar surrendered. He was taken to Cairo where shortly afterwards he was killed.

The elimination of Nizar in 1095 was to have repercussions far beyond the boundaries of Egypt. The murder of a man who many Isma'ilis saw as the legitimate Imam was an act that sent shockwaves across the Isma'ili world. Given the status of the Imam as God's proof ('*hujja*') on earth, it seemed to many of them to be a crime of the greatest magnitude. Persia had always been a part of the Isma'ili world with an independent spirit. This independence of mind and will now showed itself more clearly then ever. Large numbers of Isma'ilis in Persia and elsewhere refused to accept the coup, and regarded Nizar as a martyr. The new regime was regarded with disdain by these groups. In the absence of any obvious successor to Nizar's claims to the Fatimid caliphate, however, Persia looked for a new leader of what were to be known from now on as the Nizari Isma'ilis. Given Hasan-i Sabbah's successes to date, there was little doubt about the individual to whom the dissident Isma'ilis would look for such leadership.

The coup that brought al-Mustali power created a permanent schism within Isma'ilism. Most of Egypt eventually accepted his position as Imam (there was some resistance in the country initially but it was quickly and brutally suppressed), as did the community in Yemen, as well as the enclave that had been formed far away in India. But Persia and many of the other eastern territories refused to accept him. There was also a problem in Syria, which became something of a fault line within the Islamic world, where there was a significant party which refused to go along with the usurpation of the Imamate, something which was to create a vacuum which the Nizaris from Persia would be quick to exploit. Hasan-i Sabbah was accepted as leader of the Nizaris in the country. However, as a devout and sincere devotee of his religion, he did not appear to see his role as an opportunity for self-aggrandisement. Never once did he claim to be the Imam himself, though with his success and charisma he could surely have done so if he wished. He would accept no more that being recognized as the legitimate representative of the Imam while the latter was *in absentio*.

But the absence of a recognized living Imam to take Nizar's place did create problems. It was unfortunate that Nizar had omitted to recognize a successor before he was murdered, despite the fact that he left sons behind him. Some of these sons, several of whom resided in the Maghrib, would in fact launch revolts against the Mustalians in Egypt (a grandson would be involved in one as late as 1161) – but the lack of a clearly identified successor to Nizar weakened the Nizari cause, as it inevitably created a degree of uncertainty within the Nizari community which lessened their unity. It has been pointed out that many of the coins issued by the Nizaris after the death of Nizar did not name any successor to him, but continued merely to mention the name of Nizar himself, even half a century later.[1] This uncertainty was an unsatisfactory state of affairs and eventually a legend was developed that asserted that a grandson of Nizar had been taken from Egypt secretly and smuggled away to Alamut. However, stories which showed a line of descent for the Imamate after the death of Nizar were a long time coming, and owed more to a wish to provide a focal point for the Nizaris to rally around than any historical evidence. In the end, neither Hasan nor his two immediate successors at Alamut would name any Imams after the demise of Nizar.

Despite the tensions created by the usurpation of authority by al-Mustali, the revolt in Persia against the Turks continued with fervour. It met with some success. The Nizaris were helped as ever by the dissension among the Turks themselves, which inevitably weakened the effectiveness of the Seldjuks. The truth of the situation was that a united Seldjuk response would have been very difficult for the fledgling Nizari movement to resist but the bitter infighting of the former meant that the latter continued to thrive.

And the Seldjuks were in fact as divided as ever. Following the death of the young Mahmud in 1094, the same year as the demise of al-Mustansir, Barkiyaruq was recognized as the legitimate Sultan by the caliph in Baghdad. Despite the weakness of the caliph, his recognition was still an important gesture to the Seldjuks and Barkiyaruq may have hoped that this politically important sponsorship would cement his position. If he did indeed believe this, he was to be desperately disappointed.

Resistance to Barkiyaruq came from within his own family, as if to emphasize the disunity of the Seldjuks. His uncle Tutush began a campaign to dislodge him, though this was short-lived as he was killed in battle at Rayy in 1095. His half-brother Muhammad Tapar also attempted to dislodge him. This was to lead to a string of indecisive engagements, which was of course the worst possible outcome for the Seldjuks because, if one man had emerged decisively victorious, the tribes could have united around him. In reality, the Seldjuks were always a strongly independent group but they had in the past been held together in a loose fashion by a powerful and successful leader, which was what they needed now. But the war did not lead to a decisive outcome. In-fighting would continue right up to the death of Barkiyaruq in 1105, a position that was encouraged by the declaration of support by the regions of Khurasan and Tukharistan in 1097 for Muhammad Tapar (they were at the time ruled by his brother, Sanjar).

The Persian Isma'ilis took good advantage of this unhealthy situation. Their fighting prowess was so well recognized that Barkiyaruq eventually began to recruit some into his forces, on one occasion admitting 5,000 of them into his army. This was not a permanent situation (Barkiyaruq would soon turn on the Isma'ilis and would persecute them cruelly later in his reign) but served again to emphasize the confusion that existed within Seldjuk ranks. The Nizaris in Persia however continued with the policies that had brought them such success before the schism with Egypt. Prominent among these was of course the capture of isolated and powerful fortresses from which they could threaten the surrounding Seldjuk lands and continue to harass the Sunni enemy, striking at isolated groups of Seldjuks and then retreating behind those largely impenetrable walls when a counter-attack was launched.

One of the most important developments was the seizure in 1096 of a prominent fortress in the north-east of Persia. It dominated lines of communication from the region eastwards to Khurasan, and its capture enabled the Nizaris to threaten the Seldjuks in the region more successfully than ever. This fortress stood on a great shark's tooth of a rock, pointing jaggedly up into the sky and seeming to pierce the clouds themselves. Its rocky crags were so sharp that they seemed from a distance to be razor-thin. Its name was Girdkuh.

As with Alamut, this unassailable rock was taken not by force of arms but by subterfuge. The great *da'i* ibn Attash had converted a prominent man named Ra'is Mu'ayyad al-Din Muzaffar secretly to the Isma'ili cause. Muzaffar had many influential friends among the Seldjuk hierarchy, and he persuaded one of them, an emir named Amirdad Habashi, to seek to obtain Girdkuh from Barkiyaruq for himself. When the emir successfully obtained this gift, Muzaffar then persuaded him to hand it over to him for safekeeping. Gullibly, the emir happily assented to the request. The castle was under the control of a Seldjuk garrison when these events took place and their commander had no desire to hand the castle over but faced with the express orders of Amirdad Habashi there was little he could do. Girdkuh was therefore given over to the Isma'ilis without a single blow being struck, giving the Nizaris an isolated base away from Daylam and Quhistan.

It was of course not until Muzaffar was safely installed inside Girdkuh that his true religious affinities became apparent, and even then he managed to keep his loyalties hidden for years. In common with many other fortresses in such extreme positions, Girdkuh had many problems of supply to cope with, and Muzaffar threw himself into addressing these difficulties with great energy though limited success. The major difficulty was to find a source of fresh water for the castle. Muzaffar, who at this stage was still claiming to be a loyal Seldjuk supporter, dug a well deep into the rock but he failed to find water.[2] While Barkiyaruq was still showing signs of desiring accommodation with the Isma'ilis and accepting numbers of them into his armies, Muzaffar was happy enough to keep his Isma'ili leanings hidden.

However, come the latter years of Barkiyaruq's rule and his persecution of the Isma'ilis, such a course of action was no longer tenable. The death of his patron Amirdad Habashi in battle further exposed Muzaffar's position. He was able to smuggle a good deal of Habashi's treasure into the castle, much of which he used to finance a major restrengthening of the defences. Shortly after this was completed, he threw off his pretence of loyalty to the Seldjuk cause and openly declared himself an Isma'ili. He accepted the leadership of Hasan with enthusiasm – a state of affairs that presumably infuriated Barkiyaruq who must have been livid that he had been duped into handing such an immensely powerful fortress over to the Isma'ilis. When Muzaffar eventually died, his place was taken by his son, Sharaf al-Din Muhammad. Significantly, he had spent some of his earlier formative years at Alamut.

Other successes followed elsewhere. One of the great cities of Persia was Isfahan. Close by the city walls there was a fortress known as Shahdiz. Situated on a hill, it was in an ideal position to threaten the approaches to the city, and its capture would be a great coup for the Isma'ilis. Its importance to the Seldjuks is best evidenced by the fact that the castle had recently been strengthened by the great Sultan, Malikshah. The city had long held a sizeable Isma'ili element within its walls (proving among other things that it would be wrong to assume that the Nizaris were solely a force in the countryside); it was from here that ibn Attash had operated for much of its career. There were therefore a good number of sympathisers within the population. Ibn Attash had been forced to flee when his status had become known but in the confusion caused by the civil war between the Seldjuks, another attempt to win the city over to the Isma'ili cause was launched.

It was a hard-fought and not very subtle campaign, characterized by violence and intimidation. The Isma'ilis overplayed their hand and the populace, infuriated by the brutality that they had demonstrated, turned on them and massacred many of their supporters in the street. In some sources, it was claimed that the city's inhabitants had been infuriated by reports that an Isma'ili couple had been luring passers-by in to their house from off the street and promptly murdering them. The fact that such lurid tales could be believed perhaps offers some insight into the psychological terror that the Nizari Isma'ilis created in the minds of their enemies even in the early stages of their history. Enraged by these stories, the population grabbed hold of any Isma'ili that they could find and threw them all into a great bonfire that they erected in the middle of the town.[3]

But the Isma'ilis were resilient and they were not daunted by this reverse. When ibn Attash had been forced to flee from Isfahan his son, Ahmad, had been allowed to stay behind.[4] The authorities in Isfahan believed that he did not share his father's religious leanings. It transpired that this was a very cavalier attitude on their part, as Ahmad was actually a staunch Isma'ili; a fact that makes one ponder over the laxity of those in positions of power within the Seldjuk hierarchy at the time. Ahmad managed to obtain a position as a teacher for the garrison within the castle of Shahdiz. Significantly, much of the garrison originated from the region of Daylam, that is to say the area around Alamut, the nerve centre of the Isma'ili movement within Persia. Again, this should have alerted those in authority to the fact that, given the actions of Isma'ilis elsewhere within Persia, they were fair game for any Isma'ili who wished to trick their way into a position where they could obtain important fortresses by subterfuge.

Such was indeed the case within Shahdiz. Once he had manoeuvred his way into the castle, Ahmad started to work on the garrison. For their part, perhaps having a natural sympathy with the Isma'ilis due to their regional antecedents, the men of the garrison were willing listeners. Before he had woken up to the reality that Ahmad, the mild, unassuming schoolteacher, was in fact a dangerous revolutionary, the commander of the garrison found that he was no longer in control of the fortress. Shahdiz was taken by Ahmad for the Nizaris. Thus once more an important fortress had been won for the Isma'ilis without a blow being struck.[5] The capture of Shahdiz (which took place in about 1100) was a great blow for the Isma'ilis and against the Seldjuks. So complete was Isma'ili control of Shahdiz and the surrounding territory that they began to collect taxes from the local populace, which hit the Seldjuk treasury in the region hard.[6]

A similar coup followed. There was another castle close by Isfahan, some 20 miles distant, at a place called Khalinjan. This was also taken by the Isma'ilis, again seemingly without a fight. Some prosaic versions of its capture say that it was merely handed over, but in a more romantic description of its capture it was claimed that a carpenter had managed to ingratiate his way into the affections of the commander. According to these more exotic tales, the carpenter, once inside the castle, proceeded to treat the garrison to a party and, when they were intoxicated and incapable of any sort of resistance, the gates were opened to a group of Isma'ilis waiting outside to take possession.

Alongside this military activity, characterized more by subtle intrigues than large pitched battles, the Nizari Isma'ilis were to continue to practice the art for which the West would later christen them the 'Assassins'. Important personages within the Seldjuk hierarchy, and even leading religious figures within the Sunni community, were all legitimate targets for the knives of Shiite assassins. It is however important to keep these killings in perspective; they were an important strand of Isma'ili policy but they were far from the only one. During the reign of Hasan-i Sabbah, which lasted for approximately thirty years, the roll of honour within Alamut records about 50 assassinations. About half of them occurred during the closing years of the eleventh century. Therefore, they were by no means a frequent occurrence.

But we can still discern, albeit in a sometimes obscure way, some interesting features. Barkiyaruq's war against his half-brother, Muhammad Tapar, increased in intensity. As we have already seen, the Sultan employed Isma'ilis in his armies at this time. It appears however that he also used them in a more clandestine way. Rumours spread that some of the victims of Isma'ili assassins were friends of Muhammad Tapar and had in fact been eliminated as the result of an agreement between the Isma'ilis and Barkiyaruq. It will perhaps never be known for certain whether there are any grains of truth in these tales but we should note that throughout the life of the Nizari Isma'ili movement there were frequent claims that they had offered their services to allies from some unlikely quarters in return for help and assistance. It certainly became clear as time passed that the Isma'ilis were active on all fronts, including diplomatic and political, and were far removed from the image of fanatics inflexibly wedded to their cause and its principles that has sometimes been current.

Despite these successes all over Persia, the epicentre of the Nizari Isma'ili movement in the country remained at Alamut and the surrounding region of Daylam. It is important to remember that the Nizaris did have successes in the towns as well as the countryside. There was after all social unrest and disaffection in the former as well as the latter. But it was in remote rural areas that the Nizaris found their greatest security and these were consequently vital to their survival. Aware that the current divisions within the Seldjuks might not last for ever, Hasan-i Sabbah took advantage of the opportunity offered by the civil war to devote many of his energies to building up his strength in Daylam. Work on Alamut itself continued apace; as well as adding to the castle itself, he also worked on the adjacent countryside. Wishing to ensure the self-sufficiency of the castle, the irrigation system in the vicinity was further improved. More crops were grown as a result, and the region became something of a fertile oasis amidst the general aridity of the surrounding area.

Hasan also concentrated on building up a ring of outer defences to protect the approaches to Alamut. This was an important part of his strategy. The existence of such a ring of castles posed a major problem to any would-be invader who attempted to attack Alamut. The commander of an invading army was faced with a real conundrum. On the one hand, he could attempt to lay siege to the castles that protected the outer perimeter of Alamut's defences. Given their inaccessibility however this could take months, even years, for each castle.

It was even difficult to starve out the garrison – an important tactic in medieval siege warfare – as Hasan's attempts to provide the garrisons with adequate provisions to be self-sufficient meant that this might take an inordinately long time to accomplish. The commander of the invading force could of course choose to leave behind a force to lay siege to the castle while the rest of his force moved on, but this might weaken his main army as well as leaving the besieging army liable to counter-attack. And, although the areas around the castles were often made fertile to feed the garrison, if the defenders had received sufficient warning about the arrival of the invasion force then they would take all the provisions from the area surrounding the castle that they could carry with them and destroy the rest. On the other hand, leaving the castle intact without a besieging force to keep an eye on them left the lines of communication of the invaders dangerously exposed and also left the Nizaris with a base from which to continue their campaign to take advantage of social and religious discontent. In short, the presence of an outer perimeter of fortifications caused a major headache for enemy commanders.

To the west of Alamut stood the fortress of Lamasar. Its capture would be a useful addition to the defences of Alamut, as it guarded the western approaches to the castle. It had indeed already once been held by the Isma'ilis. Its commander was a man named Rasamuj but, after initially siding with the Isma'ilis, he had changed his allegiance and wanted to throw in his lot with the Seldjuks instead. Hasan-i Sabbah therefore sent a force under the command of a man named Buzurg-Ummid to retake the castle.[7] Buzurg-Ummid would play a large role in the future of the Nizari Isma'ilis in Persia as he would eventually succeed Hasan-i Sabbah when he died some years later.

This time there was no alternative to an all-out assault, which was duly launched. The castle fell; and, after its capture, Buzurg-Ummid followed the example of Hasan, making great efforts to improve the logistical position of the castle by building new water cisterns as well as constructing many substantial buildings and attempting to make the surrounding area more fertile. Buzurg-Ummid remained there for many years until he was eventually summoned to Alamut to take the place of Hasan-i Sabbah. After Alamut, the castle at Lamasar became the most important fortress held by the Isma'ilis in the Daylam region, the core of the Nizari Isma'ili movement in Persia.

These early successes emboldened the Nizaris, who became ever more confident in their ability to overthrow the Seldjuks and consequently more ambitious in the scale and objectives of their operations. They launched a series of attacks in south-west Persia under the leadership of Abu Hamza. Like Hasan-i Sabbah he had also spent some time in Egypt, which had presumably fired him up with a passionate zeal to extend the Isma'ili *da'wa* in Persia. He seized several important castles near the town of Arrajan in the region, and proceeded to harass and annoy the Seldjuks in the vicinity from these newly acquired bases.

The success of the Ism'aili revolt led to some surprising developments. Several Seldjuk notables in Persia were persuaded by their victories to convert to the Isma'ili cause, no doubt to the distaste of many Sunni

Muslims. In 1095, one local vizier handed over the fortress of Takrit to the possession of an Isma'ili, Kayqubid Daylami. This was an unusual development because the fortification was not in a mountainous position but rather in the middle of open country. The Isma'ilis managed to hold on to this for twelve years though it did little good to the vizier, who was murdered by his own people when they discovered what he had done.

As has been noted, Barkiyaruq was for a time prepared to tolerate, even to encourage, the Isma'ilis. This could only remain so however while their power was still limited. By 1100 their status had grown so much that many within Barkiyaruq's own court were alarmed at the danger they perceived from this quarter. This was partly because of the increased self-belief of the Isma'ilis. Some had even infiltrated their way into Barkiyaruq's own inner circle. Here they began to seek to convert the troops to their cause and, according to their enemies, they threatened any who dared resist them with assassination. It got to the stage that, according to Arab chroniclers, no one in a position of authority dared to leave his quarters unless they wore armour under their clothing. Even the vizier, Abu'l Hasan, felt so threatened that he always wore a mail shirt. By convention, courtiers were not allowed to approach Barkiyaruq if they were armed but 'now they asked for permission to appear before him armed, for fear of attack, and he granted them permission'.[8]

By this time, Muhammad Tapar had been defeated and Barkiyaruq was therefore relatively free to turn his attentions towards the Isma'ilis. The ruler of the region of Khurasan was Muhammad Tapar's younger brother, Sanjar. Barkiyaruq approached him for an alliance against the Isma'ilis arguing that in them both men had a common enemy. It was manifestly the case that each of them was threatened by the success of the Isma'ilis. Sanjar saw the sense in the proposed alliance and launched a fierce attack on the region of Quhistan. His men devastated the countryside and laid siege to the chief Isma'ili stronghold in the region at Tabas. His forces were well provided with siege engines and his great mangonels – large artillery pieces which hurled huge rocks at the fortifications – soon began to cause great damage to the walls of the city. It appeared to be on the point of surrender when the besieged Isma'ilis literally bought their freedom by bribing the enemy to go away and leave them alone.

This action only brought a short period of respite to the Isma'ilis. They knew that Sanjar was unlikely to leave them undisturbed permanently and they threw their energies into building up the defences of Tabas once more, as well as strengthening other strongpoints in the region. Inevitably, Sanjar did return three years later bringing with him a large force of his own men as well as a number of volunteers. They were obviously more determined on this occasion as Tabas was taken as well as a number of other significant fortresses. However, the terms of the final treaty were still very lenient. Sanjar asked the Isma'ilis to agree to refrain from building any more castles in Quhistan or attempting to convert new recruits. Perhaps surprised at the generosity of these terms, the Isma'ilis duly agreed to them.

Sanjar was much criticised for the perceived weakness he had shown in negotiating with the Isma'ilis. His critics argued that the Isma'ilis could not be relied upon to comply with the terms; in their view only brutal suppression of the sect was likely to be a successful policy. Many Sunni Muslims were violently opposed to the Nizaris, their attitude being well summed up in the following contemporary statement: 'to kill them is more lawful than rainwater. It is the duty of Sultans and Kings to conquer and kill them, and cleanse the surface of the earth from their pollution. It is not right to associate or form friendships with them, nor to eat meat butchered by them, nor to enter into marriage with them. To shed the blood of a heretic is more worthy than to kill seventy Greek infidels'.[9]

The stance of these ferocious critics was in fact in some ways vindicated because the Isma'ilis, left once more to their own devices, soon returned to their old ways and before long they were as strong in Quhistan as ever. But clearly in a comparatively short space of time the Nizaris had already generated a great deal of hatred among their enemies.

Barkiyaruq meanwhile sought for the easiest option to placate the angry officials that surrounded him, many of whom demanded that the Isma'ilis be brought to justice. Rather than embarking on military campaigns against the armed forces of the Isma'ilis, he vented his anger on the largely defenceless Isma'ili civilian populations that were close at hand. A pogrom was started first of all in Isfahan in 1101. Known sympathisers of the Isma'ilis were rounded up and herded to the square in the middle of the city. Neighbours were encouraged to point out any that they suspected of being Isma'ilis in their immediate vicinity. Many took advantage of the opportunity to settle old scores by disclosing their suspicions concerning their fellows, however weakly founded. Once all the Isma'ilis that could be found had been dragged to the square, an orgy of killing began. At the end of it all, the square was awash with blood.

Terrible punishment was also meted out to Isma'ilis elsewhere. In Baghdad, scores were massacred by the Seldjuks. Among their number was one of the major figures among the Nizari Isma'ilis at that time, a man named Abu Ibrahim Asadabadi. He had actually been sent to Baghdad on an official mission by Barkiyaruq himself. When he arrived, it was to find that Barkiyaruq had sent word ahead that he was now to be seized and butchered along with the other Isma'ilis in the city. As he faced death, in a city that was acrid with smoke from the bonfires on which Isma'ili holy books were now being burned, he looked his would-be killers straight in the eye. Before they martyred him, he eyed them disdainfully and proudly challenged them by saying 'Very well, you will kill me. What will you do with those that are in the castles?'.[10] A vicious circle of bloodletting had begun.

Asadabadi's heroic last words and his gesture of defiance in the face of imminent death struck home. The Isma'ilis now held so many castles in so many inaccessible places that it would be virtually impossible for any Seldjuk Sultan to dislodge them if he attempted nothing else during his entire lifetime. And the massacres did nothing to diminish the reign of terror now holding sway over Persia and Iraq. Arguably, the ferocity of the Seldjuk backlash only served to enflame Nizari passions still further, encouraging the Nizari assassins to be more determined than ever.

Although leading figures within the Seldjuk establishment were now so closely guarded that it discouraged the Isma'ilis from attempting to assassinate them, it was impractical for every public person to be so well protected that he would at all times feel safe. Soon after the pogrom in Isfahan, a leading Sunni cleric who had been outspoken in his criticism of the sect was stabbed to death in the mosque of the city. Shortly afterwards, the head of a movement known as the Karramiyya, an order that was passionately opposed to the Isma'ilis and all that they stood for, was similarly despatched in the mosque at Nishapur. Such public murders served several purposes for the Ismai'lis. Not only did they remove some bitter opponents of their cause, but the very public actions also reminded the general population that virtually no one was proof against the assassin's knife, especially when the individual wielding it had no particular care whether he lived or died as a result of his actions. Thus the reign of terror remained as vivid a reality as ever.

Barkiyaruq eventually died in 1105. When his reign ended, the Nizari threat was still a significant one. After the initial successes of the revolt its momentum had, it is true, slowed somewhat and some of the early Isma'ili gains had even been reversed. But all over Persia in particular the network of castles established by the Nizaris remained powerful and robust. They were too far dispersed to create a vice-like grip around the Seldjuk centres of power but nevertheless they were sufficiently well placed both to create major disruption along their lines of communication and to act as a springboard from which further revolutionary chaos could be launched. Barkiyaruq's place was taken by Muhammad Tapar, for so long his bitter protagonist in the hard-fought civil war that had been raging for a decade.

With the accession of Muhammad Tapar, the Nizaris may have hoped for time to regroup. They would however gain little respite from the new regime, for: 'when the Sultanate was firmly in [his] hands and no rival remained to dispute [the succession] with him, he had no more urgent task than to seek out and fight the Isma'ilis and to avenge the Muslims for their oppression and misdeeds'.[11]

His immediate priority among these targets was the castle of Shahdiz, the fortress outside of Isfahan that had fallen to the Nizaris a few years previously. Isfahan had been one of the more regular flashpoints for trouble between the Nizaris and the Sunni Seldjuks. Muhammad decided that Shahdiz must be won back from the former whatever the cost. When they became aware that he was headed for the fortress, the Nizaris tried to trick their way out of trouble. The start of the expedition, which took place in 1107, was delayed for five weeks because there had been rumours in the Seldjuk camp of imminent outbreaks of Nizari violence elsewhere; needless to say, such rumours were entirely false and had been spread around the camp by spies.

This tactic could clearly only work for so long and when the Seldjuks at last set off for Isfahan, the Nizaris changed tack. Their leader in the area was still Ahmad, son of ibn Attash. Knowing that he was in a position of military disadvantage, he started a religious debate with the Seldjuk clerics. It was an obvious attempt to prevaricate, in the hope of delaying the imminent assault by sewing confusion in the mind of the movement's enemies. Ahmad argued that the Isma'ili way was in fact the only true path to righteousness as propounded by the Prophet Muhammad. Needless to say, the Seldjuk holy men would not accept this and launched a reply of their own to his arguments. Letters were exchanged backwards and forwards. While this was going on, the military efforts against Shahdiz became desultory in the extreme. Interestingly, it appears that the religious arguments of Ahmad were so subtle that they even caused the Sunnis to argue among themselves. After a time however the contentions espoused by Ahmad were definitively rejected and operations commenced once more.

Seeing that they were so heavily outnumbered that their chances of successfully resisting the Seldjuk assault were very limited, the Nizaris in the fortress attempted to negotiate their freedom. They offered to give up Shahdiz if they were given another fortress further away in exchange. It appears that these approaches were met with some consideration, for Muhammad's vizier actually at one stage sent fresh supplies of food into the garrison so that they would not starve. However, these attempts at conciliation appeared unlikely to succeed once a Nizari assassin had tried, unsuccessfully, to murder one of the leading emirs with the Seldjuk army before the negotiations had been completed. Despite this, it was finally agreed that the garrison would give themselves up. The terms of the deal that was struck meant that most of the garrison would leave and make its way in safety to Alamut. A small garrison would stay behind when they left. Once they had received word that the first party had successfully arrived at Alamut then the second group would give themselves up, and they too would be allowed to travel to Alamut in peace.

Ahmad stayed behind with the small garrison that remained to guard Shahdiz until they knew that the others were safe. Word duly arrived that the first group had made their way to Alamut and had arrived safely. Once this news was received, it soon became clear to the Seldjuks besieging Shahdiz that they had been duped. While hostilities had ceased, Ahmad had taken advantage of the respite to strengthen the battered defences of the castle. He had successfully managed to negotiate the escape of the bulk of the garrison. Now he wished for nothing from the Seldjuks save a fight to the death. In truth, there could only ever be one likely outcome to the forthcoming battle as the odds were hopelessly biased in favour of the besiegers. Nevertheless, it was likely that the defenders would be accompanied by a large number of attackers in their forthcoming journey to paradise given their determination and bravery.

Thus it was that the castle of Shahdiz effectively became the Masada of the Isma'ilis. The Seldjuk assault was pressed home with vigour but it was repulsed. Unfortunately, there was a traitor in the Nizari ranks. He pointed out to the attackers that one of the walls, which looked as if it were heavily manned, was in fact guarded only by dummies. So short of men were the Nizaris (there were now only about 70 defenders left to defend the castle) that they had been forced to place these dummies along the walls to discourage the Seldjuks from attacking. Now that they were aware of this ploy, the Seldjuks attacked the virtually undefended section of wall and quickly broke into the castle.

Once the Seldjuks were inside the walls, the end was certain. Ahmad's wife, seeing that the conclusion of the gallant defence was not far off, dressed herself in her finest clothes and then in a final stylish gesture threw herself to her death on the rocks below. Ahmad however did not follow her example. Presumably he was overwhelmed in the battle that followed; it is inconceivable that he gave himself up voluntarily as he must have known that an awful fate awaited him. At any event, he was taken prisoner. It would have been much, much better for him if he had died in battle for his fate was a horrible one. He was taken to Isfahan and dragged in triumph through the streets of the city. The jeers of his captors, and the blows of the angry populace as he passed by, were nothing compared to the agony that followed. As a dreadful example to all other Nizaris, he was skinned alive. His skin was then stuffed with straw, and his head was sent to Baghdad as a certain sign of the Seldjuk triumph at Shahdiz. It was accompanied by the head of his son, who had also been present at the siege.

The Seldjuks were beside themselves with joy at the death of Ahmad. A letter celebrating this victory was ecstatic at his demise, cursing his activities and those of the movement of which he was a member, saying that his 'reason flew away on the path of error and went astray, and [he] took as his guide a book loaded with lies, and gave licence to shed the blood . . . of Muslims . . . cunningly catching [his] quarry, and killing them with terrible tortures and a dreadful death . . .'[12]

The fall of Shahdiz and the campaign that followed it effectively signalled the end of Nizari power in the region of Isfahan. However, it was clear that the centre of Nizari Isma'ilism was not to be found here but in the remote, mountainous region of Daylam, known to the Nizaris as Rudbar, a name that was derived from the River Shahrud which flowed through the region. An expedition was despatched to the region by Muhammad Tapar. It was led by Ahmad ibn Nizam al-Mulk. As the son of that same Nizam al-Mulk who had been assassinated by Hasan-i Sabbah's henchmen some years earlier, he had good reason to despise the Nizaris. His hatred of them was compounded by the fact that his brother, Fakhr al-Mulk, had fallen to an assassin's knife in Nishapur only a year before the campaign against Alamut was launched in 1108–9. But despite his best efforts, Alamut did not fall. Great hardship was caused by his armies, though. The fertile countryside in the region was stripped bare of provisions, and for a time famine stalked the land. So serious were the food shortages than ensued that it was said that the Nizaris living thereabouts were forced to eat grass to live.

The shortages of food struck the inhabitants of Rudbar hard. So serious was the situation that Hasan-i Sabbah sent his wife and daughters away from Alamut to the relative safety of the great rock of Girdkuh (a measure that was to be copied by a number of Nizari leaders in the future). Ahmad ibn Nizam al-Mulk tried other ways of defeating the Nizaris. He put pressure on local leaders to join him in his fight against them. However, although some sided with him at the outset, their support was neither effective nor for the longer term. They soon withdrew their assistance. Some said that this was because they were infuriated at the arrogance of the Seldjuk Sultan. However, an equally plausible reason is that they were terrified that, the moment their back was turned, an assassin's knife would be thrust deep into it. Even in their moment of greatest crisis, the Nizaris still sent their *fida'is* on missions to eliminate dangerous enemies. One such enemy was the Qadi of Isfahan, a Sunni holy man. He was well aware that he was a potential target for the Nizaris. He was surrounded by a strong bodyguard wherever he went, and he always wore armour whenever he ventured out from his home. One Friday, he made his way as usual to a nearby mosque as was his custom. While in the middle of his prayers, a man rushed forth from the crowd around him and stuck a knife deep into him. It seemed that nobody was safe from these devotees of the Nizari cause who could, it appeared, merge unnoticed into the midst of the local population and then emerge from the shadows when their attack was least expected, usually with fatal results.

When it became clear that Alamut could not be taken by a direct assault, Ahmad ibn Nizam al-Mulk withdrew the bulk of his forces. It seems that the Nizari Isma'ilis were well aware of how dangerous an enemy he was for later, when he had returned to Baghdad, he himself would be attacked by an assassin. Although he survived the attack, it was yet another example of the threat posed to Seldjuk authority by the Nizaris. Muhammad Tapar changed tack. He opted to change his tactics by wearing the Nizaris out in an extended war of attrition. From then on, for a number of years, he regularly sent armies to Rudbar to lay waste the region and attack any Nizari forces that they came across. By this approach, he hoped to exhaust their defensive energies. Finally, in 1117, a very large army was sent, led by the general Nushtigin Shirgir.

For eight years the Sultan, Muhammad Tapar, had tried to grind the Isma'ilis in Rudbar down through this strategy. But he presumably grew tired with his tactics, which were not having the effect desired. So he decided that it was time at last to force the issue to a conclusion. He therefore sent Shirgir into Rudbar, accompanied by a large train of siege engines. Soon, missiles from these were thudding into the thick masonry of castle walls, first at the outlying fortress of Lamasar, then at Alamut itself. The Nizaris were tired and, although their spirit was still willing, their strength was waning fast. It appeared that Alamut was on the point of capture. With it, the Nizari cause in Persia would effectively be dead. And then, at the decisive moment of the campaign, when it appeared that Alamut was about to capitulate, Allah himself intervened. News arrived in Shirgir's camp that the Sultan had died in Isfahan.

The loyalty of a Seldjuk warrior was to the Sultan in person and not the more abstract concept of the Sultanate in general. With the tidings that Muhammad Tapar had died, Shirgir quickly lost interest in the siege. Soon, his army was streaming away, leaving Alamut in peace. To the defenders it must surely have seemed little short of a miracle. It is easy to believe that they convinced themselves that the timing of the Sultan's death was so convenient that it could only have come about because of divine intervention. Allah was surely on their side.

Juwayni was in no doubt that a great prize had been plucked from the Seldjuks' grasp at the eleventh hour. The attack begun in 1117 was launched at a time when 'Hasan and his men were left without strength or food'. The siege had lasted for nearly a year and the Seldjuks 'were on the point of taking the castles and freeing mankind from [the Nizaris'] machinations when they received news that Sultan Muhammad had died in Isfahan. The troops then dispersed, and the Heretics were left alive and dragged up into their castles all the stores, arms and implements of war assembled by the Sultan's army'.[13]

Staring defeat, indeed oblivion, in the face, the Nizari Isma'ilis had survived. Their formative years in Persia had been fraught with danger. After their initial period of success, the inevitable Seldjuk fightback had brought them to the edge of extinction. But they lived to fight another day, weakened but not defeated, chastened but not bowed. The schism within Isma'ilism in the wider sense had itself been the cause of a diminution in the strength of their cause. There were too few Isma'ilis to allow their party to be riven with disunity. Despite their split with the Fatimid dynasty, however, the Isma'ilis in Persia had managed to form a state of their own. It was not the sort of state that most leaders would welcome. It was dispersed over a wide area and it mostly existed because it chose to place its citadels in inaccessible regions that were difficult for their enemies to conquer. It was doomed, because of its inherent weaknesses in the face of the Seldjuk threat, to suffer an existence that meant it would always be on the defensive. But the fact that any kind of state at all had been created was an achievement of which the Nizaris should have been proud.

FIVE

The Legacy of Hasan-I Sabbah

Hasan-i Sabbah led the Nizari Isma'ili movement in Persia for three decades. The strategy whereby his followers seized a string of isolated and largely inaccessible strongpoints across Persia was his. Despite the best efforts of the Sunni Seldjuks his movement was infinitely stronger at his death than it was when he founded it. This was the end result of the strategy that he so carefully crafted. Secure in their mountain fastnesses, the Nizaris would survive the Seldjuk counter-attack. This may have been the limit of his original ambition, although he also would have wished that the foundations that he laid would ultimately lead to something far greater in the longer term. Not for him idealistic but unrealizable dreams of ruling the world. He may have reasoned that, given the righteousness of his cause, in time such a wonderful outcome would be achieved. However, he was enough of a pragmatist to appreciate that this was unlikely to be in his own lifetime. Therefore, his main objective was to leave behind him the foundations of a movement that could look to the future with confidence until perhaps the unlikely dream, the unity of Islam under Isma'ili leadership, was achieved at some point in the years, or maybe even centuries, ahead. This would be his legacy to those who came after him.

Following the timely demise of Muhammad Tapar in 1117, the latter years of Hasan-i Sabbah's life were characterized by a period of relative tranquillity. The death of the Sultan proved to be a double benefit to the Nizaris. Not only did it encourage Shirgir to raise the siege of Alamut when the fortress seemed to be on the brink of capitulation, but a subsequent dispute over the succession was to lead to a violent and divisive confrontation between several of his sons. One of these, Mahmud, was proclaimed Sultan at Isfahan. One of his first acts was to punish Shirgir for failing to subdue Alamut. After the siege had been abandoned, Shirgir's woes were compounded when, during the subsequent retreat, a number of his men were lost. Rumours were rife that the driving force behind the abandonment of the attempt on Alamut was in fact the Seldjuk vizier, Qiwam al-Din al-Dargazini. Gossips asserted that the vizier was yet another secret convert to the Isma'ili cause. It is unclear whether Mahmud himself believed these stories. At any event, when he arrived in Isfahan, Mahmud had Shirgir first arrested and then executed.

This may have been an attempt on the part of Mahmud to strengthen the loyalty of others to his cause, to encourage the others so to speak; at any event, it soon became clear that the new Sultan was in desperate need of trustworthy supporters. He proved incapable of keeping the Seldjuks united, a challenge that was admittedly a formidable one. The region was soon more divided than ever and local leaders asserted ever more vociferously their right to rule independently of centralised control. The western part of Persia effectively became a self-governing region, recognizing its own Sultan. The region accepted the Sultanate, not of Mahmud, but of several of his brothers and then his nephews. Other threats also confronted Mahmud. Early in his reign, an invasion of his lands was launched by Sanjar. He was supported by a number of Nizari troops. The invasion was successful up to a point. Sanjar pushed deep into Mahmud's territories, eventually reaching Baghdad itself. A truce was agreed. Sanjar was allowed to retain a number of conquered territories, including many in the north of Persia in, or near, areas of strong Nizari influence. However, he recognized the right of Mahmud to succeed him in these lands when he died. It was a time of protracted internecine warfare: even the much weakened Abbasid caliphate attempted to re-assert its independence during the confusion.

As a result of these conflicts and the consequent diversion of Seldjuk attention away from the Nizaris, the remainder of Hasan-i Sabbah's life was lived out in relative security. A number of observers noted that Sanjar seemed particularly well disposed towards Hasan. Rumours were rife about how this state of affairs came about. Anecdotally, Hasan had sought out

Sanjar on several occasions with a view to reaching an understanding with him, but in vain. Hasan therefore decided to opt for less subtle tactics. He bribed one of the eunuchs who served Sanjar to help him. One night this eunuch made his way surreptitiously into Sanjar's bedchamber during the hours of darkness. When Sanjar awoke the next morning, it was to find an assassin's dagger planted firmly into the floor next to his bed; a clear warning that, if he were to oppose the Nizaris, then he could expect to share the fate of so many other opponents. Curiously, Sanjar did not immediately know who had been responsible for this act, and decided to keep it a secret. However, a few days later he received a message from Hasan, telling him that if he had wished Sanjar harm then the dagger would have been firmly implanted into his soft breast rather than the hard floor. It was then all too clear where the threat to his life emanated from.

According to this story, which was promulgated by the Persian historian Juwayni, Sanjar was so frightened by this event that he was terrified of upsetting the Nizaris in the future. He paid them an annual pension from then on, and even allowed them to exact tolls from travellers journeying near their great castle at Girdkuh.[1]

According to this account, this incident set the tone for relations between Sanjar and Hasan from then on: 'In short, because of this imposture the Sultan refrained from attacking them and during his [i.e. Sanjar's] reign, their cause prospered . . . During his reign they enjoyed peace and tranquillity'.[2]

Such stories make exciting reading but the truth may well have been something far more prosaic. The Seldjuks had more to worry about than the Nizaris alone. Obsessed with their own internal battles for political pre-eminence it was as easy for Sanjar to leave the Nizaris in peace as to invite their enmity at a time when their passivity would have been most welcome. In the battle between the Seldjuks and the Nizaris by this stage matters had anyway reached something of a stalemate. The blunt reality of the situation was that neither side could currently hope to score a decisive and irreversible victory. On the one hand, the Nizaris were safe enough from cataclysmic defeat holed up in their mountain fortresses. The Seldjuks had tried to shift them from Alamut and other great citadels and had failed to do so. To prolong the battle would tie up vast amounts of resource when the Seldjuk chieftains were frankly too busy fighting each other for them to wish this to happen.

But neither were the Nizari Isma'ilis in a position to win a prolonged conflict with the Seldjuks. After their early successes, they had inevitably suffered as the Seldjuks fought back. Although they had managed to retain Alamut and other major fortresses, others had been lost to the enemy. Their supporters had been ruthlessly massacred on a number of occasions, and such losses had unavoidably hit home, both in terms of their effect on resources available to the Nizaris and on their morale. Although they remained secure enough in their heartlands, and a significant but widely dispersed Nizari state had been established in Persia and beyond, the heady early days of success had not been sustainable. In many areas where they had once appeared to be in the ascendancy, particularly around Isfahan, they had been badly affected owing to persecution by the Seldjuks. They were no longer in a position to sustain a drawn-out war against the Seldjuks. They, like their Sunni foe, were exhausted. It suited both sides to reach some kind of tacit understanding which allowed both parties to co-exist, albeit in a volatile environment. Thus, the intensity of the conflict between the two parties became significantly subdued during the last years of Hasan-i Sabbah's life.

This period of rapprochement allowed Hasan to divert his attentions elsewhere. To Nizari Isma'ilis, the murder in 1095 in Egypt of the man they regarded as the rightful Imam, Nizar, nearly three decades earlier, still rankled. The loss of the Imam was an enormous blow to them, given his sacred position in their hierarchy. The Mustalian heresy, as they regarded it, still caused them great anguish. The ultimate architect of Nizar's downfall had been the vizier, al-Afdal. As such, he was reviled by all Nizari Isma'ilis. There was therefore an unprecedented outpouring of joy when, in 1121, news arrived that the vizier had been assassinated in Egypt.

There was conflicting opinion as to who was actually responsible for the murder. The Caliph al-Mustali had reigned only for a short time and had been replaced on his death in 1101 by a man called al-Amir. Al-Afdal was a dominant personality who ensured on every possible occasion that the caliph knew that he only held his position on Al-Afdal's sufferance. As a result, the caliph hated him. When news was received that Al-Afdal was dead, few were happier at the news than Al-Amir. But it was one thing to note Al-Amir's glee when he was appraised of the tidings, quite another to assert – as some chroniclers did – that he himself was the architect of the murder.

Inevitably, suspicion also fell elsewhere. The Nizaris were already past masters at carrying out such acts. When news of the death of Al-Afdal was received at Alamut, Hasan ordered that great celebrations should be enacted as a result. These were to last for seven days and nights. Copies that were made of the Nizari historical archives state unequivocally that they were responsible for the murder. Although historians argue that the Nizari Isma'ilis were often convenient scapegoats for every murder that took place in the Middle East at the time, and some are distinctly uneasy at the attribution of Al-Afdal's murder to them, it does not seem unreasonable to assume, given their record and their known hatred of the vizier, that they were indeed behind the assassination.[3]

The elimination of the vizier appeared to open up new opportunities for a renewal of the understanding between Egypt and the Isma'ilis further east. But although both parties entered into correspondence subsequently, it soon became clear that there were too many obstacles to overcome if such an outcome was to be successfully negotiated. At the outset of these discussions, a public debate was held in Cairo during which al-Mustali's claims to the Fatimid caliphate were paraded and those of Nizar rejected. This action was followed up by the despatch of a letter from the new vizier in Egypt, al-Ma'mun, to Hasan, urging the latter to see the error of his ways and return to the path of legitimacy.

A war of words began. The Fatimids in Egypt wrote a strong refutation of the claims of the Nizaris in a work entitled *al-Hidaya al-Amiriyya* or 'Guidance according to al-Amir'. It was widely read throughout the country. When it was sent to Syria it created a furious reaction. In response, the Nizaris sent back a reply of their own, rejecting in turn the claims of the Fatimids. In reply, al-Amir issued another denunciation of the Nizaris, in which he called them '*Hashishiyya*' – a term that would have interesting connotations in the future.[4]

Relations between Egypt and the Persian Nizaris deteriorated alarmingly shortly afterwards. Clearly believing that Hasan's supporters had been responsible for the murder of al-Afdal, both al-Ma'mun and al-Amir easily became convinced that they were the next target of the assassin's knife. Rumour asserted that *fida'is* had already been despatched to the country with this aim in view. The supposed targets of these assassins reacted with something akin to blind panic. The gateway to Egypt was the town of Ascalon, on the Mediterranean coast of Palestine. Al-Ma'mun removed the governor of the town, clearly dubious as to either his loyalty or his effectiveness. He then ordered that all the town's officials should be similarly dismissed unless they were well known to the local population who could therefore vouch for their trustworthiness. All visitors to Egypt who passed through Egypt were to be stopped, searched and thoroughly cross-examined. Officials in Ascalon were to try to catch them out by asking them loaded questions and by separately comparing one traveller's account with another. Anyone who had not visited Egypt before, and was therefore not known to the authorities, was to be refused entry to Egypt. Full details of all the caravans passing through were to be taken and sent on in advance of the caravan to the city of Bilbeis, which was the next major stopping off point on the way to Egypt. Here, the caravan was to be checked again to ensure that no-one had left the party or been added to it since it had left Ascalon.

The situation was even more extreme within the capital, Cairo. The Isma'ilis had survived for centuries because of their skill in operating an effective underground movement. These talents for espionage were well honed in their early, formative years when the entire movement was in constant fear of repression and had clearly not died after the formation of the Fatimid caliphate. The vizier, al-Ma'mun, set up a vast network of spies throughout the capital. Women were sent around the city to inveigle their way into the company of suspected Nizari sympathisers.

Then, without warning, al-Ma'mun struck. In a well co-ordinated action, all those suspected of being allied to the Nizari cause were arrested en masse. Suspicion fell widely, alighting in some unexpected places, including the tutor of the caliph's children. Large amounts of money were confiscated. This had been sent, it was claimed, from Persia for the purposes of fomenting revolution within Egypt. It was in every sense the establishment of a police state within the country. So successful was it that it was claimed that as soon as a would-be assassin left Alamut for Egypt every step of his progress was monitored. Understandably, relations between the Persian Nizaris and the Egyptians soon appeared as cold as the frost on a midwinter's morning.[5]

So far, we have considered the major events that took place during the life of Hasan-i Sabbah. It is appropriate at this stage to also attempt to analyse something of Hasan, the man. Sad to say, our knowledge of him as an individual is far from complete. We can glean snippets of information from the fragments of biographies and histories that have survived the ravages of time but these are all too few. Further, our knowledge of him is clouded because the works that remain were largely written by enemies, men who had little interest in, or intention of, praising Hasan. What we are left with is a tantalising glimpse of the man, incomplete and unsatisfactory but fascinating nevertheless.

His achievements in setting up a viable, albeit dangerously exposed, Nizari state are obvious enough. Such was the magnitude of this achievement alone that it fully justifies the epithet that has been awarded him of 'a revolutionary of genius'.[6] His real talent lay in, firstly, recognizing that the internal divisions within the Seldjuk territories in Persia left a great opportunity for an Isma'ili revival within the region. From recognizing the potential offered by the weakness of the Seldjuks, his greatest success was in devising a strategy that could reap the maximum benefit from the situation. The idea of setting up a chain of fortresses in mountain fastnesses, although hardly in itself revolutionary, was the perfect approach to adopt in the situation that faced Hasan. Each fortress would require huge effort on the part of the Seldjuks if it were to be reduced. Further, the terrain in which these citadels were generally situated left the besiegers even more badly exposed to the dangers of disease and malnutrition than the besieged.

Even more impressive than this though was the way in which the Nizaris adopted such a vast range of measures in their attempts to further their cause. The potential offered by the long Nizari tradition for underground activities was exploited to the maximum possible extent. Key individuals within the hierarchy of the Nizaris' enemies were the target of the efforts of either missionaries or, if this were deemed to be an unrealistic option, assassins. Men who were not likely to be converted were instead eliminated. Ironically, it is in this latter approach, the adoption of assassination as a weapon of state for which the Nizaris were to become most famous as the 'Assassins', that the success or otherwise of Nizari policies is most open to debate.

While the frequent murder of the enemies of the Nizaris did create a reign of terror, and consequent confusion, within the ranks of the Seldjuks and other foes of the Nizaris, the reaction of these terrified parties often harmed the Isma'ilis greatly. In the aftermath of an assassination, the leaders of the stricken party would thrash about wildly like a pack of so many injured animals. Their vengeance alighted, predictably enough, on any Isma'ili supporter that they could lay their hands on. In this way, hundreds of Isma'ilis were butchered, most of whom were innocent of any crime other than following the leading of their religious convictions. As a result, the Isma'ili presence in many of the less remote parts of the region was seriously affected. This did nothing to further the Isma'ili cause. There was, as we have already seen, a great deal of resentment of the Seldjuks in many of the towns and cities of the country as well as the rural areas. This social discontent was not however exploited as fully as it might have been because of the brutal repression of the Isma'ilis in many of the more urban parts of the country.

All of this tells us something of the achievement of Hasan-i Sabbah, and the effectiveness of his tactics, without necessarily telling us too much of his personality. But chronicles that have survived the centuries also describe him as a man of science, much interested in geometry, astronomy and arithmetic. Given this, it is perhaps unsurprising to find that Alamut would eventually become something of a beacon of learning, with many men – a number of whom were not even Isma'ilis – travelling from far and wide to take advantage of its outstanding library. The fact that he was academically minded should not come as too much of a revelation; Hasan was after all both middle-class and Persian and, in a region that prized learning above many other virtues, it was natural that he should be interested in the arts. But in some of the more sensational historical examinations of the sect known to the West as the 'Assassins' it is hard to find this picture of Hasan, the academic, which has largely become lost amid the more sensational aspects of the movement that he, to all intents and purposes, founded.

There is no doubt that Hasan also demanded high moral standards of himself and was equally as severe a judge of other people and their actions.

A spectacular view inside the Dome of the Rock, Jerusalem. (*A.F. Kersting*)

Exterior, Dome of the Rock, Jerusalem. The building dates from the seventh century AD and stands on the rock, the site of an earlier Jewish temple, said to be where Mohammed ascended into heaven in 632. (*A.F. Kersting*)

Louis IX at Acre receives a deputation from the Old Man of the Mountain, leader of the Syrian Nizaris. (*Mary Evans Picture Library*)

The modern city of Aleppo in Syria, seen from the ruined walls of its medieval castle. The city was never captured by crusaders. (*A.F. Kersting*)

The courtyard of the Great Mosque at Aleppo. (*A.F. Kersting*)

The castle of Masyaf, headquarters of the Syrian Nizaris. (*A.F. Kersting*)

The medieval walls of Cairo, Egypt. The minaret of the mosque of Al Hakim is seen in the background. (*A.F. Kersting*)

The courtyard of the Omayyad Mosque, Damascus. (*A.F. Kersting*)

A carved stone pocket inscription carried by Sultan Jalal al-din Khwarazm. (*The British Museum/Heritage-Images*)

Spherical brass incense burner of the Mameluke Dynasty. (*The British Museum/Heritage-Images*)

Opposite: Mausoleum of Sultan Baibars, Damascus (*by kind permission of Prof Nasser Rabbat, Massachusetts Institute of Technology, USA*)

The mausoleum of Aga Khan III at Ismailia, Egypt. (© *Gian Berto Vanni/Corbis*)

Once he took over Alamut, it was said that he never again set foot outside the castle, and only twice left his living quarters there, on both occasions making his way to the roof to see what was happening in the distance. Nor did his wives and daughters return to his side once he had sent them to the relative security of the mighty fortress of Girdkuh. He was clearly a man whose moral values far exceeded any claim on his familial devotions. Throughout his time at Alamut, it was strictly forbidden for any wine to be consumed by any of its residents. Hasan was passionately opposed to the use of alcohol, seeing it as an evil drug that dulled the senses and the morals of those who used it. At one time, one of his sons was reputedly caught partaking of wine. Hasan had no hesitation in ordering his execution.[7]

On another occasion, another son, Ustad Hussein, was accused of ordering the killing of a man without the prior agreement of Hasan. To make matters worse, the victim was a Nizari and the *fidaïs* did not usually kill their own. Again, Hasan ordered that this son too should be put to death. It subsequently transpired that these accusations were in fact groundless and another man was found guilty and executed. So that this man too might know what it felt like to lose a son, his son was put to death with him. Yet if anything Hasan's treatment of his own sons increased his prestige. In a very different world to the one in which we live, it was seen as a sign that Hasan was entirely devoted to the values that he lived by, which to him outweighed all other considerations. Such a man, it seemed, was above corruption because of his total commitment and dedication to his own inner sense of duty.

According to some accounts, Hasan realized that his actions could be used to his advantage, as it showed that he was even-handed in his approach to all his followers, even his own family: 'And he used to point to the execution of both his sons as a reason against anyone's imagining that he conducted propaganda on their behalf and had had that object in mind'.[8]

It was as a religious leader that Hasan made the greatest impact. Hasan stepped into the vacuum created by the death of the man whom the Nizaris regarded as their true Imam, Nizar, and filled the void in a way that no other man could. We should surmise that he was a humble man, given his refusal to take on the role of Imam. He steadfastly refused to be considered as such. Instead, he was known as the *hujja*, the 'proof', of the Hidden

Imam (an honorific title that the Isma'ilis had used for other leaders in the past). He was prepared to declare himself as his representative among them and, as such, he claimed to speak on his behalf. But he would not contemplate acceptance of the ultimate accolade, that of being recognized as the Imam in his own right. This suppression of ambition evidences very well the devout nature of his beliefs.

One of the reasons that the Imam fulfilled a crucial role for the Isma'ilis was for doctrinal reasons. According to traditional Isma'ili teaching, the world was destined to pass through a sequence of spiritual cycles before it reached true religious fulfilment. Each cycle was heralded by a prophet, known as a *natiq*. There had been a number of these since time began, namely Adam (the first), Noah, Abraham, Moses, Jesus and Muhammad. Between the appearance of each *natiq*, there was a sequence of seven Imams who were responsible for maintaining the faith when the *natiq* had left this earth. All of this would culminate, during the final seventh cycle, in the appearance of the Mahdi and the heralding of an age of righteousness for the earth. The position of the Imam in this vision of the world was vital, and his being was sacred. In the aftermath of the death of Nizar, it became clear that the shabby way in which he was deposed and subsequently killed meant that the Fatimid dynasty was clearly not going to fulfil many of the hopes carried in the breasts of the Isma'ilis in Persia. Now the Nizaris waited for a special Imam, the *qa'im al-qiyama* ('lord of the Resurrection') to return and proclaim the moment when the world would be spiritually reborn.

It was into this vacuum that Hasan-i Sabbah stepped, not as the Imam but as his appointed mouthpiece in his absence. But although he was never Imam, he took a lead on religious matters during his lifetime. Hasan made a number of statements on religion that were adopted wholeheartedly by his followers. So great was their impact that collectively his instructions were known as 'the new preaching', but in fact they were rather the restatement and summarisation of some much older principles. He concentrated particularly on the doctrine of *talim*, which related to the importance of authorized teachers within the Isma'ili world. Such teaching was a vital ingredient in Isma'ili doctrine, because the Isma'ilis, it may be remembered, argued that not only the outward meaning of the Qur'an needed to be considered but also the hidden, inner meanings.[9] These esoteric interpretations of what was known as the *batin* of the Qur'an gave recognized religious teachers immense influence within Isma'ili society. Naturally enough, Hasan argued that only the Isma'ili Imam had the right to be recognized as the authoritative teacher of the Qur'an and its hidden inner meanings.

Hasan was explicit in his designation of over-arching spiritual authority to the Imam. Juwayni says that he stated that: 'the knowledge of God was not to be attained through reason and reflection but through the teaching of the Imam, for most of mankind were possessed of reason and everyone had views on the ways of religion. If the use of reason were sufficient for the knowledge of God, the members of no sect could raise objections against other sects and all would be equal, assuming that everyone was possessed of religion through the use of reason. But since it was open [for men] to object and repudiate and some felt the need to imitate others, this was nothing else but the doctrine of instruction, namely that reason was not sufficient and there had to be an Imam in order that in every age the people might be instructed and possessed of religion through his teaching'.[10]

Hasan committed his detailed ideas to writing, which fortunately for us has survived through the works of a man named al-Shahrastani (who may well have been an Isma'ili himself). According to these, there were four fundamental elements within his teaching. The first was a simple restatement that all men needed a teacher; accompanying this was a statement that reason alone could not lead men to find religious truth, because faith also was needed. In this he was perhaps rejecting the position of many of the philosophers who were then (and had always been, in the East) prominent in the region, who argued that man could find his way to spiritual fulfilment through the use of reason alone.

The second element perhaps went to the heart of Isma'ili teaching on the importance of the Imam, in that it stated categorically that there was only ever one true teacher in the world and that would be the Isma'ili Imam. This was juxtaposed to the Sunni position, which allowed for a host of religious scholars to offer doctrinal opinions at any one time. In this, Isma'ilism showed itself to be diametrically opposed to the Sunni branch of Islam and all that it stood for. It also of course put Hasan in a very strong position among his followers as, although he himself was not the Imam, he was his appointed representative. The third and fourth elements detailed by al-Shahrastani were further statements about the authority of the Imam, which again served to emphasize his importance.

Hasan's teachings touched a chord among his followers. By creating the image of the supreme religious authority on earth who must be obeyed and whose instructions were infallible, Hasan formed a vision of someone that men would give up much to follow, even life itself. The Fatimids had failed in their attempts to win all Isma'ilis to their cause, and their failure was exacerbated when their dynasty became more and more a secular rather than a spiritual force. This diminution of the spiritual element in their attitudes left a void which Hasan was able to exploit successfully.

Finally, Hasan never forgot what he believed to be his duty to carry on the *da'wa* throughout the Islamic world. The Isma'ilis had from the outset been enthusiastic about evangelizing their beliefs to as wide an audience as possible as part of their strategy of non-violent conversion. Since their earliest days, the continuation of this mission had been a fundamental part of Isma'ilism. It might be thought that Hasan had far too many problems in Persia to carry on the mission outside of the country during his life but in fact this was not the case. During his period of leadership such missions were launched on his initiative in regions like Azerbaijan. However, it was the despatch of missionaries to Syria which was to have some of the most important repercussions for our story,[11] as it brought the Nizaris into contact both with other Seldjuk rulers and also to the West European Crusader knights who arrived in Palestine shortly before the *da'wa* in Syria was launched. From these contacts, the legends of the 'Assassins' would eventually implant themselves in Western consciousness.

Hasan was a quite remarkable man and it may have seemed impossible for his supporters to imagine life without him. But he was, in the end, mortal. In 1124, he fell ill. Aware that he, like all other men, must die, he arranged for his succession in a typically meticulous fashion. He sent for his trusted deputy, Buzurg-Ummid, telling him to make his way to the great mountain fortress of Alamut from that other impregnable citadel, the castle of Lamasar. When he arrived, Hasan told him that he had been chosen to take his place as the head of the Nizari Isma'ilis. No doubt the redoubtable old man lectured him for a time on the importance of retaining his humility even though he had been awarded this great honour. He probably also emphasized that Buzurg-Ummid was not a great man in his own right, rather his role was to prepare the way for the Imam when he returned.

The new leader of the Isma'ilis would have a great deal to contend with. The Seldjuks would undoubtedly try to destroy the Isma'ilis again at some point in the near future, and there were many other enemies to watch out for. After the attempts to rebuild relations with the Fatimids had failed, Hasan had directed that another effort be launched in Egypt to convert the people there to support the Nizari cause, but these had largely petered out after very little success had been achieved. There was therefore much to do in an evangelical sense, and Hasan's replacement would also need to drive forward the *da'wa* around the Islamic world if the ultimate end of the Nizari movement, that is the conversion of all Muslims to the Nizari cause, were to succeed. It was a very full and demanding agenda for Buzurg-Ummid to be faced with on his accession to power.

Aware that his successor would be stretched by all these competing demands on his time and energy, Hasan also arranged for a council of three to be set up to support Buzurg-Ummid. Dihdar Abu' Ali Ardistani, a *da'i* of great experience was one of the three, along with Hasan Adam Qasrani and Kiya Ba Ja'far who was the military leader of the Isma'ili army. Dihdar Abu' Ali Ardistani was to have a particularly important role, as he was to take charge of the *da'wa*.

Having made these final arrangements to ensure that all that he had striven so hard to build would remain after he departed this world, Hasan prepared himself for his end. He was by now a very old man, who could look back on a life of achievement amidst great personal hardship and self-sacrifice. He had effectively turned his back on the world for decades, his existence being largely lived out within the four walls of his room at Alamut. Rashid al-Din says of him that he spent most of his time after he arrived at Alamut 'inside the house where he lived; he was occupied with reading books, committing the words of the *da'wa* to writing, and administering the affairs of his realm'[12] – in short, he lived a life of self-sacrifice and devotion to the cause he espoused.

His family life had to all intents and purposes been non-existent for years, and his great sense of duty had even led him to execute two of his sons. He may have appeared, by the standards of many, a harsh and unlovable man, but he had won the respect of his people in a way that few other men could have hoped to achieve. By an accident of history, the West would become much more familiar with one of his successors, Sinan, the leader of the Syrian Isma'ilis who lived in the second half of the twelfth century but there was no doubting that Hasan was the greatest of all Nizari leaders. When he died, his supporters must have believed that the world had come to an end because he had led them so long and so far. For his enemies, feelings were somewhat different. One of them noted quite simply that 'in the night of Friday, 23 May 1124, Hasan hastened off to the fire of God and His hell'.[13]

There was however an alternative epitaph which, coming as it does from a 'neutral' source, has greater objectivity. The Patriarch of Constantinople had some time before sent an envoy to Hasan, in itself a strong indication of the legitimacy of the Nizari state. The envoy recorded his impressions of Hasan for posterity:

'His natural dignity, his distinguished manners, his smile, which is always courteous and pleasant but never familiar or casual, the grace of his attitudes, the striking firmness of his movements, all combine to produce an undeniable superiority. This is fundamentally the result of his great personality, which is magnetic in its domination. There is no pride or arrogance; he emanates calm and good will'.[14]

For his people there was great grief when he died (no doubt accompanied by a sense of foreboding about the future). Heavy of heart, they buried the man they called Sayyidna – 'Our Master' – reverently in the place where he had spent so much of his life. There, in the craggy, unconquerable eyrie of the eagles they erected a shrine to his memory. For over a century, it would be a place of pilgrimage for the Nizaris until an enemy that might have proved too strong even for him threatened to exterminate the movement he was devoted to, one which owed all that it had achieved to his sacrifice and vision.

SIX

The Syrian Dimension

The momentous events in Persia were echoed elsewhere in the Middle East, notably in Syria. The Seldjuk incursions that struck Persia also had a profound effect further west. The situation was particularly confused in Syria. By the close of the eleventh century, many city-states in the area had their own emirs who ruled to all intents and purposes autonomously. Some of them were Seldjuk warlords, who constantly plotted against each other, but there were other influences present in the region as well. Some cities, such as Tripoli on the Mediterranean coastline were ruled by local Arab chieftains who managed to retain a semblance of independence by constantly playing off one local warlord against another. What exacerbated the situation still further was that effectively Syria lay on a fault-line where the Fatimid world bordered the Sunni Seldjuk regime. As a result, the region around Syria, particularly in Palestine, became one of the major battle zones between the two major Islamic power blocs. In the confusion created by these tensions, there was great potential for independently minded local leaders to assert a degree of autonomy, and also for radicalism to take root. In short, Syria made an ideal recruiting ground for the Isma'ilis.

This was particularly so as the town of Salamiya, for many years the heartbeat of the Isma'ili world before the creation of the Fatimid caliphate, was to be found in Syria. As such, the region had a special place in the hearts of the Isma'ilis. The long-lived caliph of the Fatimid dynasty, al-Mustansir, clearly thought so, as in 1051 he sent his chief *da'i*, a man

named al-Shirazi, to Syria to preach the *dawa*. We may be sure that in
addition he would have been charged with the responsibility of fomenting
dissent against the heretic Caliph Abbasid in Baghdad.

There were other possible reasons why the local population might feel
animosity towards the Abbasids in Baghdad. Before the installation of the
city as the capital of the Abbasid caliphate in the eighth century, the centre
of the Islamic world had been in Damascus, which continued to play a
vital role in the politics of Islam long after this time. It remained an
important centre of learning and culture, although much of its previous
prominence in these fields had transferred eastwards to Baghdad. There
were also other important cities in the region, such as Aleppo and Homs;
while the strategic role of Syria was equally important because it abutted
on to many areas of traditional Byzantine influence. It was a frontier
territory and, like most regions of that type, it could prove immensely
difficult to control.

Such a range of tensions inevitably attracted dissentient groups to target
the area for their activities. In the first part of the eleventh century, the
Druze, supporters of the discredited al-Hakim, had made their home in
their mountain retreats in Lebanon. This hints at another feature that
characterizes the area; in common with Persia, wide areas of plain were
broken up by sizeable, difficult-to-access mountain ranges; ideal territory,
in fact, as a base for groups similar to those that had been set up by Hasan-i
Sabbah in Persia.

The Muslims in Syria were so involved fighting each other that they
failed to notice a grave threat forming far to the west. If they
communicated with the remnants of the Umayyad dynasty in Spain, they
would have been aware that parts of that country had been reconquered by
Christian knights after decades of Islamic rule. Slightly further to the east,
on the island of Sicily, what remained of the Muslim kingdom there was
mopped up by an aggressive army of Norman warriors in 1072. The
Christian territories in Western Europe were starting to become more
expansionist and ambitious in their policies. Perhaps this all seemed quite a
remote sequence of events to the Muslims in Syria who were, after all,
hundreds of miles away from where this action was taking place. In the
longer term however these trends were to be of profound significance to
them.

There was perhaps also another reason for disregarding the increasing assertiveness of Western Europe as well as its geographical remoteness. The greatest power in Christendom had for centuries been the Byzantine Empire. Certainly, this appeared to be the most likely Christian foe for the Muslims of Syria and the wider Levant. But it appeared that the power of Byzantium was broken. Crushed by the Seldjuks on the field of Manzikert in 1071, it seemed that the old empire was shattered, its power destroyed irrevocably. The traditional heartland of Byzantium, Asia Minor, was wide open to Turkish settlement. The Muslims in the rgion may have surmised that the empire was irrelevant and its days were numbered. Content that the most likely source of Christian aggression was effectively no longer a prominent player in the politics of the region, the Muslims of the Levant were happy enough to concentrate on their own internal debates and succession crises.

But by the strangest of ironies it was the very weakness of the Byzantine Empire at that time that was to facilitate the crisis that was to throw the Mediterranean coast of the Islamic world into turmoil. No longer able to provide its own armies, and unable to recruit extensively in Asia Minor (as it always had done in the past) Byzantium looked to the West for salvation. Initial plans by Pope Gregory IX in Rome to send an army to the East came to nothing but then, in 1095, a fresh appeal was made by the Byzantine Emperor Alexius Comnenus to Pope Urban II asking for the help of Christian warriors to defeat the Muslim Turks.

Alexius ideally wanted an army of mercenaries to come and operate under his direction and reconquer the lost lands of Asia Minor for him. However, the response to the appeal was so overwhelming that no one, not Alexius, nor the Pope himself, could control it. Inspired by an intense outpouring of religious emotion, numbers of Western warlords committed themselves to a great Crusade to recover the heartland of Christendom for their faith. The target for the expedition quickly changed. No longer was it intent on recovering Asia Minor for Byzantium. Nothing less than the reconquest of Jerusalem would suffice for these warriors – a city which, at the time, was in Turkish hands (although by the time that the Crusade eventually arrived at its destination it would be held by the Fatimids once more). This inevitably put the Crusade on a collision course with Islam, for whom the city was also holy.[1]

In advance of the main party of armed knights (to be more accurate, a number of different groups of such men set out more or less independently) a large number of ordinary folk, their emotions whipped up by the spiritual frenzy created by the preaching of the Crusade, set out for the East. They were little more than a rabble. Their discipline was largely non-existent and they fell out with the inhabitants of the Christian states through which they passed on their way towards Asia Minor with alarming ease. They arrived in Constantinople in 1096. The Byzantine Emperor, Alexius Comnenus, could not contemplate them remaining in the vicinity of his capital, Constantinople, for any length of time (they had already tried to pillage several Byzantine towns and cities) and had them shipped over to Asia Minor at the earliest opportunity. Once there, they were quickly entrapped by a large army of Seldjuks led by the greatest warlord in the region, Kilij Arslan I, and destroyed.

The irony of the disasters that overwhelmed these early expeditions was that they actually benefited the Christian cause. The well-armed forces that set out long after these misguided poor folk were much better prepared. They had taken longer to assemble their forces but this was an inevitable consequence of the amount of preparation they had engaged in prior to their departure. Predictably enough, they soon showed themselves to be independently-minded individuals who had little intention of being mere puppets of the Byzantine Empire. Eventually, these better-armed groups also made their way into Asia Minor. When news of their arrival was received, however, Kilij Arslan was slow to react. No doubt judging the danger they posed by the completely erroneous benchmark of the poorly armed forces that he had defeated so easily a short time before, he let them lay siege to his capital, Nicaea. By the time that he did respond to the threat, the moment had passed him by. When he eventually tried belatedly to force the Crusaders to retreat, his attacks were beaten off. Now thoroughly aware of the predicament that he was in, he was powerless to intervene as Nicaea was lost to him in June 1097.

The Crusaders pushed on, down the Syrian coast. Their greatest barrier was the ancient Christian city of Antioch, currently in Muslim hands. It was enclosed by vast fortifications; so great was the acreage contained by the walls that large market gardens kept the besieged well supplied with food while the besiegers sought about vainly for provisions. But here, as elsewhere in the Muslim world, Islam was divided. The city was under the command of a man named Yaghi-Siyan. He had played off the two leading Seldjuk warlords in the area against each other with great skill. One of these was named Duqaq of Damascus, the other Ridwan of Aleppo. The two men vied to achieve dominance in the region with great venom, their desire to achieve local supremacy at the expense of each other apparently not reduced one iota by the fact that they were brothers.

Yaghi-Siyan desperately asked for help; Duqaq responded but Ridwan, still seething after being duped by Yaghi-Siyan not long before, refused to send one man to his aid. The siege dragged on for ages; the besiegers suffered great deprivation and hardship but, helped by treachery from within the city itself, the Crusaders eventually broke in and overwhelmed the defenders. An orgy of bloodletting followed. The lack of a unified response from the Islamic leaders in the region had played straight into the hands of the West European armies.

Worse was to follow as far as Islam was concerned. The weakness of the fragmented Syrian coastal region meant that the Crusaders' advance was difficult to stop. Individual cities either paid tribute to the Crusaders to avoid the horrors of a siege or were overwhelmed after initial resistance. A united response from Islam might have caused great difficulties for the Crusaders, who had suffered enormous losses due to attrition from battle, famine or disease, but such a reply was for the moment virtually non-existent. Eventually, the Crusaders reached Jerusalem itself. The garrison of Fatimid troops (the city was by then in Egyptian hands) resisted for a while but eventually, on 15 July 1099, the walls were breached. The defence quickly collapsed but the fall of the city was followed by dreadful massacres of the Islamic and Jewish inhabitants.

The capture of Jerusalem had several major effects on the Middle East. Four Crusader territories were created in the region. Two were based on Antioch and Edessa, both of which had been captured by the Crusaders before Jerusalem. Another was later set up around the city of Tripoli on the coast. The most prized of all was, naturally enough, based on Jerusalem. The Crusader states introduced another major player into the politics of the region. The loss of Jerusalem was an enormous blow to Islamic morale and it was to affect the confidence of the regions abutting the new Crusader territories, especially Syria, particularly badly.

More specifically, the formation of this Christian, West European enclave was to have a significant impact on the story of the so-called 'Assassins'. When Nizari communities were set up in Syria soon after these events took place, they would come into contact with the Crusader kingdoms and their acts would be recorded by Western chroniclers. The effect on the development of the Assassin legends would be great. Writing only of what they knew from their own experience, Western chroniclers would write of the Assassins in Syria as if they were the only Nizari group that existed. Largely unaware (until later years at least) of the presence of the group in Persia, Western chroniclers would create the illusion that the Assassins sect, as they eventually came to call them, existed mainly in Syria. The reality was that, for most of the history of the Nizari movement, the headquarters of the sect remained in Persia and during Medieval times the heart of the Nizari movement always remained in the country. But the Western chroniclers were to paint a picture that suggested that exactly the reverse of this situation was the case.

At about the same time that the Crusade arrived in the East, preparations were finalized for a major Nizari initiative in Syria. The long-standing radical traditions of the area and the existence of Isma'ili groups there already (for a time Syria had been part of the Fatimid empire) inevitably attracted them. Even the topography of the region offered assistance, with several large mountain ranges within the protective folds of which the group could hide themselves away from the violence of their enemies. A party was despatched to Syria from Persia, led by a *da'i* named al-Hakim al-Munajjim, which means 'the physician-astrologer'. Their aim was to take the *da'wa* to Syria. They arrived there at some time around the year 1100.

They announced their arrival in the region in typical fashion. The town of Homs was an important and fairly large place. One of its leading citizens was a man named Janah al-Dawla Husain. His prominence in society was undoubted; for a time he had been the guardian of Ridwan of Aleppo when he was younger. However, it appears that the two men had subsequently had a falling-out. He was effectively the ruler of Homs, and also a man who took his religious devotions seriously. What happened next was related by Ibn al-Qalanasi, a Muslim chronicler, who told how when Janah al-Dawla descended from his citadel to the mosque for Friday prayers 'surrounded by his principal officers with full armour, and occupying his place of prayer according to custom, [he] was set upon by three Persians belonging to the Batiniya [Nizaris]. They were accompanied by a shaikh, to whom they owed allegiance and obedience, and all of them were dressed in the garb of ascetics. When the shaikh gave the signal they attacked the amir with their knives and killed both him and a number of his officers'.[2]

In the ensuing panic, a number of people were struck down in revenge for the killings, including ten sufis who were, according to Ibn al-Qalanasi, innocent. But the tenuous hold of the Turks in the area was evidenced soon after when 'most of the Turks amongst the inhabitants fled to Damascus, and everything fell into confusion.' The outcome however did little good to al-Hakim al Munajjim, the man who was the first leader of the Syrian Nizaris, as he died at more or less the same time as the assassination, news of his demise being received within fourteen days of news of this event. But the Nizaris had announced themselves in the region in spectacular fashion and had, crucially, found themselves a powerful and influential patron in Ridwan of Aleppo.

Ridwan was a controversial figure. His religious tolerance shocked many of his more devout compatriots. He was not himself overly interested in spiritual matters. Thus he had no compunction in taking the Nizaris under his wing, even though he himself was not an Isma'ili. He had a number of opponents in the area (his quarrels with Duqaq of Damascus have already been noted), and the fear induced by the Nizaris could well be a very powerful weapon indeed. So he invited them into Aleppo, and provided them with sanctuary. It was an excellent base for the Nizaris. Its citadel, massively proportioned, epitomised the power of the city. The strength of Aleppo is best evidenced by the fact that, although it stood astride the new Crusader kingdoms in the region, which were to remain in West European hands for nearly 200 years in one form or another, never once did it fall to them, despite frequent plans to capture it. But al-Hakim al-Munajjim, the Nizari *da'i*, would not live long to savour his initial success, as he died in 1103 shortly after arriving in Syria. Another Persian *da'i*, Abu Tahir al-Sa'igh, took his place.

There were some high mountains not far from the city of Aleppo. In line with their policy in Persia, the Nizaris sought to establish bases among them. However, they clearly did not enjoy the same strength that they did further east (or else their opponents in Syria were stronger) as their attempts to capture several strongpoints in the area met with failure. For several years they carried on their efforts, without success, until finally their fortunes seemed to turn for the better. Some thirty miles to the south-west of Aleppo stood a castle at a place called Afamiya. Its lord was a Fatimid supporter, Khalaf ibn Mula'ib. As such, he was no friend of the Nizaris. He also had little time for Ridwan of Aleppo, who had owned the castle until Khalaf had seized it from him some years earlier. Not only that, once he had possession of the castle he used it as a base to launch frequent raids on the surrounding countryside, making a thorough nuisance of himself.

The Nizaris, keen to ingratiate themselves with Ridwan and also to gain a base from which to launch their operations, plotted to capture the place. After all, they were involved in a *dàwa*, a mission to convert the world to their cause, and they could not merely rest passively on their laurels in Aleppo. Such complacency was alien both to their creed and their character. Once again, if the chroniclers are to be believed, their flair for subterfuge asserted itself. In February 1106, a party of them approached the castle, leading a great war-horse, bearing a suit of Frankish armour. They shouted up to the men guarding the gates that they had killed a great Crusader knight, and they were now bringing his horse and armour to Khalaf as a mark of their respect.

The men were granted entry – after all there were only six of them. Khalaf received them warmly (we may assume that an opportunist such as he would often receive offers of help and friendship from men who would be only too keen to share in his gains). He fed them, entertained them and lodged them in comfortable quarters. Sadly for him, he was obviously fooled completely by their ruse. The quarters that they were housed in were right next to a wall. Under cover of darkness, they dug a hole through this wall. Large numbers of their allies, who had been waiting patiently outside, came through the gap. Before the garrison was remotely aware of what was happening, they had been overwhelmed. Khalaf was resting in his room. Ibn al-Qalanasi says that 'when they approached him and he became aware of them, he faced them boldly, but one of them dashed at him and drove a dagger into his belly. He then threw himself into the tower, trying to reach one of the harem apartments, but another of them delivered a second blow, and he died in a few minutes'.[3]

The leader of this group of Nizaris, a man named Abu'l-Fath, triumphantly sent news to Abu Tahir in Aleppo, who hurried over from the city to take up residence in Afamiya, the first significant conquest of the movement in Syria. However, any triumphalism that may have been felt was decidedly premature. There were other forces in the area, and they were not all Muslim. When the Crusaders had arrived in the East, one of their foremost leaders was a man named Bohemond.[4] He was a politically astute Norman adventurer who it appears cut quite a romantic figure in his day. Accompanying him was his nephew, Tancred, who had inherited much of his flair for intrigue with little of his charm. Bohemond had returned to Italy some time previously, and the city of Antioch was ruled in his absence by Tancred. Tancred was apparently well aware of what was going on at Afamiya (perhaps he too had been troubled by raids launched from there in the past). Soon after the castle was captured by the Nizaris, Tancred arrived outside the castle. He had with him as a bargaining chip a Muslim captive – the brother of that same Abu'l Fath who had first taken the castle.

On his first visit, Tancred was happy enough to be bought off. However, the reprieve consequently granted to the Nizaris in Afamiya was to prove a very short-term one. In September of the same year, 1106, Tancred was back. This time, he was determined to take the castle. Most sieges were decided by the painful, drawn-out process of starving the garrison out rather than all-out assault. Tancred blockaded the town so thoroughly that the Nizaris soon surrendered, seeing that their position was hopeless. For Abu'l Fath whose intrigues had been responsible for the castle's capture, the result of the siege had awful personal consequences. Tancred was in league with a man named Mus'ab ibn Mula'ib, who was the brother of Khalaf, the former ruler of Afamiya who had been murdered by Abu'l Fath and his men. Aby'l Fath's fate was therefore an inevitable one – 'when [he] fell into his hands, he put him to death by torture, and carried away Abu Tahir the goldsmith and him companions with him as prisoners'.[5]

It was a bitter pill for the Nizaris to swallow. Their frustration at seeing the cup of victory dashed from their lips when they had been granted so little time to drink from it must have been immense. For a time thereafter, they struggled to make any impression in Syria. In contrast to the early years of Hasan-i Sabbah in Persia, their first steps in Syria were generally faltering ones. They do not seem to have achieved enough popular support to re-create the great impact that they had made further east. There was however still the occasional assassination attempt that reminded the world of their continued presence in the region. In 1111, they launched an attack (which was unsuccessful) on a leading Persian citizen in Aleppo who was passionately opposed to their cause. But one thing that was clear enough was that, although they enjoyed the patronage of Ridwan, the inhabitants of his city did not approve of his choice of allies. On several occasions, there were outbreaks of violence directed at the Nizaris in the city. This did not augur well for their long-term prospects beyond the lifetime of Ridwan.

But in 1113, their involvement was claimed in an act which, if it did belong to them, was their most significant in Syria thus far. One of the greatest of the local warlords was the Seldjuk emir of Mosul, Mawdud. He was much feared by many, including Ridwan of Aleppo, who had not let him enter his city when he had been in the vicinity two years earlier. Mawdud visited the great city of Damascus where he stayed with the ruler of the city, Toghtekin. When he was about to enter the Great Mosque of the city, an assassin threw himself on him and attacked him. Mawdud was stabbed in the stomach. He managed to stagger away from his assailant but collapsed shortly afterwards. He was clearly dying. Offered food, he reputedly refused it, as he did not want to break his fast before facing God. Soon after, he expired. Mawdud was a powerful man, who had brought a great army to Syria to lead a counter-attack against the Crusaders. His killing was a significant event.

It was not inconceivable that Mawdud's army might be used against other opponents, even Aleppo itself. Some historians point out that the Nizaris are not the only suspect for this particular murder.[6] While it is true to say that virtually every killing of the period was blamed on them regardless of their guilt or not, Mawdud was a natural enemy of the Nizaris. He was also at odds with Ridwan, effectively their patron, who might also have been disconcerted by the friendly relations between Mawdud and Toghtekin, a potential rival. There were, in short, very convincing motives for their participation in the act, so there is some evidence of their involvement, albeit largely circumstantial.

1113 was also a significant year for the Nizaris of Syria in another respect, for in December of that year Ridwan died. Given the fact that his patronage was a personally motivated act of policy on his part, there was no guarantee that the Nizaris in Syria would enjoy the same degree of protection from his successor. Ridwan's son, Alp Arslan, took his place and at first continued to protect their interests. But he was not a strong character and when a letter was received from the Seldjuk Sultan Muhammad in Persia warning him to strike against the Isma'ilis, he followed his orders. Aleppo had never, as a whole, warmed to the Nizaris, and the inhabitants of the city supported a purge against the sect. The action that followed was brutal and decisive:

'Abu Tahir the goldsmith [was arrested] and all the adherents of his sect, about 200 souls. Abu Tahir the goldsmith was immediately put to death, along with the missionary Ismail, and the brother of al-Hakim al-Munajjim, and the other leaders in their movement who have been referred to. The remainder were imprisoned and their properties were confiscated. Some of these were interceded for, some were set free, some were thrown from the top of the citadel and some were executed. A number escaped, fled to the Franks and dispersed throughout the country'.[7]

Surprisingly, even after this pogrom the Nizaris still retained a degree of influence in Aleppo. Indeed, their greatest enemy in the city, a man named Ibn Badi', who was instrumental in urging the purge against them, was ejected in 1119. The Nizaris were to obtain absolute revenge on him shortly afterwards. They received word that he was on his way from the city, and had worked out in advance the route that he was likely to take. Consequently, as he was about to cross the Euphrates, he fell straight into an ambush and was killed, along with his two sons. But these were the last flickering embers of a dying fire. By 1124, Aleppo had another ruler, who opted to expel the Nizari *da'i* in the city and all his followers. It was effectively the end of the movement in Aleppo.

The Nizaris continued to find it difficult to establish themselves in Syria. They attacked the castle of Shaizar on an Easter Sunday, while the garrison there had gone out to witness the Christian celebrations. The force, a hundred strong, succeeded in capturing most of the castle but the defenders sought safety in a tower. Here, the defenders 'pulled up the women . . . by ropes so that they remained safely under their care.' They then launched a counter-attack and, their war cry of Allahu Akbar inspiring them to greater efforts, they began to force the Nizaris back. Then 'the Batinis [Nizaris] became disheartened and subdued and the men of Shaizar attacked them in increasing numbers, put them to the sword, and killed them to the last man'.[8]

By this time, however, they had already found themselves a new home and a new patron in Syria. Toghtekin of Damascus, recognizing in the Nizaris both a potentially dangerous enemy and a possibly useful ally, decided that it was in his interests to offer the Syrian Nizaris his protection. It was again an alliance of convenience, and the residents of Damascus, just like those of Aleppo, did not on the whole approve of the relationship. However, they were but bit players in the politics of the region, and they were for a time powerless to do much about their antagonism, other than indulging in some subdued complaints among themselves. In 1126, the presence of the Nizaris was noted (as was their conspicuous bravery) in a campaign, ultimately unsuccessful, conducted by Toghtekin against the Crusaders. Perhaps in recognition of their gallant involvement in the episode, the leader of the Syrian Nizaris, another *da'i* from Persia named Bahram, was invited to take up residence in Damascus.

Shortly afterwards, Bahram approached Toghtekin for his help in obtaining a fortress in the region from which the Nizaris could launch their *da'wa* afresh. Toghtekin gave them a castle close to the border with the Crusader kingdom of Jerusalem at Banyas. No doubt Toghtekin reasoned that from their base here the Nizaris could disrupt the affairs of the Crusader state, at least locally, and therefore saw mutual benefit in the arrangement. It was at any rate an important step for the Nizaris. Because of its strategically sensitive position, the castle would lead a chequered life and would change hands on many occasions. As well as the castle, the Nizaris were also given a 'palace' (or so it has been described, but we should not perhaps read too many grandiose implications into this) in Damascus, a move as important in its symbolic connotations, confirming the support of Toghtekin for the Nizaris, as for its practical effects.

There were soon rumours that this improvement in the fortunes of the Nizaris was not as a result of the approval of Toghtekin himself but rather his vizier, al-Mazdagani. The latter was not an Isma'ili but he recognized well enough the advantages to be accrued from enlisting the support of the Nizaris in Syria. And the Nizaris were quick to provide more spectacular proof of their talent for assassination, reminding the local warlords that it would be wise to court their friendship. The current emir of Mosul, il-Bursuqi, was a Turkish soldier of fortune and an adventurer who had seized power in the city. He was through and through a warrior. When he was not at war with fellow Seldjuk nobles, his favourite pastime was honing his military skills against the fledgling Crusader states in the region.

In 1126, he set out on a campaign against the Franks. Success in such ventures often rested on the element of surprise; if the Crusaders were caught off guard then much profit might accrue to il-Bursuqi but if they were prepared for him, their fighting skills should be sufficient to resist his assault. Man for man, the superior armour of the Frankish knights made up in quality for what they lacked in numbers – they were almost invariably outnumbered in any battles that they fought against the Muslims – although this superiority was frequently negated by tactical naïveté and indiscipline in battle. The current King of Jerusalem, Baldwin II, was an astute statesman and a capable general and he was ready for il-Bursuqi and his men when they arrived. As a result, stalemate ensued; the subsequent campaign was a desultory affair with neither side willing to risk much in open battle. After a short period of tactical manoeuvring and posturing, a truce was agreed and both armies returned home.

For il-Bursuqi, the homecoming was to be an inauspicious affair in more ways than one. He was of course hardly returning covered in glory (though such indecisive outcomes to military campaigns were regular occurrences and this one was not at least blemished by any great loss of life among his men), but this was incidental compared with the events that happened soon after his return.

One of il-Bursuqi's first acts when he arrived back in Mosul on 26 November 1126 was to attend Friday prayers in the mosque of his city. There was a small party of Sufis in the building, who did not attract any undue attention. All of a sudden, eight of the Sufis (who were really Nizari assassins) fell on il-Bursuqi and stabbed him to death. All but one of the assailants were killed in the attack, but this did not matter much to them, as it seemed in their eyes to be an act of martyrdom which would reap its own rewards in the life to come.

The chronicler Kamal al-Din, a historian from Aleppo, relates an interesting tale with regard to this event which gives an insight into the psychology of the Nizaris. When news of the successful assassination was received by the families of the murderers, great rejoicing ensued as it was thought that their future in paradise was assured. However, one of the *fida'is* escaped. His mother's reaction was revealing, for: 'when she heard that Bursuqi was killed and that those who attacked him were killed, knowing that her son was one of them, she rejoiced and anointed her eyelids with kohl and was full of joy: then, after a few days her son returned unharmed, and she was grieved, and tore her hair and blackened her face'.[9]

The aftermath of il-Bursuqi's death generated more instability in the region (a continuing state of affairs that incidentally did much to protect the vulnerable Crusader states in their early fragile years of existence). It illustrated perfectly how the Nizaris, through their use of a weapon that brought terror to their enemies, managed to exert an influence out of all proportion to the size of the movement. Each successive murder added another paragraph to the story of the movement, a development that cumulatively created a picture of Nizari assassins waiting to emerge from the shadows and strike down any enemy dead with impunity. It was an unorthodox tactic, but in terms of prolonging the longevity of the sect it is hard to dispute that it was by now fairly effective. Further disturbance to the political coherence of the Islamic states of the region was caused when il-Bursuqi's successor, his son Mas'ud, died shortly afterwards. He had quarrelled with Toghtekin not long before and rumours asserted that his death was brought on by poisoning (though this time the finger of suspicion pointed at Toghtekin himself, rather than the Nizaris. It is interesting to note that there almost no alleged Nizari assassinations that involved any weapon other than a knife).

Although such acts were the events for which the Nizaris were subsequently best remembered in the West, there were other developments taking place which were much more important in protecting the future of the Nizaris in the region. Bahram is, like most Nizari *da'is*, a shadowy figure; the lack of detailed histories of the Nizaris and the desire of such men to avoid too much public scrutiny, make this inevitably the case. Ibn al-Qalanasi notes that 'he lived in extreme concealment and secrecy, and continually disguised himself, so that he moved from city to city and castle to castle without anyone being aware of his identity'.[10] He had made his way from Persia (evidencing that the Nizaris in Persia still provided the overall leadership of the movement), concealing his movements during his journey westwards.

Now that Bahram had succeeded in improving the position of the Nizaris in Syria, he worked conscientiously to protect his gains, particularly at the castle of Banyas. He planned to make this the base for his mission in Syria: 'he set about fortifying it and rebuilding what of it was in ruins or out of repair. In all directions, he despatched his missionaries, who enticed a great multitude of the ignorant folk of the provinces and foolish peasantry from the villages . . . Their evil power was thereby increased and the true nature of their false doctrine made manifest'.[11]

He substantially improved the state of the defences, and then used it as a base for a concerted effort to preach the *da'wa* in the surrounding countryside. It was in many ways perfect territory for such a mission. There were many Druzes and other factions in the area who offered great potential for conversion. But his efforts were to prove short-lived. His followers were implicated in the murder of a local chieftain. Soon after, Bahram was involved in a battle with the dead man's brother, who had sworn to avenge him. The battle went badly for Bahram; his men were defeated and in the course of the battle he was killed. As a mark of respect to the Fatimid caliph, Bahram's head and one of his hands were removed and sent to Cairo for the Fatimids to gloat over.

All in all, 1128 (the year in which Bahram was killed) was a bad year for the Nizaris in Syria. In the same year, Toghtekin of Damascus, their protector, also died. All was not lost however as al-Mazdaqani, the vizier who had supported their cause in the past, was still the chief adviser of Toghtekin's successor, Buri. But the vizier's days were numbered. Buri did not share his hopes and aspirations, and perhaps also had no wish to be under al-Mazdaqani's restrictive influence for too long. He soon felt confident enough to arrange for al-Mazdiqani's murder. Once he was removed, it was fairly clear that the Nizaris, al-Mazdaqani's allies, were also likely to be repressed.

In the aftermath of the vizier's murder the people of Damascus, who as a rule despised the Nizaris, vented their fury on them. The ferocity of the populace was unconstrained and in the massacres that followed, it was said that 6,000 Nizaris were killed. Ibn al-Qalanasi describes the events in some detail, stating that 'a large number of individuals among them who had taken refuge with various high quarters in order to protect themselves, and who hoped for safety through their intercession, were forcibly seized and their blood was shed without fear of consequences.' For one man in particular the end was terrible:[12]

'Among those who were captured was the man known as Shadhi the freedman, the pupil of Abu Tahir the Batini goldsmith who was formerly at Aleppo. This accursed freedman was the root of all the trouble and evil, and was repaid with the severest punishment, at which the hearts of many of the Believers were comforted. He was crucified, along with a few others of the sect, on the battlements of the walls of Damascus . . .'[13] Ismail however, who had taken the place of Bahram, was not in the city but was at Banyas, but the events that took place at Damascus affected him greatly. Soon afterwards, he surrendered Banyas to the Franks, and went to live in their lands. In 1130, he died of dysentery.

His demise seemed to mark the beginning of the end of the Syrian diversion of the Nizaris but in fact it led to a change of direction in their tactics. Their ejection, first from Aleppo and then from Damascus, had effectively ended their hopes of forming a militant group in the cities. As a result, they were forced to seek their salvation by setting up more bases in remoter areas. The irony of this of course was that it was exactly the tactic that had proved so successful an approach in Persia. The radicalism of the movement meant that, when times were difficult, the local population were always likely to turn on the Nizaris and vent their frustrations on them. This was easy enough in a city where the normally outnumbered Nizaris had few places to run or hide. It was however quite a different proposition if the Nizaris were to revert to their time-honoured approach of seeking refuge in remote and powerful mountain fortresses.

The Nizaris were not slow to exact their revenge. Shortly afterwards, Buri was attacked by two *fida'is* sent from Persia (perhaps a suggestion of the current weakness of the Nizaris in Syria itself was that they were not

Syrian assassins). He was stabbed in the neck and hip. His assailants were overwhelmed and killed but, although Buri survived for a time, a year later the hip wound reopened and he died.

The Nizaris in Syria were perhaps due a change in fortune given this difficult period for them in the country and it duly arrived after their terrible sufferings in Damascus. In the years that followed, a number of important fortresses were taken, which collectively became known as '*qila al-daʿwa*' or 'the fortresses of the *daʿwa*'. The first of them, the castle of Qadmus, was in fact bought from an Islamic warlord in 1133 rather than conquered (it had been captured by him from the Franks the year before). Under the leadership of another energetic *daʿi* in the region, a man named Abu'l Fath, this became the epicentre of a series of Nizari conquests. The Crusaders had failed to exploit their early successes on the coastal plain by pushing into the hinterland and, aided by their lack of success, the Nizaris were able to make a number of gains. Other fortresses followed, such as Kariba, which was captured from the Franks in 1137.

That these assaults were attended with extreme violence is clear from some of the accounts that survive. In a Nizari attack on Shaizar, one of the defenders, named Hammam al-Hajj, found himself in hand-to-hand combat with a Nizari. In the fight that followed, 'the Ismailite held in his hand a dagger, while al-Hajj held a sword. The Batinite rushed on him with the knife, but Hammam struck him with his sword above his eyes. The blow broke his skull, and his brains fell out and were scattered over the ground. Hammam, laying the sword from his hand, vomited all that he had in his stomach, on account of the sickening he felt at the sight of those brains'.[14] The intensity and terror of movements such as these, and the bloody and intimate nature of medieval warfare, are a powerful antidote to any excessively romantic views of the Nizaris that their mythology might encourage.

Their greatest success so far, however, was still to come. About forty miles to the north-east of Homs, on the edge of a mountain range known as the Jabal Bahra, stood a fortress at a place called Masyaf. It was captured by the Nizaris in 1140. From a position amidst rugged cliffs, it looked down imperiously on the plains below, its massive walls seemingly impervious to assault. Resonant of many similar positions in Persia, it was an ideal base for the Nizaris to continue their *da'wa* in Syria. It would become their focal point in the region, and eventually the Syrian equivalent of Alamut, the great, the unconquerable. The Nizaris had at last begun to establish themselves in Syria. It marked part of an important upwards trend for the Syrian Nizaris; by the end of the twelfth century, the Western chronicler William of Tyre would claim that they held ten castles in Syria, and had 60,000 adherents there.[15]

Against difficult odds, the Nizaris survived in Syria and then started to expand. Frequent attempts to destroy them, particularly by the emir of Mosul, Zengi (who ejected the Crusaders from one of their greatest conquests of the First Crusade in the city of Edessa), were resisted. In the middle of the twelfth century, the Syrian Nizaris started (in relative terms at least) to feel secure in the region. On the bedrock laid during these years the Syrian Nizaris were about to enjoy their most productive, or to the West, at least, their most evocative, years.

But the image of the Nizaris was about to change. Events were about to occur which would bring them much more to the forefront of Western minds, and in so doing the myth of the 'Assassins' was about to assume an altogether more exaggerated level than had previously been the case. So far, the Nizaris had on the whole avoided targeting prominent Crusader figures in their assassination attempts, although they did from time to time come to blows with the Franks in pitched battle. Perhaps the Nizaris had more important targets elsewhere to concentrate on, or had merely ignored the Crusaders except when they directly stood in the way of advancing Nizari interests.

Indeed at times the Nizaris acted in concert with the Crusaders, though not always with success. In 1148, a Kurdish chief of the Assassins, Ali ibn Wafa, joined the Franks under the leadership of Raymond of Antioch in a campaign against Nur-ed Din, a rising Sunni star in Syria. Ali ibn Wafa saw great benefit from the enterprise, as he recognized in Nur-ed Din an enormous threat and consequently, according to Runciman, 'hated Nur-ed Din far more than the Christians'.[16] Their mission met with some success, catching Nur-ed Din off his guard.

But when Nur-ed Din besieged the fortress of Inab in the following year and the Franks, with their Nizari allies hurried to the rescue, the outcome was very different. The Muslim forces were larger than those of the Franks but despite the advice of Ali Raymond decided to attempt to reinforce the besieged garrison at Inab. On 28 June 1149, the Franks and their Nizari allies camped overnight close by the fortress at Inab, at a spot in a hollow known as the Fountain of Murad. When they awoke in the morning, it was to find that during the hours of darkness they had been surrounded by the forces of Nur-ed Din.

There was little option but to attempt to fight their way out but it was a hopeless contest, with the odds against the Franks and the Nizaris lengthening even more when a sandstorm blew up in the faces of the Frankish heavy cavalry, the only real hope of survival for the allied force. The resultant battle was in reality more of a massacre. Nur-ed Din pressed home his advantage to the full. Ali was killed, along with Raymond of Antioch. The latter was a particularly important prize for Nur-ed Din who sent the skull of Raymond, placed in a silver case, to the caliph in Baghdad as a token that the Infidel had been crushed.

Yet despite this reverse and the loss of Edessa to Zengi in 1144 (after which the Crusader county around it effectively withered away, ultimately to nothing), the Crusader territories elsewhere continued to prosper reasonably effectively. One of these was the county of Tripoli. By 1152, its Count, Raymond II, was experiencing marital difficulties. Attempts were made by the King of Jerusalem to patch up their differences, seemingly with success. His wife, the lady Hodierna, was to take a vacation in Jerusalem, after which she would return to her husband's side.

Looking every bit the devoted couple, Raymond escorted Hodierna to the city gates to wish her a comfortable journey. As he returned to his headquarters through the city streets, he was set upon by a band of men who had approached him surreptitiously. In the mêlée that followed, he was struck down and killed. A hue and cry went up in the city. Every Muslim that could be found (for the killers were definitely men of Eastern extraction) was killed on the spot in retribution but of the real killers no trace was found. They merely disappeared back into the shadows from which they had come. Men had no doubt that they were Nizari *fida'is*, though what their purpose was in murdering Raymond few could explain.[17]

It was the first time that the Nizaris were accused of murdering a Crusader noble. Throughout the entire history of the Crusader kingdoms only a handful of Western knights were assassinated in this way, far fewer than the number of Islamic notables killed elsewhere. But the murders would, understandably enough, strike a chord with Western chroniclers who would embellish the myth of the 'Assassins' until they were perceived as spectral, unprincipled killers, ghosts who would vanish into thin air once their heinous crimes had been committed. The stage was set for the first great flowering of the 'Assassins' myth in the West, the image that lives on in so many vivid imaginations to this day.

SEVEN

The Resurrection

After a shaky start in Syria, the Nizaris began to consolidate their position in the country. However, at this stage the Nizari mission to Syria was not the main focus of the movement's activities. The epicentre of the movement was still to be found in Persia. While the Nizaris had been attempting to establish themselves in Syria, much had also been happening in Persia. Fundamental changes were taking place, which had a profound impact on the movement.

Kiya Buzurg-Ummid, who succeeded Hasan-i Sabbah in 1124, had been a loyal supporter of the Nizari cause, remaining as custodian of the important castle of Lamasar for nearly thirty years before his appointment as chief *da'i*. His limited experience of wider affairs may have appeared to have made his succession a time of potential instability for the Nizaris. But Hasan had fulfilled his duty to the cause that he believed in so passionately to the last, for he recognized in Buzurg-Ummid a capable, efficient and loyal administrator who would give of his best to further the interests of the Nizaris. He would prove to be an able leader of the movement, perhaps lacking the inspirational qualities of his predecessor and certainly not emulating his early successes (though circumstances had changed much since those first heady days of triumph) but someone who at least provided stability and a degree of continuity. His greatest achievement was to lead the Nizaris through a period of consolidation in Persia while, further west, the *da'wa* in Syria at last took root and began to show profit.

The Seldjuks badly misjudged the temper of the Nizaris when Hasan died. They reckoned that the Nizaris would be at their weakest now that Hasan had perished. Sanjar's vizier, Mu'in al-Din Kashi, was instrumental in launching a fateful assault on the Nizaris. He gave orders to 'kill them, wherever they were and wherever they were conquered, to pillage their property and enslave their women . . . he despatched troops against every part of their possessions, with orders to kill whatever Isma'ilis they encountered'.[1]

However, the assumption that there would be instability among the Nizaris now that Hasan-i Sabbah was dead was erroneous. Hasan's influence was so strong that few Nizaris felt inclined to ignore his choice of successor. The Seldjuks however seemed to be unaware of this. Massacres of Isma'ilis took place in 1124 (the year of Buzurg-Ummid's accession to the throne) and two years later two larger-scale offensives were launched against the Nizaris.

Neither of these achieved very much. In the east, Sanjar had left the Nizaris largely to their own devices for many years, perhaps suggesting a truce (official or unofficial is not clear) between him and the group. However, he took advantage of what he assumed to be the weakening of the Nizari position after Hasan's death to renew his old territorial aims in Quhistan, the isolated, desert province in the distant east of Persia. He sent a large force aggressively into the region, massacring Isma'ilis in several centres. In one of them, an Isma'ili village called Tarz, the population was virtually wiped out. The leader of the Nizaris in the village killed himself by throwing himself headlong from the top of the minaret of the mosque rather than surrender himself to the very dubious mercies of his enemies. But, again, Quhistan proved not to be fruitful territory for Sanjar. Except for a few very minor gains, nothing was achieved for all his efforts.

The campaign launched by the Seldjuks in the north proved even less fruitful. The district of Rudbar (from which, incidentally, Buzurg-Ummid originally came), in which Alamut was situated, was again their target. A large army set out for the region, led by Asil, a nephew of Shirgir who had abandoned the siege of Alamut nearly a decade before when so favourably placed. Not only did the Seldjuks fail to make any gains of significance, they were driven back, no doubt suffering much at the hands of the local Nizaris of Rudbar who were far more experienced in taking advantage of the rugged local conditions. A great deal of plunder was taken by the Nizaris in this reverse, as well as a number of prisoners taken.

Among these captives was an important emir, Tamurtughan. Sanjar was so deflated at his capture that he personally humbled himself and negotiated with the Nizaris for his release. Neither was this the end of the Isma'ilis' revenge. The campaign against them, as we have seen, had originally been the brainchild of the Sultan's vizier, Mu'in al-Din Kashi, who had led the recent expedition to Quhistan. In 1127, he took on two new grooms in his household. As the Persian New Year approached, he summoned them into his presence. He wished to ingratiate himself with the Sultan by presenting him with two fine horses and he wanted the grooms to pick out the most suitable pair for him. On the morning of 16 March, they came to see him. Before he knew what was happening, they had grabbed hold of him and stabbed him to death. The grooms were in reality Nizari *fida'is*. It was another useful reminder from the Nizaris to their enemies that the latter should leave them in peace or personally look out for the consequences.

The Nizaris made other gains in this period. As well as seizing several less notable fortifications, they also constructed for themselves a large castle at Maymundiz. With its size and position it reflected well enough the continuing confidence and morale of the Nizaris. With their situation considerably enhanced after these abortive Seldjuk campaigns against them, other important warlords in the region reasoned that they should seek to remain on good terms with the Nizaris. In 1129, one of them, Mahmud – at the time the Seldjuk sultan of Isfahan (the days when the Seldjuks had one all-powerful Great Sultan had long gone) – sent messages to Alamut, asking Buzurg-Ummid to despatch envoys to Isfahan to discuss the terms of a peace treaty.

This proved to be a fatal move for the Nizari envoys. The population of Isfahan seized them after they had left Mahmud and murdered them. Mahmud was apologetic towards the Nizaris but did not feel strong enough to punish the leaders of the lynch mob. As a result, the negotiations fizzled out. The Nizaris took their revenge by attacking the town of Qazwin, killing 400 inhabitants in the process. Inevitably, tit-for-tat retaliation followed, with Mahmud sending an expedition against Alamut, though predictably with no more success than his predecessors. Another expedition against the powerful fortress of Lamasar also failed.

But this was effectively Mahmud's last campaign against the Nizaris, for he died in 1131. Unsurprisingly, his succession was bitterly disputed, giving the Nizaris another chance to recover their strength. This particular succession dispute lasted longer than most (the new sultan was eventually to be Mahmud's brother, Mas'ud), and one of the men who sought to take advantage of the ensuing confusion to further his own ambitions was the Abbasid caliph, al-Mustarshid. The caliphate was a pale shadow of what it had once been, its power effectively destroyed many years past. Al-Mustarshid made efforts to remedy this by entering into an alliance with a coalition of emirs against the new sultan. The subsequent campaign however eventually ended in failure and defeat for al-Mustarshid. He was captured by the sultan and, in 1135, was taken as his prisoner to the town of Maragha. Maragha was not unfamiliar with the Nizaris as, a short time previously, the governor of the city had fallen victim to an assassin's knife.

Representations were made to the sultan, particularly by the veteran campaigner, Sanjar, not to punish the caliph too severely. The sultan agreed not to harm him and treated him well. He was kept within the confines of Mas'ud's camp, however. Shortly after, a party of assassins made their way into the camp. The attack that followed was particularly frenzied. Twenty-four assailants laid about al-Mustarshid, 25 wounds being inflicted on him in the attack. His abdomen was slit open, his nose cut off, and he was decapitated. His corpse was stripped, and two of his servants killed. This was an overwhelming attack, and it seems clear that the guard placed over the caliph was wholly inadequate, although a party of soldiers set off after the escaping assassins and killed a number of them.

At the time there was much speculation that the Nizaris were not in this instance the perpetrators of the crime. Certainly, Mas'ud had no reason to protect the caliph other than to maintain good relations with Sanjar. As a result, many said that he was either himself the instigator of the murder or that he had deliberately been lax in keeping guard over al-Mustarshid, who as the Sunni caliph was reviled by the Nizaris. Even Sanjar was not above suspicion of complicity, so much so that Juwayni felt it necessary to act as apologist for him, stating that 'his respect for all that related to the caliphate and compassion are too plain for such false and slanderous charges to be laid against his person'.[2]

Whatever the truth of these theories (and the Nizaris were often convenient scapegoats for virtually every murder in the region at the time) when news of the caliph's death was received at Alamut, wild rejoicing ensued. In accordance with Nizari convention on such occasions, the celebrations lasted for seven days and seven nights. Certainly, it appears that the Nizaris were quick to claim the credit for this particular assassination.

Buzurg-Ummid's reign was characterized by a far smaller number of such assassinations than Hasan-i Sabbah's (though those who were killed were sometimes extremely important individuals). Buzurg-Ummid spent much of his reign consolidating the Nizari position in and around its base in Daylam. There was another significant Shiite group present in the region, the Zaydis, with whom the Nizaris had long enjoyed an acrimonious rivalry. In 1131, a Zaydi named Abu Hashim claimed to be the Imam of the Isma'ilis, a boast that was effectively considered as heresy by the Nizaris.

Buzurg-Ummid resolved to stamp on such sedition quickly. He sent letters to Hashim, rebuking him for his false claims and informing him that he would be made to answer for his blasphemies. Shortly afterwards, a Nizari army was despatched to punish Hashim for his heretical proclamations. In the ensuing campaign, Hashim was captured and brought back to Alamut. Here, Buzurg-Ummid berated him for his heresy and attempted to persuade him that his doctrines and beliefs were misguided. According to some accounts, his persuasion was successful for Hashim abandoned his previous claims and opted instead to become a Nizari. It did him little good, however, as he was burned alive as his punishment.

During Buzurg-Ummid's reign, which lasted until 1138, there was some action in areas away from the Nizari heartland (for example, the Nizari assassins were occasionally active in Georgia) but generally efforts were concentrated on their power bases, now Daylam and the region around Alamut, the area of Quhistan in the east of Persia and the Nizari enclave in Syria. On one occasion a former enemy of the Nizaris, Yarankush, sought sanctuary at Alamut. Buzurg-Ummid gave him the protection that he required. Even when Yarankush's arch-enemy, the Shah of Khwarazm, who had for many years enjoyed good relations with the Nizaris, asked Buzurg-Ummid to hand him over, he was rebuffed. Buzurg-Ummid argued that it would be wrong for the head of a state who had offered another man his protection to subsequently go back on his word. Buzurg-Ummid was clearly a man with a well-developed sense of honour.

Buzurg-Ummid's long life ended on 9 February 1138. He had been a prominent figure in the Nizari movement for at least four decades, and had shown himself to be a worthy successor to the great Hasan-i Sabbah. His supporters reverenced his memory, burying him next to Hasan at Alamut. His enemies of course were ecstatic, describing the day of his death as the time 'when he was crushed under the heel of Perdition and Hell was heated with the fuel of his carcass'.[3] They were also encouraged by what they thought would be the succession dispute that they believed would follow but again their expectations in this respect were to be disappointed. Three days before his death, he had nominated his son Muhammad as his successor. The degree of control and organization then enjoyed by the Nizari leadership among their followers is nowhere better evidenced than by the fact that this nomination was accepted, as far as can be ascertained, without a murmur. The trappings of power were transferred seamlessly to Muhammad in accordance with Buzurg-Ummid's last wishes.

This was an interesting development. The Nizaris had not previously practised a hereditary form of succession (although the Nizari movement, as opposed to the Isma'ilis more generally, was still very young) but in fact it did set a precedent for the future. It also perhaps reflects Isma'ili tradition, which asserts that the Imamate passed from father to son.[4] Muhammad's reign was to be ushered in by another significant assassination, almost as if the new incumbent of the seat of power at Alamut was seeking to stamp his mark at the beginning of his reign. Al-Mustarshid, the slain Abbasid caliph, left behind him a son, al-Rashid, who succeeded him. He was naturally as despised by the Nizaris because of his position as his father had been. He had also fallen out with the Seldjuks, so much so that they deposed him. He travelled from Iraq to Persia to seek support in the struggle for his re-instatement, but was taken ill in Isfahan. There, in June 1138, a group of Nizari assassins fell on him and killed him. The deed was once more celebrated with a week of festivities in Alamut, a fitting beginning to Muhammad's tenure.

Yet in many ways, this violent start to his reign was not representative of what was to follow. There were fewer assassinations while Muhammad was the chief *da'i* of the *da'wa* in Persia than there had been in previous reigns, substantially so when compared to the reign of Hasan-i Sabbah. Again, several of those killed by *fidai's* were men of some stature and importance, so the Nizaris still made their mark on the societies that surrounded their isolated provinces. Apart from al-Rashid, the other victim of great prominence to fall to them, in 1143, was Da'ud, a Seldjuk sultan. He was the target for four assassins who eliminated him while he was in the north Persian town of Tabriz. Some pointed the finger at Zengi, the emir of Mosul, to whom Da'ud was a potential rival but the Nizaris had equally good reason to want him out of the way, as he was the leader of a faction that was despised both on religious and political grounds (in truth, the two were thoroughly intertwined within the Islamic world) by the Nizaris.

These significant victims aside, the total number of recorded assassinations (14 in the 24 years of Muhammad's reign) represented a small sum of victims when compared to the much larger numbers of enemies eliminated in similar fashion in the past. It may be thought that this represented an inevitable part of the evolution of the Nizari movement. After all, many states that are originally built on revolutionary and radical roots eventually have had to learn to live with their neighbours. Constant warfare and attrition may, in the longer run, be beyond the resources and the energies of such movements, who have to learn to compromise, to practise the art of politics, to make their way in the world. In this context, there was nothing particularly surprising in the fact that the number of such murders tailed off as, on political grounds, there was good reason to seek a greater accommodation with one's neighbours (or at least antagonize them less than had been the case in the past). However, with a radical movement such as that of the Nizaris, with sometimes fanatical devotees (and such radicalism is usually the most immovable, least open to compromise, motivation of all), many members of the movement were unhappy at this less assertive attitude towards their natural enemies.

There were other signs that the place of the Nizaris in the world was undergoing something of a sea change. The documents of the movement that survive from the period deal almost exclusively with minor and relatively trivial issues. They are far more likely to discuss local cattle raids and boundary disputes than they are the wider issues affecting Islam and the Muslim world in its broader sense. This is a fundamentally important

111

clue to the way that Nizari paradigms of the world were changing to reflect altered circumstances. The early years of conquest, inspired by visions of winning the world for Islam (at least in its Nizari form) had been replaced by a much more limited perspective, one which recognized that the Nizaris were not going to conquer the world (at least in the short term) and had better get used to a more restricted vision, one that barely looked beyond survival or, at best, consolidation. Nizari Isma'ilism had lost its ambition. In short, it had become localized.

This was reflected in its territorial holdings, which were now largely isolated to two widely separated chunks in Persia and the newly-won territories in Syria. But this was not without its benefits as far as the Nizaris were concerned. For the most part, the Seldjuks round about were content to leave them to undisturbed by this time, as their own dominance was increasingly under threat and they had many distractions elsewhere to divert them from what they perceived to be the heretical Nizari movement.

There were however local confrontations between the Nizaris and their near-neighbours. The two major localized opponents of the Nizaris at this time were the ruler of the region of Mazandaran (which lay on the south shore of the Caspian Sea) and the Seldjuk governor of Rayy, Abbas. It was said that both of them delighted in nothing more than massacring Isma'ili heretics and erecting towers made of the skulls of their victims. The latter had made a dangerous enemy; the seemingly immortal Sanjar, who was a major player in the region for decades. In 1146 or thereabouts, Sanjar arranged for the murder of Abbas while the governor was on a visit to Baghdad. Abbas was then decapitated, and his head was sent to Khurasan as irrefutable proof that he was dead.

During this relative period of tranquillity, Sanjar appears to have continued with his ambivalent policy towards the Nizaris, at some times at odds with the movement, at others assisting them. This probably reflected nothing more than the fact that Sanjar was an inveterate opportunist, always ready to adopt the policy which seemed to offer him the greatest prospect of gain. Elsewhere, the Nizaris did not completely abandon their attempts to gain a foothold in the wider world. There was even a mission to Afghanistan during Muhammad's reign.[5] But these initiatives were limited in scope and ambition, a pale reflection of the much more adventurous projects entered into during the reign of Hasan-i Sabbah.

There were murmurings of discontent among some Nizaris who looked back at the days of Hasan-i Sabbah as a kind of halcyon era, when nothing was impossible for the fledgling movement. There also appears to have been an increasing level of frustration at the fact that there appeared to be no imminent return of the Hidden Imam, long awaited since the death of Nizar, which had occurred nearly half a century before. Throughout the long years of struggle while the Nizaris sought to establish themselves, the prospect of the resurrection of the Imam (the *qiyama* as it was known to the Isma'ilis) had been a consistent source of encouragement to the movement. As time passed, however, with no sign of his imminent coming, dissatisfaction and disillusionment among some of the Nizaris grew.

All these problems were about to come to a head. Muhammad appeared to be a devout and committed man, stern in his beliefs and his adherence to the *sharï'a* (Islamic law) but not, it seems, charismatic in his leadership. Unfortunately for him, his son, Hasan, was from a distinctly different mould. From a very early age, he showed a deep interest in the writings of Hasan-i Sabbah, whose zeal and fervour appear to have exercised a certain magnetism for the adolescent Hasan. As he grew older, it became clear that he was destined to be a persuasive orator, whose skill and intelligence would win many supporters to his side.

Hasan began to develop doctrines which appeared to some of the more traditional Nizaris to be heretical; doctrines concerning for example the importance or otherwise of the *sharï'a* and the likely return of the Imam in the near future. Muhammad it appears was a man of little imagination; he was certainly an individual who adhered rigidly to the strict teachings of the Islamic law. There were rumours that Hasan had been drinking wine, which would have incensed Muhammad. He was extremely perturbed by the radical ideas of his son, and he determined to stamp on them before they undermined his authority and threatened the stability of the Nizaris. He asserted emphatically that: 'this Hasan is my son, and I am not the Imam but one of his *daïs*. Whoever listens to these [Hasan's] words and believes them is an infidel and an atheist'.[6]

His harsh words were followed by even harsher action. He resolved to make an example of those who agreed with his son's unorthodox teachings in a way that could not possibly be misinterpreted. In a vivid and unmistakable assertion of the legitimacy of traditional Nizari adherence to

113

the *sharī'a*, 250 of Hasan's followers were executed. Another 250 were exiled from the castle at Alamut. Each one was forced to make their way out from the castle with the corpse of one of those executed tied to their backs.

It was a blunt warning to Hasan that his views were unacceptable to Muhammad. Hasan quickly moderated his views. He was perhaps lucky to survive; after all, Hasan-i Sabbah had not hesitated to kill two of his errant sons. His change of heart apparently appeared to convince his father, who accepted him back into the fold, so much so that he nominated Hasan to succeed him on his death. But Hasan maybe had studied the early teachings of the Nizaris, particularly the doctrine of caution, or *taqiyya*, which allowed an Isma'ili to hide his true beliefs to protect himself. For the evidence that emerged soon after Hasan succeeded his father was to demonstrate that, rather than moderating his views, if anything they appeared to have become more extreme.

Muhammad died in 1162 and was succeeded by Hasan, then a man of some 35 years of age. At the start of his reign, there was little obvious sign that he would exercise an approach that was very different than that of his father. There was the occasional hint that certain aspects of the *sharī'a* would not be applied with the rigidity that had been the case while his father led the Nizaris. But this relaxation was very general in its application, and did not seem to presage any significant change in overall Nizari attitudes and beliefs.

Those who believed that Hasan had meekly opted to adopt the ways of his father however clearly did not know him well. The change of tack, when it did come, would be huge, ushering in a new epoch for the Nizaris (Hasan himself believed that it would herald a new dawn for the entire world). Hasan had been at the head of the Nizari movement for some two and a half years when he summoned his supporters to Alamut where, he told them, he wished to address them on a subject of the greatest possible importance. This required a good deal of organization; summonses were sent out to Nizaris across Persia. A great number of them dutifully made the journey towards the mountains of Daylam, and the unconquerable citadel of Alamut, perched menacingly on its eyrie, watching over the plains far below as an immense trail of people made their way up the winding path which led to the castle on the summit.

A large congregation assembled in the castle courtyard. The date was 8 August 1164. It was of significance to the Isma'ilis for two reasons: firstly, it marked the anniversary of the day that Ali, focal point of the Shiite movement, had been killed. Secondly, it fell in the middle of Ramadan, a time when the Muslims generally were required to fast during the hours of daylight and eat only a very restrictive range of foods during the hours of darkness. In the middle of the courtyard, facing west towards the holy city of Mecca, was a pulpit that had been especially erected for the occasion. It was festooned with great banners, one at each corner, one white, one red, one yellow and one green.

The whole proceedings were brilliantly stage-managed. The congregation was organized meticulously, split up according to where they had originally come from, those from the eastern Nizari territories to the right of the pulpit, those from the western regions to the left and those from the north directly in front of it. In a symbolic statement that those in the congregation could not at this stage possibly have been fully aware of, they were all standing with their backs towards Mecca. It was just before noon when Hasan made his grand entrance.

He slowly made his way to the pulpit, proceeding with majesty and solemnity, an ethereal, almost ghostly figure, dressed in a robe of white, his head covered by a turban of the same colour. Deliberately and respectfully, he bowed to each segment of the crowd, all the time holding in his hand a sword, a symbolic declaration of his power of life and death over all men. Then he began, his audience hushed, waiting with bated breath for their leader to preach to them and offer them his vision of the future.

Confidently and loudly, he spoke. He had, he said, been in communication with the Hidden Imam himself. The time for compromise had passed. No longer would the Nizaris have to suffer a prolonged period of agonized anticipation, waiting in frustration for the moment (they knew not when) that the Hidden Imam would return.

Addressing himself to 'the inhabitants of the worlds, both men and angels', he told his enthralled audience that a message had come to him from the hidden Imam, with new guidance that 'The Imam of our time has sent you his blessing and his compassion, and has called you his special chosen servants. He has freed you from the burdens of the rules of Holy Law, and has brought to you his Resurrection'.

The waiting was over. The Hidden Imam had returned, and now spoke directly to his people through the mouthpiece of Hasan himself. He explained himself further. In the past, Hasan-i Sabbah had been the Imam's representative on earth, but Hasan was more than this; he was the caliph in person.[7] The moment of Resurrection, *qiyama*, was here and now. In recognition of this, the strict adherence to *shari'a*, the letter of the religious law, that had previously been practised by the Isma'ilis was no longer necessary. Such rigorous application of the law was only necessary to prepare the world for the moment when the true Islamic way would once more be restored to the world. Now that this moment had arrived, the law was no longer required.

So that none should be in doubt as to his spiritual status, the Imam had also sent word that Hasan is 'our vicar, *da'i* and proof. Our party must obey and follow him in both religious and worldly matters, recognize his command as our command and know that his word is our word'.[8] The Hidden Imam wanted everyone to know that Hasan's authority was absolute and unchallengeable.

Such pronouncements might seem somewhat vague to the modern mind; to the Medieval Nizari mind it was the most radical and revolutionary statement that could be imagined. It was as if, at a stroke, the whole of the world had been turned on its head. Nothing would ever be the same again. There must surely have been a range of emotions present in the crowd. For so long, the Nizaris had been taught that the only way to salvation was adherence to the law, albeit that the concept of *batin* had allowed much flexibility in its interpretation. To be told that everything they had practised in the past with such religiosity and reverence was now redundant must surely have come as a shock to many. But they had also been told that their leader was to all intents and purposes infallible in his comprehension of spiritual matters and his announcement to them therefore offered a wonderful prospect of a new golden age.

In order to emphasize the point that the *shari'a* was no longer relevant to them, he ordered the congregation to indulge themselves in a great feast that had been prepared for them (something that would have been unthinkable during the period of Ramadan previously). Messengers were despatched post haste across Persia to spread the incredible news throughout the Nizari community. Other aspects of the *shari'a* were abandoned. Previously, Islam had required that all Muslims should pray five times a day. Now, this was no longer required. In the light of the resurrection, the coming once again of the true age of Islam, man was effectively in communion with Allah all the time; as a result he could speak to Him whenever and wherever he wished.[9]

The stage management of this momentous event was all-important, especially the date that it took place. Hodgson recognizes that 'it was perhaps suitable to pick the day of Ali's death to proclaim a resurrection of the dead'.[10] It would transpire however that those who wished to believe that this ushered in the beginning of an age when the Nizaris would conquer the world in a physical sense were sadly mistaken. In fact, Hasan's vision of the coming of Islam was more subtle than this. He reasoned that, now the moment of resurrection had arrived, the ultimate spiritual world, paradise itself, now existed within the physical world. All those who wished to accept the doctrines of the Nizaris could find the spiritual world here and now on this earth, while all those who did not were condemned to live in Hell, also within the physical world (the definition of Hell being the unfulfilled and miserable nature of all those who refused to accept the Nizari way). The *qiyama* was, in the words of one commentator, the 'final judgement against [the Nizaris'] opponents – whoever is not now saved, never will be'.[11]

It was a subtle argument, which naturally enough appeared to the enemies of the sect as being naïve, self-deluding and heretical. The *qiyama* was, as has been noted, a 'declaration of independence from larger Muslim society'.[12] But it also recognized two other facts of life. The first of these was that the physical conquest of Islam, or even Persia, by the Nizaris increasingly appeared to be an impractical and unachievable ambition. Such an outcome appeared well beyond the reasonable limits of Nizari ambitions at this moment in time. This being so, it was perhaps as well to change the definition of what were the primary objectives of the movement. Otherwise, the morale of the Nizaris might be irretrievably damaged. Secondly, it recognized implicitly the geographical limitations of the Nizaris, confined as they generally were to limited spheres of influence within Persia and Syria. Effectively, the doctrines espoused by Hasan were to increase the insularity of the Nizaris, particularly so in Persia. From this moment on, the Nizaris would, for a time, turn their backs on the outside world, which was in their eyes both living in a state of darkness and also, as a result, largely irrelevant to them.

A similar ceremony took place in Quhistan a short time later. At the fortress of Mu'minabad the chief called the congregation together and addressed them in a similar fashion to that adopted by Hasan at Alamut. Preaching from a pulpit that was also facing the wrong way round, his message was, according to the chroniclers, ecstatically received, so much so that the 'assembly played harp and rebeck and openly drank wine upon the very steps of that pulpit'.[13]

It has been argued that Hasan's radical ideas, which ultimately led to him openly claiming to be the Imam himself, were generally accepted by the Nizaris, both in Persia and in Syria, at least outwardly.[14] However, it is difficult to believe that all the Nizaris willingly accepted his teachings. After all, the movement had previously become very conservative in its attitude to the *sharï'a* (Hasan-i Sabbah's execution of his own son for drinking wine being just one example of how seriously breaches of religious law were taken). It is probable that, even if outwardly many subscribed to the radical concepts espoused by Hasan, inwardly a number of them were left uncertain and confused by this complete volte-face regarding the doctrinal beliefs of the Nizaris. Certainly, such was the view of Juwayni.[15]

That there was indeed dissent within the Nizari community was soon to be evidenced in the most spectacular way possible. A group of dissidents were enraged by what they saw as Hasan's heresy and his sacrilegious assumption of semi-divine status. Prominent among these men was his own brother-in-law, Hasan ibn Namawar. Certainly, the cause of these rebels was to be helped by Hasan's fierce resolve in eliminating those who refused to accept his teachings. Any who refused to accept the reality of the Resurrection were condemned to die a brutal death by stoning.[16] A plot was hatched by a group of conspirators who wished to remove Hasan before he committed any more blasphemies. It was led by his brother-in-law. On 9 January 1161, in the great castle at Lamasar, Hasan was stabbed to death. His reign had been short but, in a religious sense, momentous.

As it happened, the assassination of Hasan would do his brother-in-law little good. Dynastically, the leadership of the Nizaris was continued by the assumption of power of Hasan's son, who became Muhammad II. He would continue his father's policies. One of his first acts was to order the execution of his father's murderer and most of his family with him. His succession was, from what we can ascertain, largely unopposed. The perceived heresy therefore outlived Hasan himself, which means that whatever uncertainty there was within the Nizari community was not strong enough to overthrow the established leadership of the movement. The murdered Imam was much reverenced by many Nizaris, who awarded him the title of Hasan *ala dhikrihi'l-salam* – Hasan, 'on his mention be peace'.

Muhammad was only nineteen years of age when he assumed leadership of the Nizaris in Persia. Partly because of his youth when he inherited this role, he was to be the longest serving leader of the movement. For nearly fifty years he would be Imam of the Nizaris. But it was to be a time when the insularity of the Persian Nizaris would become increasingly marked. During his period of office, the Syrian Nizaris would effectively go their own way. They would be led by a man who was to become, to the West, the most famous Nizari of them all, who was enshrined in Western legend as the 'Old Man of the Mountain', leader of the mysterious and murderous sect of the 'Assassins'. His personality would dominate the story of the movement like no other – at least in the consciousness of Western Europe.

Rashid al-Din Sinan was born in Iraq near the city of Basra. He later claimed to his biographer that his father was a wealthy man in a village on the road from the city. The exact year of his birth is unclear, some sources giving the impression that it was in 1133 but others that it was 1135. His early religious upbringing is slightly ambiguous. There are traditions current that he started life as a 'Twelver' Shiite. There were however a number of radical Shiite groups in the area where Sinan was brought up. He was therefore likely to have at least known of the existence of less conservative Shiite ideology from very early on in his life.

Given the important position that his father must have held in local society, Sinan maybe looked forward to a rewarding and comfortable life. However, there are hints that early on in Sinan's life there was a serious domestic quarrel within his family. Sinan told his biographer that something happened between him and his brothers which ended with his exile from the family home. It was an acrimonious departure. Sinan's biographer simply claims that he said: 'something occurred between me and my brothers which obliged me to leave them, and I went forth without provision or a mount. I made my way until I reached Alamut, and entered it'.[18]

By this time, Sinan was apparently already either a convert to the Nizari movement, or considering becoming one. It would not have been mere chance or coincidence that led him to make his way to Alamut. Here he sought, and was offered, sanctuary. The *da'i* at the time, Muhammad I, took the youth (for such he must have been at this stage) under his protection. He was entered into the school in the citadel. One of his classmates was Hasan, the same man who would later proclaim the *qiyama* at Alamut. It appears highly probable that the two developed a close bond, for on his accession to the leadership of the Nizaris one of Hasan's first acts was to give Sinan a very prominent position. Soon after Hasan's assumption of power, Sinan was given a task that was to change his life completely. There was not at this time unanimity among the Nizaris in Syria and Hasan decided that Sinan was the man to restore a sense of unity and coherence to the movement there. He was therefore commanded by Hasan to make his way to Syria and await further instructions.[19]

It was a fateful decision. It would certainly give the Syrian Nizaris unity, but one of the major results of this would be to increase their level of independence from Persia. Rather than bringing the Nizaris closer together, it would actually drive them in some respects further apart. But it would have other results as well. Sinan was no blind zealot. He was a politician of immense skill and vision. He would make friends with those who were by inclination his enemies in order that they could make common cause against mutual foes. This would bring the Nizaris into the orbit of a number of different groupings; other Isma'ili sects in Syria, the Fatimids in Egypt, Sunni Muslims throughout the Levant. He would also bring the Nizaris more closely into contact with the world of the Crusaders. It was this latter relationship that would move the Nizaris in the Middle East firmly out of the realms of reality and deep into the world of myth.

EIGHT

The Old Man of the Mountain

Sinan travelled from Persia to Syria adopting a clandestine route. He made his way as discreetly as possible, avoiding as far as he was able the towns along the way. He had letters of introduction and instruction with him, which he would need to establish the legitimacy of his credentials with the Syrian Nizaris. He did on occasion however stop for a short time in safe houses inside some of the towns en route to his destination, where there were Nizari sympathisers. He stayed for a night in Mosul, visiting a building known as 'The Mosque of the Carpenters' in the city.

Once leaving Mosul he again opted to travel on out of the way tracks where his security was more assured until he reached the border between Iraq and Syria at the town of Raqqa. From there, he made his way to the first bastion of Nizari Isma'ilism in Syria, the great city of Aleppo. It was currently ruled by Nur-ed Din, the son of Zengi, a great warrior and implacable enemy of those he regarded as heretical Shiites. When he arrived Nur-ed Din was currently away on a military campaign and Sinan took advantage of his extended period of absence to spend a short time in the city itself. He made contact with some of the Nizaris still remaining in the city, handing them letters from Hasan to prove his authenticity. He probably also acquainted himself with the current state of affairs in Syria, and most especially the position of the Nizaris within the country.

Much had changed during the course of the twelfth century. Although there was still, inevitably as it seemed, constant strife and turbulence in the area, there were signs that some of the major players were becoming more

121

powerful at the expense of others. There were tangible manifestations of an increase in Muslim power in the region, although from a Nizari viewpoint not from a source that they would have found particularly palatable, as the Islamic fightback against the West European Crusader incursions was being led by the Sunnis of Syria.

The first great Sunni leader to strike a major blow for the Islamic cause was Zengi,[1] who captured Edessa from the Crusaders and put most of the Latin Christian population there to the sword. But although it seemed that his power was in the ascendancy, his campaign to recapture the Holy Places of Palestine for Islam was cut short. Zengi was a tempestuous personality, quick to lose his temper and fearsome when he did so. He also indulged frequently in drinking bouts (something which would have shocked many conservative Muslims). During one of these, he awoke from a stupor to find one of his eunuchs drinking from his gold cup. Muttering curses at the servant who had shown such temerity, he threatened to punish him severely for his nerve. He then promptly fell back into his stupor. Probably, when he awoke he would have forgotten what had taken place, so drunk he had been, but this must remain a speculation, for he never woke again. The servant involved was terrified. He therefore killed Zengi while he slept rather than risk his wrath when he woke.

There then followed a rather unsavoury scramble by Zengi's sons to succeed him. So afraid of Zengi were the majority of his retinue that his body was left for a time before anyone dared approach it. When they did so, it was to pull the ring of state from his fingers – whoever held this would have a powerful claim to the throne. Eventually, the succession settled on Nur-ed Din. He was in many ways the antithesis of his father. In mid-career, he became devoutly religious and abstemious in his habits to the point of asceticism. From then on, he lived simply, rejecting the fripperies and excesses that sometimes characterized the courts of the rulers of the time.

But he was also a man of decision, capable of inspiring intense devotion and loyalty. He was above all supremely focussed; he sought for absolute power in the region not, it seems, for his own sake but for the sake of the religion that he held so dear. He would intensify the Muslim world's attempts to drive the Crusaders back to the place from whence they came, laying the foundations from which his ultimate successor, Saladin, would launch a decisive Muslim fightback against the Crusaders from the west. He also perceived that the Fatimid caliphate was effectively dying, and in its weakness he caught a glimpse of a tremendous opportunity to advance the cause of what he saw to be the legitimate form of Islam.

His cause would ironically be greatly helped by the incompetence of the Crusaders themselves. The loss of Edessa had left a deep wound in the West, and another Crusade was launched, led by King Louis VII of France and the Emperor Conrad, ruler of the Holy Roman Empire. After a disastrous crossing of Asia Minor (where much of the army was cut to pieces by ferocious attacks from the Seldjuk Turkish tribesmen who had made their home in the region) the remnants of the Crusade finally arrived on the Mediterranean seaboard of Syria. They could not then decide where to launch their next attack; although the loss of Edessa had given impetus to the Crusade, its recovery was clearly not the only, or even the main, objective of the expedition. Aleppo was seriously discussed as a possible target, but this was eventually overlooked for another Syrian city further south: Damascus.

It was an illogical, almost nonsensical, choice. The city was then ruled by a man named Unur who had entered into an alliance with the Franks. Damascus was a major objective for Nur-ed Din – he would certainly need to capture it if he were to hold complete sway in the region – and the alliance that Unur had formed with the Franks formed a strong barrier against his achievement of this aim. The decision of the Franks to attack Damascus changed all this. Unur was forced into the embrace of Nur-ed Din; once there, he would be unlikely to escape from it again. The siege of Damascus that followed was a fiasco, lasting for three days before the Franks gave up an unequal struggle against a city now heavily reinforced by the soldiers of Nur-ed Din. They achieved nothing save the loss of an invaluable ally in the region. These events took place in 1148. Unur managed to retain a degree of independence following the defeat of the Crusade but Nur-ed Din of course would not slacken off in his push for the city. By 1154, Damascus – and most of Syria – was his.

In the decade following this, Nur-ed Din consolidated his position in Syria. It also became abundantly clear that the Fatimid dynasty was unlikely to survive for much longer. Like a pack of wolves sensing a badly injured prey, predators closed in on Egypt. Assisted by their proximity to the country, the Crusader kingdoms of the Levant invaded it several times, though with limited success. Alarmed at the prospect of the country falling into Christian hands, and also wanting it for his own Empire, Nur-ed Din responded by demonstrating an increasing level of interest in Egypt. His power continued to grow, threatening both Christian invader and Nizari alike. But the Nizaris continued to cling on tenaciously in Syria, enjoying a degree of security behind their solid castle walls, perched on the mountain tops of the country.

One such was the castle of Kahf and it was to this Nizari citadel that Sinan made his way at the end of his journey from Persia. However, it was to be some time before he was able to play a very active role in Syria. The Nizaris in the region already had a leader, Abu Muhammad. His role can be barely discerned through the mists of time. He led the movement in Syria through a difficult period when the security of the young mission in the country was constantly threatened by larger and powerful enemies. But what exactly his role was is largely a matter for conjecture as, generally speaking, we only catch an occasional glimpse of him acting behind the scenes. Yet although he was a shadowy figure he cannot have been completely ineffective, for it was not Sinan's role to overthrow or replace him. According to tradition, Sinan was in Syria for seven years before he became leader of the Nizaris in the region.[2] He presumably spent most of his time getting to know the local population, winning friends and influencing others to help him when the time was right and generally forming an understanding of the Nizaris' position in the country.

When Abu Muhammad died it was far from clear who would succeed him. In fact, the disputes that arose at this time suggest that the unity of the Nizaris, in Syria at least, was not at all complete. Without express instructions from Alamut, his place was taken by a man named Ali ibn Mas'ud. This appointment was however a controversial one (not least perhaps because it had not been sanctioned by the headquarters of the movement at Alamut). Some opponents were so outraged by his assumption of power that they resolved to eliminate him. The two main leaders of this conspiracy were Abu Mansur and another Nizari named Fahd. As Mas'ud was leaving his bath, he was stabbed and killed. The conspirators were not strong enough to step into the breach created by his murder and were arrested. Advice was sought from Alamut as to what should be done with them. Eventually, Abu Mansur was executed but Fahd, for whatever reason receiving more clemency, was subsequently released.

It was in these slightly unsatisfactory circumstances that Sinan took control of the Nizari movement in Syria. Given his prominence in Persia previously, and indeed the nature of his personality, it is inconceivable that he had just lain low during all the time that he had so far spent in the country and he had presumably already built up a groundswell of support in the region. There is no reason to doubt that his appointment was to the satisfaction of the leadership at Alamut (who had, after all, held him in high enough esteem before his departure and had marked him out for this special mission to Syria) and he was therefore soon accepted as the leader of the Syrian Nizaris.

One of his first tasks was to announce the *qiyama* in Syria. It has been pointed out that there was a strange contrast between responses to this momentous religious development between Persia and Syria.[3] In the former region, the Nizaris recorded the event meticulously while their Sunni enemies virtually ignored it. In Syria, the reverse was true. While there is little mention of it from a Nizari standpoint here, the Sunnis in the region had a field day with the radical argument that the *shari'a* could now be abandoned. In their vivid imaginations, it meant that all kinds of depravity and libertinism now took place within the still largely secret world of the Nizaris. In a tale that echoes those told of the Qarmatis a few centuries previously, a Sunni chronicler wrote with relish that 'he had heard that Sinan allows them [i.e. the Nizaris] to defile their mothers and sisters and daughters'[4] while also accusing them of the slightly less erotic sin of abandoning the ritual of fasting during Ramadan.

Sinan quickly took stock of the situation. Surrounded by enemies as he was, he clearly needed to strengthen the position of the Nizaris in the country. Fundamental to the achievement of this aim was that they should first of all enjoy unity among themselves. He therefore threw his energies into healing the rifts that had opened up between the various factions within the Syrian Nizari movement. He also sought to increase the Nizaris' security by strengthening existing castles, building new ones and even on occasion seizing them from the Crusaders. But he did not forget the Nizaris' oldest weapon. He recruited men of courage and strength to the ranks of the *fida'is* (who in contrast to those in Persia appear to have lived as a separate corps within the Nizari movement in Syria) with a view to unleashing them on any particularly powerful and obstinate enemy should the need arise.

But to Sinan it was clear that the primary short-term objective for the movement was to find friends in Syria and the surrounding regions. Syria was situated at a point where different worlds collided. Here, the Byzantine Empire met the Muslim world, Shiites lived cheek to jowl with Sunnis, the Seldjuks' lands bordered on those of the Fatimids and the Christian Crusader kingdoms in the Levant lay adjacent to Islam. With all these political complications present there were both threats and opportunities for the Nizaris. The threat was that the movement would be so dominated by its neighbours that it would be swamped by them. Numerically, the Nizaris were no match for many of their rivals, whom they could realistically never hope to best in battle relying on their own resources. But the opportunity was that, if they were politically astute, they could take advantage of the complicated geo politics of the region to play off one neighbour against another. Sinan came to realize that in this latter approach lay the Nizaris' best hope for long-term survival.

In order to bring this policy to a reality, it was necessary for Sinan to cast his net out in an attempt to make some unlikely allies. There was one group in particular that attracted the attention of the Nizaris fairly early on in Sinan's period of control in Syria. The Crusaders had come to the East fired up with intense religious emotion. The religious motivations that led to the First Crusade created an aura of invincibility in the Crusaders' own minds. Convinced of the righteousness of their cause (after all, in their eyes had God not honoured their enterprise by granting them the capture of Jerusalem, His Holy city?) the Crusaders believed that the establishment of the Kingdom of Jerusalem, and indeed their other territories in the region, presaged the beginning of a Golden Age for Christendom. It seemed to many Christians that this really was the beginning of the establishment of God's kingdom throughout the world.

The early signs appeared to be very promising for the Western invaders. Soon after Jerusalem was captured in 1099, a large Fatimid relieving force had been sent packing back to Egypt after a serious reverse. There were of course occasional setbacks even then for the Crusaders, but to them they seemed like God's reminder that they were not to become proud because of their success, or to punish perceived sins committed by the Crusaders. But these early hopes soon began to fade. Although the fall of Jerusalem was indeed followed by a period of some success throughout the first decade of the twelfth century (cities such as Acre and Jaffa were to fall to them after Jerusalem was captured) the conquests then began to dry up. The loss of Edessa was a bitter blow to the morale of the Franks in Outremer, and the debacle of the Second Crusade added to the general air of depression.

There were other worrying factors for the Franks to consider. The Byzantine Empire, which observers thought was finished after the cataclysmic Byzantine defeat at Manzikert, began to re-assert itself. Most worrying of all from this perspective, the Byzantine Emperor John Comnenus turned up in front of the walls of Antioch with a large army to claim the city back for Byzantium. By subterfuge, the Franks avoided handing it back to him but his renewed interest in what had once been Byzantine territories was a very worrying portent for them. Partly because of these factors, the Crusader leadership in Outremer began to realize that it needed to co-exist with at least some of its neighbours if it was to thrive, or even survive.

In 1173, discussions began between the Franks of Outremer and the Nizaris with a view to forming a mutual understanding between the two. The Franks had not always been on good relations with the Nizaris. The murder of Count Raymond of Tripoli by men believed to be Nizaris had of course done nothing to endear the movement to the Franks. And there had been occasional border disputes between the two groups, as well as intermittent raids by one against the other, although these had been interspersed with occasional bouts of co-operation, such as the Inab campaign in 1149. But the need for friends in the region on the part of both groups led to an attempt to resolve the differences of the past, and to construct a more positive relationship for the future.

Such an alliance would prove particularly advantageous for the Nizaris. Their territories in Syria broadly formed an ungainly and dangerously exposed salient into the Frankish territories. To form an alliance of sorts with the Franks would therefore offer significant strategic attractions to the Nizaris. Sinan therefore resolved to send a delegation to the court of Amalric I, the King of Jerusalem, to see if such an understanding could be reached. Negotiations seemed to go well. The chronicler William of Tyre, a local resident and perhaps the finest historian ever to write an account of the Crusader kingdoms, says that the Nizari ambassadors were even prepared to accept Christianity as the price of their friendship, though in this he is surely wrong. It may be that the Nizaris attempted to explain to the Franks the importance to them of Jesus as a prophet, to stress common understanding. It is probable that something of the Nizaris' arguments was lost in translation, with the result that the intentions of their ambassadors were not fully understood.

Nevertheless, the Nizari negotiators returned homewards well satisfied with their efforts so far. Although no firm agreement had been reached, there had been a number of positive signals given out which encouraged both parties to be optimistic about future developments. There was however another factor which had not, as yet, entered into the equation. A perennial problem for the Franks in Outremer was their shortage of manpower. After the euphoria of the First Crusade had died down, it proved difficult to obtain recruits to protect Outremer and settle in the Kingdom. Groups of Crusaders often made their way on pilgrimage to Jerusalem but these were usually transient visitors, who were more likely than not to return home once they had fulfilled their pilgrims' obligations, normally by visiting the Church of the Holy Sepulchre in Jerusalem.

This was a major headache for the leaders of Outremer, who were hugely outnumbered by their Muslim neighbours. In an attempt to establish a standing army of sorts to strengthen the Kingdom's security, radical measures were adopted. These consisted of forming groups of knights, run along the lines of monastic orders, whose primary purpose, though initially to protect bands of pilgrims en route to Jerusalem and the other holy places of Outremer, eventually became the protection of the kingdom itself. Two of these groups eventually achieved far greater prominence than the others. One of them, the Knights Hospitallers, had been in Jerusalem from a time pre-dating the First Crusade by several decades, though their initial role had been a non-aggressive one. The other group, the Knights Templar, was founded in Jerusalem itself in about 1120 (historians do not agree on the exact date).[5]

As the twelfth century progressed, both Orders (and indeed others less well-known in modern times) became more prominent players in the defensive strategy of Outremer. Surrounded as it was by potential enemies, it was natural that a ring of castles should be erected to protect it from hostile incursions. A chain of such fortifications was duly constructed around the borders of the Kingdom. Providing sufficient forces to garrison these was such a major drain on the very limited manpower resources of Outremer that radical answers were called for. In an attempt to address the problem, many such castles were handed over to the Orders. Given their position, often right on the frontier lands of Outremer, some were in close proximity to the Nizaris, which resulted in relationships that on occasion proved to be far from friendly.

Nothing exemplified these difficult relations more than the reaction of the Templars after the murder of Count Raymond of Tripoli in 1152. Their response was to attack the Nizaris who were their neighbours and to demand tribute as punishment for the crime. The Templars were powerful warriors and the Nizaris accordingly agreed to pay them the sum of 2,000 besants per annum. A key requirement of the Nizari offer of support for King Amalric some twenty years later was that this tribute should no longer be demanded of them. The King agreed to this request.

There was unfortunately a complication which confused this seemingly straightforward arrangement. The Templars (and the other military Orders for that matter) owed allegiance not to the King of Jerusalem but to no less an authority than the Pope himself. This put them literally above the law of the land in which they lived. For their part, the Templars were incensed at the proposed accommodation with the Nizaris. They were keenly aware of the importance of their Order to the kingdom; an awareness which, in the eyes of their critics (who would eventually be numerous and powerful) would border on ostentation and pride.

Undoubtedly, the loss of tribute would be something of a financial blow to them, although they were already accumulating vast stores of wealth across Christendom and could bear the loss. As religious men (they were after all serving as knights as a means, as they saw it, of fulfilling a Christian duty) they may also have been incensed at what they perceived to be an unacceptable compromise of Christian principles. It is also possible that they were angry that Amalric had surrendered one of their rights when he had no authority to do so. Whatever the motive, the subsequent actions of the Templars were clear enough. As the Nizari delegation made their way back home, they were waylaid by a party of Templars and killed.

Amalric was incensed. He demanded that the knight responsible for the outrage should be handed over to him. The Templars had no intention whatsoever of doing so: they did not answer to the King, and consequently completely ignored his demands. But they misjudged their man. Amalric was not prepared to countenance their actions, which compromised the strategic interests of Outremer. Ignoring the legal niceties – the Templars had no legal obligation to obey his commands – he took matters into his own hands. He laid siege to the castle of the guilty knight responsible for the murder, a one-eyed Templar named Walter of Mesnil, in the port of Sidon. Subsequently captured, he was flung into a dungeon. Amalric had far exceeded his authority in doing this, although he undoubtedly felt justified in doing so for the sake of his Kingdom. He sent word to Sinan subsequently denouncing the Templars, and disowning himself from their actions.

Whether or nor Sinan was convinced of his sincerity is unclear, although Amalric's prompt and draconian reaction against the Templars appears to prove conclusively that he indeed had no part in their attack on the envoys. But from this point on, negotiations were desultory. They eventually fizzled out completely when Amalric died in 1174. The man appointed to be regent of the kingdom until Amalric's son came of age was Raymond III, Count of Tripoli. As it was his father that the Nizaris had murdered at Tripoli some twenty years previously, the abandonment of discussions between the two groups is perhaps understandable.

That these negotiations came to nothing was a great pity, both from the perspective of the Nizaris and the Franks. Both sides desperately needed allies at this stage, for there was a rising power in the Levant, one that provided a greater threat to both parties than either had previously known. To understand how this position of danger had come about it is necessary to return once more to Fatimid Egypt. It had been obvious for a while that the ruling dynasty here was decrepit and effectively in a state of terminal decline. This transparent weakness made the country a tempting target of the predatory states adjacent to the country. Matters came to a head in 1160. The death of the caliph al-Fa'iz in this year led to a dynastic dispute. The eventual loser was the commander of the Fatimid armies, Shawar. However, Shawar refused to accept the finality of his defeat. He approached Nur-ed Din for help. In response, Nur-ed Din despatched the governor of Homs, a famed warrior named Shirkuh, to his aid.[6]

This was a dangerous move on the part of Shawar. Personally, he perhaps had little to lose from the alliance. But for the Fatimid dynasty itself it was a potentially fatal initiative. Nur-ed Din was the foremost political figure of the Sunnis in the Middle East, and he was furthermore a devout man who would like nothing more than to see the Shiite heresy in Egypt destroyed, and replaced by a Sunni government. Shawar was well aware of the threat and showed himself to be a master of intrigue. There was of course another power in the region, the Christian kingdom of Outremer. Always ready to made gains at the expense of the Muslim world, the Franks responded positively to initiatives from Shawar asking for their help to remove the forces of Shirkuh once they had successfully restored him to power. He played this particular hand like a master at first. Several times, he managed to play off the Franks against the Sunni forces of Shirkuh. However, in the end he did not know when to stop and alter his tactics.

In 1168, Shawar called the bluff of Nur-ed Din once too often. In this year, he again asked for Nur-ed Din's help, this time to remove the troublesome Franks from his country (they had been trying, with limited success, to conquer Egypt). When Nur-ed Din responded on this occasion, he made sure that it was with sufficient force to ensure that the stay of his troops would this time be more permanent. At the head of this force, as well as the redoubtable Shirkuh, was a man destined to be one of the most famous Muslim warriors of all time. His name was Salah al-Din Yusuf ibn Ayyub, but he would be much better known to the West as Saladin.

Once Shirkuh's army had ejected the Franks from Egypt, they quickly turned their attention to the overthrow of the Fatimid caliphate. An early victim was Shawar, who was killed on the order of Saladin. Shirkuh became vizier of the country but when he died shortly afterwards Saladin himself assumed this position. He soon manoeuvred himself into a situation from which he could completely destroy the Fatimid military machine, which was almost surreptitiously dismantled. A revolt by Nubian slaves was put down with great violence.

In 1171, Saladin felt strong enough to show his hand openly. In that year, the name of the Abbasid caliph was read out in Friday prayers in the great mosque of Cairo. Previously the Fatimid caliph had been granted this honour, but instead a litany of supposed crimes against the dynasty was read out. It was as clear a sign as it was possible to give that the Fatimid age was over.

It perhaps spoke volumes for the weakness of the dynasty that the changeover took place with little more than a ripple of protest. It was true that Saladin identified the key players in the Fatimid hierarchy and imprisoned them. But in response to the suppression of the Fatimid caliphate, and indeed the widespread destruction of libraries containing Fatimid literature, there was little sign of public unease. One thing that Saladin's actions illustrated abundantly well was that he was no friend of people that he regarded as heretics, being himself a devout Sunni. The fact that the Fatimids in Egypt had adopted a different form of Isma'ilism than the Nizaris in Syria would prove of little comfort to the latter group, as their beliefs and practices were as blasphemous and heretical in Saladin's eyes as those of the Fatimids. It appears that the Nizaris knew this well enough, as there were rumours of the restoration of contacts between them and the Egyptian Fatimids shortly before Saladin's coup, though these ultimately came to nothing.

Saladin was officially Nur-ed Din's representative in Egypt but as time went by he began more and more to assume the air of a man who was ruling in his own right. At one time it looked as if he and his theoretical master would actually come to blows but open conflict was avoided, albeit with some difficulty. It was no surprise when, on the death of Nur-ed Din, Saladin staked his claim to rule both Syria and Egypt. Nur-ed Din left as his successor a young son, Malikshah, who was not old enough to rule in his own right.

In 1174, Saladin marched into Damascus and took control of the city. This posed an enormous danger to many groups in the region, not least of whom were the Nizaris. In order to resist the threat that this posed, some unpalatable decisions had to be taken. Malikshah was given sanctuary by the emir of Aleppo, Gumeshtekin. Saladin marched north to the city, capturing Homs en route, and laid siege to it. Gumeshtekin was frantic for help, and looked about for suitable allies. He eventually resolved to seek out assistance from an unusual source. An offer was sent to the Nizaris offering them land and money if they would assassinate Saladin. The offer of money alone would not have been enough to induce the Nizaris to respond affirmatively to this request for help, but there were enormous strategic advantages to be gleaned from the alliance. The Nizaris therefore confirmed that they would attempt to assassinate Saladin. So began one of the stories that was to lie at the core of the mythical tale of the Assassins.

The first attempt on Saladin's life occurred when he was laying siege to Aleppo in December 1174 or January 1175. Even in the Middle East, this could be a cold time of year and the region was in the grip of winter. A group of assassins in disguise attempted to approach Saladin. Unfortunately for them, their luck was out. With Saladin was a local emir. As a resident of the country, he was well acquainted with many individuals including the Nizaris. When the group made their way towards Saladin, the emir recognized some of them. Realizing well enough what their purpose for being in the camp was, he raised the alarm. It was a fatal move on his part as he was killed in the mêlée that followed, but he did succeed in preventing the Nizaris from fulfilling their murderous intentions. Saladin himself, no doubt grateful for the self-sacrifice of the emir, survived.

The Nizaris regarded this as only a temporary set backand resolved to try their luck again. They saw their chance when Saladin was besieging the citadel of Azaz in 1176. On 22 May of that year, another party of would-be assassins made their way into Saladin's camp. This time his bodyguard was unprepared for the attack. The assassins made their way close enough to Saladin to actually start striking him with their knives. Unfortunately for them, he was well protected by the armour that he was wearing and their blows only wounded him. Before they could complete their mission, they were overpowered. But if the chroniclers are to be believed, the attack made a great impression on Saladin. Soon after, according to their accounts, he surrounded himself with a greater number of guards than ever and had a tower especially erected in which he could sleep safely. The psychological effect of being a known Nizari target was clear for all to see.

Soon after this attempt on his life, Saladin resolved to eliminate the Nizaris from Syria once and for all. Up to this point, there had not been too many overt signs of active aggression on the part of Saladin against them. There were, it is true, reports that he had taken advantage of the Nizaris' problems a year or so earlier. At that time, a large force of anti-Shiite radicals had raided Nizari territory in Syria. In the aftermath of their vicious assault on the Nizaris, in which 13,000 reportedly perished, a great cloud of confusion descended on the region. Saladin had taken advantage of this uncertainty by raiding the Nizari territories himself, taking a great deal of plunder and killing a number of Nizaris in the process. These however were opportunistic manoeuvrings on Saladin's part, when he had profited from temporary weaknesses of the Nizaris to further his short-term interests. What he had in mind now was something far more significant – nothing less than the subjugation of the great Nizari fortress of Masyaf and with it the crushing of the Syrian movement in its entirety.

The castle at Masyaf had effectively become the headquarters of the Nizari movement in Syria. It was a strong and well-defended fortification, in a position that made it difficult for any attacking army to assault. Saladin was by this time well experienced in warfare (though at this stage in his career he was far from the finished article as a military strategist). He laid a close siege around the castle, bringing up his great engines of war to weaken the fortifications and prepare the way for a final attack on its battered walls. Soon after the siege began, there were a few desultory skirmishes. Then, after barely a week, the siege was abruptly raised.

A variety of theories were put forward to explain this about-face on the part of Saladin. The more extreme of them argued that supernatural powers were at force. There were rumours that Saladin had awoken in his tent one morning to find that a poisoned dagger had been placed next to his pillow, alongside an oatmeal cake of a variety only made by the Nizaris. There was also a slip of paper, on which had been written a threatening verse. The implication of these particular tales was clear: Sinan, or one of his henchmen, had slipped through the large cordon of bodyguards as if he were a phantom and could, if he wished, have killed Saladin there and then. Saladin, shocked that his guards could be bypassed so easily, hastily sought Sinan's forgiveness and good relations were restored between them.[7] As well as the sheer sensationalism of this tale, which makes it extremely difficult to credit *per se*, such commentators did not adequately explain why the would-be assassin had not availed himself of such a wonderful opportunity to kill Saladin, given the chance, when on two previous occasions the Nizaris had done everything in their power to achieve just such an end.

This quasi-mythical story mirrored other such tales that were to attach themselves to the Nizaris, and cloak their relations with Saladin in a sometimes impenetrable cloud of fable and intrigue. One of the more chilling of them concerns an envoy that Sinan had sent to Saladin with a message that he was to give to Saladin in private. After the envoy had requested a private audience Saladin understandably suspected a trap, but when the messenger insisted that the message was for his ears alone, he decided to compromise. He sent all of his guards away from his tent, apart from two whom he trusted more than the others. When the envoy insisted that these should also be sent away, Saladin refused to comply with his request. The envoy asked why he had refused to send these two away also. Saladin replied that he knew these men better than any other – according to the chronicler who tells the tale Saladin thought of them as 'sons' – and there were no other men in the world that he would trust more.

The messenger then turned to the two men. He asked them point blank whether, if he instructed them to do so, they would kill Saladin. In reply, the two guards drew their swords and said to the envoy 'command us as you wish'. The envoy then told Saladin that, on this occasion, he could keep hold of his life. He then left the tent accompanied by the supposedly loyal bodyguards. Saladin was awe-struck. If men whom he trusted so implicitly were in fact retainers of Sinan, then in whom could he have confidence?

The story is in its own way an entertaining tale of subterfuge and conspiracy but in fact the reasons for the raising of the siege of Masyaf were probably far more prosaic. Some commentators asserted that a peace deal had been brokered between Sinan (who was absent from Masyaf, where he normally lived, while the siege took place) and Saladin by the latter's uncle, the governor of Hama.

This is by no means an impossibility. Hama bordered the Nizari lands and it was understandable that the governor of a city situated in this potentially sensitive position would not wish to experience any unnecessary unrest which would destabilize the region. Maybe too Saladin thought that he had made his point. He could not be pushed around with impunity and any further threats from Sinan would be reacted to in the strongest possible way. An equally convincing reason put forward however was that a raid by the Franks on Saladin's lands elsewhere made a cessation of hostilities desirable. The exposed position of Syria, at a crossroads adjacent to so many groups fundamentally antagonistic towards each other, meant that on many previous occasions military campaigns in the region had been abandoned when half-finished because of such strategic considerations.[9]

Whatever the true reason for the abandonment of the siege, the after-effects were clear enough. From that point on, the Nizaris never again made an attempt on the life of Saladin. For his part, Saladin left the Nizaris in peace. There were even claims that, when Saladin led a highly successful campaign against the Franks of Outremer a decade later, which nearly ended with the latter ejected from the Levant for good, he was accompanied by the Nizaris. The fact that both parties left the other untroubled from that point on hints at several things. Firstly, it suggests that the Nizaris and Saladin each recognized the powerful position that they held. There was, it is true, a strange imbalance in this relationship – the Nizaris would have been annihilated in any open battle against the far stronger forces of Saladin. But the movement could not be eliminated at this time without a substantial expenditure of time and effort on the part of Saladin, and he had other objectives to fulfil before he concentrated on their destruction.

But it also tells us something of the character of Saladin and Sinan. Both were devout men, passionately devoted to their cause, which they believed to be undeniably righteous. And the cause of one was diametrically opposed to that of the other. But neither was a fanatic. There was room in their view of the world for pragmatism and compromise. The truce between the two held, which was highly beneficial to supporters of both parties, but perhaps a pity to those who love tales of mystery and intrigue.

There is also another possible hypothesis to explain the improved relations between Saladin and the Syrian Nizaris. Sinan had already sought to reach an understanding with the Franks. However, despite the willingness of the then King of Jerusalem, Amalric I, to respond positively to these approaches, the Templars had violently intervened. The military orders became increasingly powerful in the Kingdom, with ultimately catastrophic results. Not only did they threaten to become all-powerful, they were frequently at odds with the Nizaris in Syria. Their border castles, standing guard over the volatile frontiers of the Kingdom, frequently abutted on to Nizari territories. As such, they threatened the Nizaris, a situation that was dramatically exacerbated in 1186 when the Hospitallers made the castle of

Krak Des Chevaliers, barely a dozen miles distant from the Nizari stronghold of Qadmus, their military headquarters. As Saladin was hostile towards these aggressive and sometimes violent Christian knights, it was logical that the Nizaris should seek to ally themselves to him.

Sinan developed a highly successful rapport with a number of his neighbours, such as Saladin. This enabled the Nizaris in Syria to become largely self-sufficient from the Nizaris in Persia. To what extent this developed into full-blown independence from Persia remains a matter for conjecture. Some chroniclers suggest that Sinan continued to recognize that ultimate authority for matters affecting the Nizaris vested in Alamut.

Abu Firas,[10] admittedly writing some 150 years later, describes Sinan as the deputy of the Imam in Alamut. Of course, this sobriquet (if indeed accurate given the time lapse between the lifetime of Sinan and the time at which Abu Firas wrote) may well have been honorific rather than a genuine reflection of Sinan's attitude towards Alamut. Later writings of the Syrian Isma'ilis award Sinan semi-divine status, treating him as something of an Imam in his own right. These latter writings however date from a time when there had been a schism between the Isma'ilis of Persia and those of Syria, so they may not accurately reflect the reality of the situation during Sinan's lifetime.

Given all these caveats, consideration of the nature of the relationship between the Syrian Nizaris and their Persian counterparts is inevitably speculative. However, there are certain facts that can be relied upon and we also know something of the personal characteristics of Sinan (at least in an implied fashion) from the nature of his policies. Those policies were dynamic; he did not rigidly adhere to alliance with one party or another. He adapted his policies to changes in circumstances, reacting quickly to events and amending his stance as appropriate (the understanding reached with Saladin soon after the siege at Masyaf began is a perfect example of this).

Such evolutionary politics do not fit well with a high degree of centralized control, especially when exercised from Alamut, which was many days' travel away from Syria across territory which, to add to the difficulties of communication, was largely held by men inimical to the Nizari cause. And indeed, it would be true to say that, although Alamut traditionally appointed the *da'is* operating in its territories, the dispersed nature of the lands held by the Isma'ilis had always led to a considerable degree of local independence, even in Persia. The sense of introspection current during Sinan's lifetime among the post-*qiyama* Nizaris in Persia, which naturally encouraged them to lose some interest in the outside world, may also have created the conditions whereby Syria could more easily assert a degree of independence from Persia as far as the movement in the former was concerned. All these factors suggest that throughout most of Sinan's time in Persia, the Nizaris there operated to all intents and purposes autonomously from Alamut.

There were indeed some suggestions that those at the headquarters of the Nizaris at Alamut were not altogether happy with these developments in Syria. One account went as far as to suggest that the former tried to take draconian action to bring them to an abrupt halt, stating that: 'the Chief Minister sent emissaries from Alamut a number of times to kill him [Sinan], fearing his usurpation of the headship, and Sinan used to kill them. Some of them he deceived and dissuaded from carrying out their orders'.[11]

This is not to say however that the Syrian Nizaris were always so united that there was never any hint of internal dissension. There was indeed one very serious example of this during the period that Sinan led the movement in the country. A group called the 'Sufat' (which literally means 'The Pure') developed very extreme tendencies. There had always been tension within the movement between the hidden meanings of the Qur'an (the *'batin'*) and its outward teachings (the *'zahir'*). This tension had always been present to an extent among the Nizaris and, within Islam in its wider sense, it was one of the greatest areas of contention between the Sunnis and the Shiites. But the Sufat argued that all of the outward teachings of the Koran could be abandoned completely now that the *qiyama* had been proclaimed.

Sunni historians of the time ascribed all kinds of promiscuity to the Sufat, reflecting earlier tales of incest and sexual depravity. They were also accused of abusing alcohol. Some of the Sufat reputedly even claimed that Sinan was God. But the bias of the sources should be noted; allegations of such excess had been routinely levelled against radical groups on previous occasions. What is clear however is that the movement adopted some policies that were too extreme even for Sinan to tolerate. Perhaps afraid of outside interference (at one time an army from Aleppo was actually despatched to the region with the express aim of extirpating the heresy), Sinan reacted promptly and ruthlessly to suppress these extremist tendencies. Many of the Sufat had placed themselves as they thought well out of the way of danger in the mountains but Sinan was not to be so easily avoided and he advanced on them, killing a large number and effectively decimating the movement.[12]

Aleppo's attempts to intervene directly, independently as it seems of Sinan, suggests that relations between the city and the Nizaris were strained. Shortly after the situation deteriorated. Whether or not this was a direct result of the understanding reached between the Nizaris and Saladin is debatable, but it may safely be assumed that the authorities in Aleppo would not have been best pleased at the news. Saladin had tried to take the city by force not long before, and it would not have been unreasonable if Malikshah, the ruler of Aleppo, regarded the nature of this changed relationship as an act of treachery on the part of his former allies. These tensions came to a head in 1177. On 31 August, Shihab-al-Din ibn al-Ajami was murdered by Nizari assassins in Aleppo. He was an important man, being Malikshah's vizier as well as having previously held the post when Nur-ed Din was alive. Rumourmongers asserted that this act had been carried out because of a ruse on the part of Gumeshtekin. He had, it was claimed, forged the signature of Malikshah on a letter sent to Sinan asking that the latter should send assassins to Aleppo to eliminate the vizier.

Whatever the truth or otherwise of these claims, Gumeshtekin was overthrown soon afterwards. But the incident can have done little to endear the Nizaris to Malikshah, a young man perhaps conscious of his own vulnerability, however much the Nizaris protested their innocence of al-Ajami's murder. In the following year, open hostilities broke out between Aleppo and the Nizaris. The castle of al-Hajira was seized from the Nizaris by Malikshah.

They were of course furious about this but were not strong enough at the time to recapture the castle. Nevertheless, they did not let the outrage go unpunished. Shortly afterwards, a great fire broke out in Aleppo, destroying much of the city's market place. There was no doubt that this was arson, and there was equally little question who was behind it. Despite the scale of the damage, which suggested that a good number of arsonists were involved, not one was captured, which suggests that the Nizaris' skill for subterfuge (and perhaps their links with elements of the local community) was still strong.

In the succeeding years, much was to change in the fragile political infrastructure of the region, especially in the Crusader kingdoms adjacent to the Mediterranean. The situation of these territories, hundreds of miles away from mainland Christian Europe via a difficult sea crossing that it was only possible to make at certain times of the year, left them dangerously exposed. It would be difficult for reinforcements to be rushed to the aid of the Kingdom if it were under heavy attack, a state of affairs that was exacerbated by an alarming growth in apathy regarding the region on the part of Western Europe. These strategic weaknesses were made even greater by a resurgent Islamic world, at the head of which was Saladin.

Saladin had already united much of Syria and Egypt, essentially forming a vice-like grip around the Crusader kingdoms. His conquests went hand-in-hand with his diplomatic overtures towards other Islamic groups, such as the Nizaris, in the region. Suppression of such heretical sects (as Saladin regarded them) was less important to him than the recovery of Palestine for Islam. He was enraged by the actions of some of the Crusader barons in Outremer, who flagrantly broke truce after truce and attacked caravans of Islamic pilgrims in cold blood. His foremost priority was therefore the elimination of the Western forces occupying Palestine. For a number of years, he launched frequent raids on Outremer. These reached a climax in 1187 when Saladin led a huge army on a massive incursion into the kingdom.

His Christian enemies played right into his hands. With a tactical naïveté that it would be hard to exceed, they did everything to place themselves at a disadvantage. Their command riven by internal disputes, the greatest army that they had ever assembled was marched through desert-like conditions at the height of summer, straight into a trap laid by Saladin. The resulting battle, at Hattin, was a disastrous and total defeat for the Crusaders. The finality of this defeat was absolute, the manpower resources of the Kingdom of Jerusalem (always a source of weakness for the Crusaders) had been denuded to form the army raised to defend the kingdom. The disaster at Hattin left all of Outremer wide open to Saladin.[13]

Saladin sought to exploit his victory. City after city fell to him. His triumph seemed complete when Jerusalem itself was recaptured by his army. Although the territories of Tripoli and Antioch remained mostly intact, of the Kingdom of Jerusalem virtually nothing remained. Virtually nothing, that is, save the port of Tyre. As the only city of note left to the

Crusaders in the Kingdom of Jerusalem (although some isolated castles remained in their possession) any Christians who wished to fight on made their way here. Saladin for a time laid a close siege to the city, which seemed destined to fall. Yet, in one of those moments of fate which can have a massive impact on future history Saladin, perhaps confident that he could capture the port at any time that he wished, did not vigorously push home his advantage.

Even so, it seemed that Tyre was living very much on borrowed time. But although its position seemed hopeless, this would change dramatically with the arrival of a ship on 14 July 1187. On board was a man named Conrad of Montferrat. He had just sailed into the annals of Crusader history and right to the heart of the 'Assassin' legend. Conrad was an adventurer and something of an unlikely hero. A man of sometimes dubious moral virtues (he divorced his first wife for no better reason than he wanted to marry another woman, something which in the moral climate of the world in which he lived shocked many to the point that some felt he committed bigamy by so doing), the effect of his arrival was electric. His presence energized the defence of the city. Its end, once seemingly just a matter of time, became less certain. Nothing that Saladin could do would lessen his resolve. This included Saladin's threat to kill Conrad's father (whom he had captured in the Hattin campaign) if he did not hand over the port. Eventually, the siege was raised.

As a result, a bridgehead was formed from which a counter-attack could be launched. The Crusaders did their best to ensure that their chances of success were minimized. A bitter dispute broke out among them over who should be King of the emaciated Kingdom of Jerusalem. It might have been better to leave such arguments until they had a Kingdom to fight over.

There were two rival claimants to the throne. The previous incumbent, Guy of Lusignan, was a weak man whose legitimacy had always been in question. Many were unhappy with his ineffective rule, and turned to Conrad as their chosen candidate in his place. But this infighting could not disguise the fact that a terrible reverse had hit the Crusader territories, especially the Kingdom of Jerusalem. This rump was barely viable. A great Crusade was therefore launched from the West, which had been shaken from its apathy by the loss of Jerusalem. It made its way to the vital port of Acre, where the Crusaders had been laying siege to the city. At the head of this Crusade were King Philip Augustus of France and Richard I, King of England.

Acre eventually fell to the Crusaders in 1191. Philip considered that this fulfilled his Crusading obligations and returned to France, leaving Richard effectively in command of the Crusade. Although Jerusalem remained an elusive target, something of an enclave was carved out by the Crusaders in the region once more. They then returned to the taxing problem of who should be king. Guy of Lusignan was a vassal of Richard through the territories that he held in France, and Richard naturally enough supported his claim. However, when he asked the other leading men of the kingdom who they supported, he found that he was effectively in a minority of one in his views. Almost unanimously, they wanted Conrad to be king.

Richard accepted the decision, albeit reluctantly. The news was despatched to Conrad (who was currently in Tyre) where he received it joyfully but humbly. He expressed great humility in his acceptance of the decision, and prayed that if he were not worthy of the prize, then God should take it from him. His request would be answered in spectacular fashion. There were two young men in the town, who had made their way to Tyre some time before. Although of local extraction, they were Christians and men of learning who spoke the language of the Franks well. They later became monks and developed a good relationship with Conrad.

On the evening of 28 April 1192, shortly after he was offered the Kingdom of Jerusalem (but before his coronation had taken place), Conrad was irritated to find that his wife had not yet prepared for dinner. Not in an especially pleasant mood he made his way through the streets of the city towards the house of his friend, the Bishop of Beauvais. In the course of his journey, he was approached by the two recently-arrived monks. They engaged him in polite conversation. Then, in a fraction of a second, the mood changed completely. The two men suddenly produced daggers that they had concealed within the folds of their robes. Whether or not Conrad recognized the men in that moment for the Nizari assassins that they truly were, we shall never know. But the outcome of their attack was clear enough. Conrad: 'immediately fell from his horse and was rolling on the ground, fatally wounded. One of the murderers was immediately cut down while the other ran straight into the next church. In spite of this he was dragged from it and dragged as a condemned man through the middle of the town until his last treacherous breath'.[14]

Before he died, the captured assassin confessed that he had been sent by Sinan. However, he also introduced an intriguing and unexpected piece of information into his confession. He claimed that the instigator of the crime was Richard, King of England. It was a startling revelation. Richard, it is true, was no ally of Conrad. He had after all advocated the cause of Guy of Lusignan in the contest for the Kingship.

But if he were really behind the crime, it was an extraordinarily inept move politically. The removal of Conrad threatened the security of the Kingdom; unity was essential if it were to survive. Richard himself was aware that he could not tarry indefinitely in the region before returning to England. There were many who found the involvement of Richard hard to credit. However, some of his enemies were convinced enough of his involvement. During his journey back to England, Richard landed in the lands of the Austrian Duke Leopold (a man he had previously insulted during the course of the Crusade) and was flung into prison for months. Among the crimes levelled at him was the murder of Conrad of Montferrat.[15]

However, another suspect also emerged. Aspersions were soon cast in the direction of Saladin.[16] Muslim accounts refer to Saladin's involvement. Saladin, in the account of Ibn al-Athir, was responsible for Conrad's death:

'the cause of his death was Saladin's negotiations with Sinan, leader of the Isma'ilites, to send a man to kill the king of England: if he then killed the Marquis he would get 2,000 dinar . . . .' Sinan decided to go along with the plan: he sent two men dressed as monks, who introduced themselves to Conrad. They waited for six months, successfully winning Conrad's confidence. However, they were just waiting their moment:

'after this time the Bishop of Tyre held a banquet for the Marquis. He went, ate at his table, drank his wine and then left. The two Batinites then fell on him and inflicted mortal wounds upon him, then one of them fled and went into a church to hide. When he realised that the Marquis had been brought into the same church to have his wounds bandaged, he fell on him and killed him. After his death the two assassins were also killed.' Ibn al-Athir records that the Franks attributed the murder to Richard.[17]

Saladin's involvement seems highly unlikely; there were reliable reports that Conrad had for a time been trying to come to terms with him and on occasion his envoys had been seen making their way into Jerusalem, possibly to discuss such an understanding. The rumours of Saladin's involvement only make sense if it is assumed that Saladin disliked the thought of Conrad as King because he would be a threat to him. But, after he had revived the Kingdom's fortunes following his timely arrival at Tyre, Conrad's performance had not been impressive. Rumours of Saladin's desire to eliminate Conrad nevertheless persisted.

There are in fact other accounts in existence that assert that there was a far more likely reason for Sinan himself to aspire to the elimination of Conrad. Some time before, Conrad had captured a ship carrying a valuable cargo, as well as a number of Nizaris. The cargo was confiscated and the passengers were thrown over the side to drown. It is probable that the motivation for Conrad's murder was nothing other than a good old-fashioned desire for revenge. As an incidental side-effect, it presumably did the Nizaris little harm to keep the Crusaders divided among themselves; if they were too busy sorting out their own internal affairs, then they would be distracted from interfering with those of the Nizaris too much.[18] There was certainly much to gain for the Nizaris from the confusion arising after the murder of Conrad. Despite his poor showing since his initial successes at Tyre, he was the overwhelming choice of the Frankish nobility, who saw in him a strong king. His death was a shock to Outremer and the weakened Kingdom that resulted posed a lesser threat to the Nizaris than would otherwise be the case.

The murder of Conrad was the last major act of Sinan's period of tenure in Syria. It was a fittingly spectacular end to his reign as it registered more significantly in the consciousness of the West than any other single action of the Nizaris. It added to the mythical power of the Nizaris greatly, although even before Conrad's murder, there were certainly some Crusaders well aware of the threat posed by the Nizaris, as evidenced by the greatest of all their chroniclers, William of Tyre: 'If for example there be a prince who is hated or mistrusted by this people [i.e. the Nizaris], the chief gives a dagger to one or more of his followers. At once whoever receives the command sets out on his mission, without considering the consequences of the deed nor the possibility of escape. Zealous to complete his task, he toils and labours as long as may be needful, until chance gives him the opportunity to carry out his chief's orders'.[19]

Soon after, in or around 1193 (the date is not completely clear) Sinan died. His time as leader of the Syrian Nizaris had been a remarkable one.

Whether he deserved to be remembered above Hasan-i Sabbah is a moot point but, in the eyes of the West, this was an inevitable consequence of the fact that he had been in far closer contact with the Crusaders than Hasan was. But his achievements were nevertheless impressive. Surrounded by potential enemies, the Nizaris in Syria appeared superficially to have little chance of survival, but by a judicious mixture of the terror tactics employed by the Nizaris in the past and subtle diplomacy they had clung on to their territories in the region. Sinan had made friends of those who appeared destined to be his enemies, while at the same time occasionally alienating those who had once been his friends. In the uncertainty that his tactics created among his potential opponents, as well as the ability of the Nizaris to terrify their enemies and create for themselves an influence out of all proportion to their size, lay the salvation of his people.

Inevitably, the remarkable nature of his achievements added to the growing quasi-mythical status of the group that he led in Syria. Great, almost supernatural, powers were ascribed to the Nizaris as a result of his reign. They were also applied to him personally. To the Franks, he was known simply as 'The Old Man of the Mountain'. Later groups of Nizaris in the region would extol his virtues above all other Imams.[20]

But for whatever reason, the transfer of power from Persia to Syria was only a temporary one. The pre-eminence of the former was soon re-asserted shortly after his death. We must therefore turn our attention once more to what had happened, and what was about to happen, in Persia. Sinan's reign was, for the Nizaris in Syria, a golden period in their history, but it was in many ways an Indian Summer. Events were about to unfold that would leave the movement facing cataclysm and complete destruction.

NINE

Re-integration

The personality of Sinan, and his deeds in Syria, inevitably attracted attention away from the Nizaris in Persia. This trend was reinforced by the character of Muhammad II, leader of the Persian Nizaris and nominally the movement as a whole, who assumed leadership in 1161 following the murder of his father. He was to be ruler of Alamut, and of the Nizari movement in its wider sense, for longer than any other *daʿi*. Paradoxically, we know less of his period in power than we do of any other leader of the Nizaris. Under his auspices, the Nizaris became insular to the point of virtually disappearing from Sunni histories of the Middle East.

As few of the Nizaris' own historical records are available, this puts the modern historian at a distinct disadvantage. This is particularly so when considering the development of the concept of the *qiyama* within the movement. There is no doubt that this was one of the most theologically explosive doctrines developed by the Nizaris. It was, to use a modern colloquialism, religious dynamite. But it passes without a mention in any of the contemporary Persian Sunni chronicles of the time. It was not until a century later, when Alamut at last passed into the hands of the enemy, that Sunni historians seem to have become aware of the doctrine in Persia. Only then did they describe it at any length and they wrote as bitter enemies of the movement, whom they regarded as heretics. This of course seriously calls into question their objectivity.

Muhammad accepted the doctrine of the *qiyama*, proclaimed by his father so spectacularly at Alamut, with enthusiasm. He regarded him as a martyr for the Nizari cause and, as we have seen, punished his murderers ruthlessly. However, he not only accepted the *qiyama* in the form that his father had proclaimed it, he developed it further.

As we have seen, Hasan-i Sabbah refused to proclaim himself Imam. But as time passed with no sign of the Hidden Imam appearing, the Nizari rank and file must have become increasingly disquieted by this apparent lack of urgency on his part to return once again to earth. It was possibly this nervousness which led Hasan II to proclaim the Resurrection at Alamut. During the course of his short reign, Hasan hinted that not only was he the heir to the Imam in a spiritual sense, he was also his direct descendant in a physical capacity. Muhammad II went further. He was not content just to make such subtle hints, he resolved to develop a far stronger case that he was the legitimate successor to Nizar, both by divine assent and by right of physical descent.

Several stories developed to support such a claim. Two of them claimed that Hasan II himself was descended from the Imam who had given the movement its name, Nizar. One of these tales asserted that the grandson of Nizar, al-Muhtadi, was smuggled out of Egypt by a faithful Nizari, Abu'l Hasan Sa'idi. He was taken to Alamut itself, where he took up residence, in secret, in the village at the foot of the rocky outcrop on which the great citadel stood. Only Hasan-i Sabbah himself was aware of the true identity of the mysterious new arrival in the village. The most popular variant of what happened next claims that when the wife of Muhammad I had given birth to a son, he was secretly exchanged with a descendant of al-Muhtadi, a baby boy who grew up to be Hasan II. The second version suggests that, instead of this surreptitious swap, a woman in the village who was pregnant was handed over to the protection of Muhammad II. The woman gave birth to a boy who became Hasan II (the child was also a lineal descendant of al-Muhtadi in this latter tale).

Both stories may appear inherently unlikely. It is easy of course to claim a prestigious ancestry when it is argued that such secrecy had attended the situation that knowledge of an individual's antecedents was vested only in one person, that is the chief *da'i* of the Nizaris, at any one time. The story about the swapping of the children at birth in particular is a classic motif found in several cultures, not just the Nizari. The weakness of all the various arguments put forward to claim such an exulted heritage was that the status of Hasan II, and by definition his son and successor, rested solely on the authority of Muhammad II, who had much to gain if such stories were believed. Yet the credibility of the chief *da'i* of the sect – who now became its Imam as well – was such that these stories – which may appear inherently unlikely – were widely accepted, and from then on the Nizaris traced their line of Imams from Hasan II.

These developments served perhaps to enhance the status of Muhammad but this was in an environment where the Nizaris as a movement became increasingly introspective. During Muhammad's reign, the outside world was largely (though not, as will be seen, exclusively) forgotten about. There were hardly any assassinations of note taking place throughout his long period in office, which extended from 1166 to 1210. The only noteworthy exception to this was the murder of the caliph's vizier in Baghdad. There was one tale of significance that the chroniclers did relate however, and it is worthy of mention as it adds another strange story to the lengthening collection of romances attending the sect.

This story revolved around a famous theologian of the time. His name was al-Razi (also known as Fakhr al-Din), a Sunni teacher who taught his students in a religious institution in Rayy. He was a devout Muslim who was renowned for being particularly outspoken in his criticisms of the Isma'ilis, whom he regarded as being heretics worthy only of contempt and vilification. His lectures in fact became famous for their violent assaults on the misguided principles and dogmas (as he saw it) of the movement.

These verbal attacks apparently upset Muhammad, and he sent a *fida'i* to Rayy to put a stop to them. The man sent to perform this task successfully sought a place as one of al-Razi's students. The Nizaris, and particularly the *fida'is* employed by the sect, were renowned for several qualities that they developed during their lifetime as a major political force. The first of these was the ability to conceal themselves, to integrate themselves chameleon-like into any environment within which they wished to operate. The second was patience. For seven months, the *fida'i* dutifully attended lectures, carefully avoiding the tendency to react aggressively when his tutor launched into yet another diatribe against the movement of which the student was secretly a member.

At last, an opportunity for retribution presented itself. The subject matter of one particular lecture led to an especially complicated theological debate.

148

The *fida'i* asked to see al-Razi in private at the end of the lesson. Not unnaturally assuming that he made this request for the purposes of further clarification, the tutor readily assented. However, when the two men were alone in the classroom together the real motivation for the meeting suddenly became ominously clear to al-Razi. The *fida'i* produced a knife, which he showed threateningly to his tutor. When the latter asked what he planned to do with it, the student graphically replied that he 'wanted to slit his belly from the breast to the navel. because you have cursed us from the pulpit'.

The obvious danger that he was in prompted al-Razi to attack his would-be assailant. A fierce struggle ensued but the student, being the younger and fitter man, proved too strong for his tutor. He sat on al-Razi's chest but he gave him at least a chance to beg for his life. The latter asked the Nizari what the price of his life would be. The *fida'i* told him that, from this day on, he was to refrain from all further attacks on the Nizaris and their beliefs. To further encourage him, he drew a purse from his pocket containing 365 gold pieces (one must assume that the purse must have been unnaturally large). He handed it to al-Razi, telling him that a further payment would follow annually if he kept up his side of the bargain. From that day on, the tutor modified both his language and his tone towards the sect. The change did not pass unnoticed. One of his students asked him why he was so moderate towards the Nizaris when he had formerly been so passionately opposed to them. The response came quickly; al-Razi replied that it was as well to listen carefully to the arguments of the sect as they were 'both weighty and convincing'.[1]

The story of al-Razi lends colour to a period of Nizari history which is, in terms of known historical events, something of a closed book to later historians. However, it was one thing for the movement to wish to be left to its own devices in a world of its own, it was quite another for such an ambition to be fulfilled. Such an attitude might seem like a luxury that the Nizaris could barely afford but in practice they broadly achieved their aim of being left in peace and quiet by the potentially hostile Sunni states around them. To understand why this was so, it is necessary to consider the broader situation in the Middle East during Muhammad's reign.

Since the beginning of history, the Middle East has been the world's battlefield. In its highly strategic position as the hub in the wheel between Europe, Asia and Africa, it was in many ways the true centre of the Ancient World. For millennia, the region had resounded to the marching feet of vast armies, often it is true using the region as a thoroughfare on their way to greater conquests but inevitably leaving chaos in their wake. Further, it had been exposed to tidal waves of humanity unleashed on the unsuspecting people of the Middle East as tribal expansionism spilled over into the region. The latest of these had of course been the Turks from Central Asia. The greatest of these Turkish incursions so far had emanated from the Seldjuk dynasty. At first, the dynasty appeared to be unbeatable. But as time progressed the Seldjuks, as we have seen, started to fall out among themselves. Over time, these internal pressures grew, eating away at the vitality of the dynasty like a malignant cancer, until at last it became terminally ill.

So it was that, during the reign of Muhammad II, great uncertainty was present in Persia and Iraq, as surely as it was in Syria and Palestine. For it was during his lifetime that the diseased Seldjuk dynasty reached a state from which there was no hope of recovery. This of course was manna from heaven for Muhammad, for it meant that the chances of his movement being left to its own devices were that much greater than they might otherwise have been, as his potential enemies were too busy defending the scraps of what they already held to pay much attention to the Nizaris.

The last powerful Seldjuk sultan, Tughril III, was killed in battle in 1194. In effect, the united Seldjuk state that he claimed to rule had passed away some time before. In its place, a number of smaller, autonomous territories had been set up, often ruled by independent Turkish chieftains who maintained many of the old structures (and indeed their Sunni Islamic beliefs) of the now-defunct Seldjuk kingdom, albeit on a much reduced scale. Although these smaller Turkish territories were still capable of creating considerable instability in the area, the demise of the Seldjuk dynasty did leave a vacuum in the region which an ambitious new power might hope to exploit. One such force that was to rise in the Middle East emanated from Khwarazm, on the eastern shores of the Caspian Sea.

Under the leadership of a man named Tekish, Khwarazm came relatively to resemble a haven of tranquillity and stability amid the upheavals taking place across the Middle East. This stability was to put Khwarazm at a significant advantage in relation to its neighbours. In response to an appeal from the Abbasid caliph, al-Nasir, Tekish entered into an alliance against the Seldjuks. It was his army that was responsible for the death of Tughril III at Rayy. However, his plans to dominate the caliphate in the same way that the Seldjuks had previously done proved over-optimistic. In al-Nasir, the caliphate had found a man of a far greater stamp than the procession of nonentities that had generally held the post of caliph in the preceding years and decades. Now that Tekish had helped him eliminate the last of the Seldjuks, al-Nasir had no further need of him. Inevitably, conflict broke out between Tekish and the man he assumed to be his ally when it became clear that the Khwarazmians were redundant to the caliph's plans. But al-Nasir in response sought around for new allies, something that would have a significant impact on the medium-term development of the Nizaris.

Later on in the reign of Muhammad II, the Nizaris once more became embroiled in border disputes with their neighbours. The region of Rudbar, in which Alamut was located, was adjacent to Tabaristan. There had long been tensions between the two regions, and these were exacerbated during the final part of Muhammad's reign. Frequent raids into Tabaristan accompanied the occasional murder of some important figures of the ruling hierarchy within the area. But the expansionism of the Khwarazmians inevitably impacted on the Nizaris, who were geographically too close to Khwarazm to escape the attentions of the rising power in the region completely. Miyajiq, a Khwarazmian general, captured and killed a number of Nizaris from Alamut in 1205. This is difficult to understand as two years earlier the Nizaris had assassinated the vizier of Tekish reputedly at the request of the Khwarazmians themselves. This at least demonstrated that although the Nizari *fida'is* were not so prolific as in earlier times, they could still strike the occasional dramatic blow against some important, and presumably well guarded, individuals within the Middle East.

Further east, the Nizaris in Quhistan were faced with another significant threat to their continued independence. An attack was launched on Quhistan by the Ghurids, bitter rivals with the Khwarazmians in an ongoing struggle for supremacy in the east of Persia. Quhistan was devastated by these attacks, and the Nizaris there were forced to submit to the Ghurids. This left the Nizaris in an ambivalent position in relation to the Khwarazmians. Although they had been threatened in Rudbar by the growing menace of the Khwarazmians, on the other hand both parties had a mutual enemy in Quhistan in the shape of the Ghurids. Clearly, the increasing ambition of the Ghurids threatened both the independence of the Nizaris in Persia and the quest for dominance of the Khwarazmians. The Nizaris decided to throw in their lot with the Khwarazmians. Showing that the old ways had not been completely lost to the Nizaris, they attempted to ingratiate themselves with the Khwarazmians by assassinating a prominent member of the Ghurid ruling dynasty in 1206.

These manoeuvrings hint that during the latter years of Muhammad's reign it became apparent that the Nizaris desire for splendid isolation was no longer a tenable policy. There were too few changes of note during this period to suggest that this represented a radical alteration in the policies of the Nizaris in general, and the isolated examples of their interference in the affairs of the outside world were probably reactive in nature. Such subtle changes in stance were perhaps inevitable given the interference of the Khwarazmians in Rudbar and the Ghurids in Quhistan; aggressive action on the part of these growing powers forced the Nizaris to modify their policy. These acts intimate a change in attitude on the part of the Nizaris. But when Muhammad II died in 1210 (it was rumoured that poison was the cause of his demise) and was succeeded by his son, Jalal ad-Din Hasan, who became Hasan III, few if any could have expected the spectacular about-face that was to ensue shortly afterwards.

Hasan had been declared Muhammad's successor when he was still a child. Intriguingly, his mother was a Sunni Muslim and it is difficult to avoid speculating that he was affected by this in his subsequent attitude to the wider world of Islam. He was reputedly at odds with his father from early on in his life, and he clearly felt uncomfortable with a number of the religious and political policies that had been adopted by the Nizaris. Even before he inherited leadership of the movement, he had been in secret communication with a number of important individuals throughout the region, expressing the hope that it might prove possible one day to heal some of the breaches that had developed within the wider world of Islam.

Juwayni says that Hasan, 'whether because of the orthodoxy of his beliefs or because of hostility towards his father . . . conspired against Muhammad and sent secretly to the caliph of Baghdad and the sultans and rulers of other lands to claim that, unlike his father, he was by faith a

Muslim and that when his turn came to reign he would abolish the Heresy and reintroduce the observance of Islam'.[2]

Among the recipients of these clandestine approaches were, as well as the Abbasid caliph in Baghdad, Shah Muhammad, of the Khwarazmians. These secret discussions were to stand Hasan in good stead when he eventually assumed his position as head of the Nizaris but, while his father was still alive, there was no possibility of these approaches leading to any tangible results. It appears that in later life Muhammad II became aware of these illicit contacts, of which he naturally disapproved strongly, and for a time relations between him and his son were decidedly chilly.

There is no conclusive evidence to confirm whether or not Muhammad really was murdered, and consideration of Hasan's role in his killing (if indeed that is what it was) must of course be speculative. Hasan certainly had motive enough to remove his father, both because he stood to inherit a great deal of power when Muhammad died and also because the political beliefs that he held were markedly different. But motive alone does not provide incontrovertible evidence of guilt, and it is an equally feasible explanation that there were other members of the movement who were unhappy at Muhammad's rule and wished to see a new injection of energy to the leadership of the Nizaris, given his exceptionally long period in office.

The end result of the change in leadership was clear enough though. Hasan's attempts to build links with the outside world were reciprocated, particularly by al-Nasir, the Abbasid caliph. Al-Nasir was an astute politician. He realized that to return the caliphate to the position of supremacy that it had once, centuries before, held in the Islamic world was a totally unrealistic objective. Although there were some serious divisions within the established order, which an assertive and strong power could realistically hope to exploit, the days had long passed since the caliphate had the resources at its disposal to be such an entity. Realizing this well enough, al-Nasir instead decided to create a small but viable state within Iraq, which he could realistically hope to control. The achievement of even this limited objective however relied on his ability to create meaningful alliances with other key players in the region, and he was therefore very amenable to the friendly approaches made by Hasan.[3]

In this respect, the preliminary approaches Hasan had made before assuming power presumably stood him in good stead. They gave him a personal credibility that might have been lacking if he had suddenly rejected all the Nizaris' teachings with no prior warning. For the approach that he now adopted was diametrically opposed to that which had been advocated by the Nizaris for the best part of half a century. He castigated the movement for accepting doctrine which he regarded as heretical, and emphasised that from now on rigid adherence to the *sharīa*, the sacred law of Islam, was to be the rule. It was said that he 'professed Islam, and severely rebuked his people and party for their adherence to the Heresy, and strictly forbade them continuing . . .'.[4]

Al-Nasir was presumably delighted at this change in stance as, although it did not presage overnight the elimination of all differences between the Sunnis and the Nizaris, it offered the potential to radically lessen the impact of such variances. Later commentators asserted that this period, an interlude of reciprocity between the Nizaris and the caliphate (and to an extent the Islamic world in its wider sense), was in fact an extreme example of the Isma'ili practice of *taqiyya* and that effectively the change in policy reflected nothing more than a tactical ruse. Such an interpretation requires both that Hasan was a strategic genius and that al-Nasir was a man who was easily fooled. As such, such a convenient explanation seems unlikely, although not of course impossible.

Understandably, the complete rejection of everything that the Nizaris had believed in during the recent past was greeted with some scepticism on the part of the movement's neighbours. After all, the Nizaris had survived thus far by a combination of ruthlessness, luck and the frequent employment of tactics that were politically expedient. The citizens of the nearby city of Qazvin had frequently been at odds with the Nizaris. In an attempt to win their trust, Hasan sent a delegation to the rulers of the city. He invited them to respond by despatching their own representatives to Alamut. There, they would be given free rein to inspect the library. Anything that they found that they did not approve of, he undertook to have destroyed.

The party was duly sent. There were, predictably enough, a number of writings that inflamed their religious sensibilities. Among these were works written by the immediate predecessors of Hasan, as well as some by no less a person than Hasan-i Sabbah himself. To demonstrate his sincerity and the authenticity of his apparent conversion, Hasan had a great pyre erected of the errant documents in the courtyard at Alamut. Once it was complete, he ordered that it be set alight.[5]

The flames that consumed these old, and previously sacred, works represented not only the practical destruction of some ancient and revered doctrines but the symbolic abandonment of the policy of isolation from the rest of the Islamic world that had recently become associated with the Nizaris. Nor, according to Juwayni, did this mark the end of Hasan's attempts to prove his credibility. The chronicler claimed to have seen a letter dictated by him and sent to the authorities in Qazvin. In this, he attested to the legitimacy of his recently-declared change in direction as well as emphasizing his total acceptance of the over-riding authority of the *sharī'a* and condemning the previous leaders of the sect as heretics. As if to further demonstrate the totality of his adherence to orthodox Islamic ways, he appended a hand-written note, personally abusing the past leaders of the Nizaris, adding the curse 'may God fill their graves with fire!'.

There was other circumstantial evidence by which Hasan sought to prove to potentially cynical Muslim powers that the Nizaris had changed their ways for good. One of the most obvious outward manifestations of adherence to orthodox Islamic beliefs was participation in the *hajj*, the annual pilgrimage to Mecca, the spiritual home of the Muslim religion. A couple of years after his accession, his mother took part in the pilgrimage. She was admittedly a Sunni but even so such an act would have been difficult to imagine during the reign of Muhammad. En route, she stayed awhile in Baghdad, where she was received generously and respectfully by the caliph.

Unfortunately, her subsequent visit to Mecca proved to be less satisfactory. While she was there, the cousin of the Sharif of the city was murdered. Reportedly, the murdered man bore a striking resemblance to the Sharif himself, who therefore not unnaturally assumed that he may have been the intended target. The presence of relatives of the Nizari leadership in the city at the time presumably raised his suspicions that they were responsible for the murder.[6] The sharif turned on the pilgrims from Iraq and Persia who were in the city at the time and levied a large fine on them. In the event, much of this was subsequently paid by Hasan's mother personally.

To demonstrate still further the extent to which his movement had abandoned the old ways, Hasan built new mosques and bathhouses – symbols of conventional Islamic life – in many of the places inhabited by the Nizaris. The caliph, al-Nasir, was clearly convinced by these moves, because in 1211 he formally recognized the Nizaris as Sunni Muslims. Soon after, Hasan sought to legitimize his rule still further by commencing negotiations with the dynasty ruling the neighbouring state of Gilan for the hand of four of the daughters of the current ruler. The caliph was happy to approve the match, demonstrating his confidence in the authenticity of Hasan's more accommodating stance towards Sunni Islam. The marriages subsequently took place. The symbolism of these events was profound; it evidenced the acceptance of the Nizaris back into the wider Islamic world. One of these wives subsequently gave birth to a son and heir, who was given the name of Muhammad.

Hasan ingratiated himself still more with his neighbours by committing some of his forces to military expeditions, something that had not taken place for many a long year. Generally speaking, the participation of the movement in secretive assassination attempts was largely (although not totally) abandoned. Instead, Hasan was content to declare his support of some parties, and animosity towards others, in a far more open manner.

A particularly fruitful relationship was developed with the ruler of Azerbaijan, a man named Ozbeg. In 1213–15, Hasan helped him to suppress a revolt led by one of his principal lieutenants. In return for his help, Ozbeg willingly subsidized the expenses of the army while it was assisting him. Ozbeg was successful in destroying the power of his rebellious aide and reclaiming the territories that he had lost as a result of the revolt. However, he does not seem to have been blessed with a great deal of judgement as regards his choice of confidants. The governor he appointed to rule over the reconquered lands, Ighlamish, proved as untrustworthy as his predecessor. In 1217, two years after the campaign with the Nizaris, Ozbeg again asked for Hasan's help in suppressing opposition to his rule. On this occasion, Hasan was able to demonstrate that the Nizaris had not completely lost their old skills. *Fida'is* were sent against Ighlamish, who was successfully eliminated.

Soon after this act, in 1221, news came of a great force that had appeared on the extremities of Persia. A huge army of migrant tribesmen had swept across Asia from the furthest corners of the world. They had already brushed aside anyone foolish enough to resist with a ferocity that was unique, even for those violent times. Great empires, in some cases seemingly as old as the world itself, had been blown apart, tossed about like chaff in the teeth of an uncontrollable hurricane. These tribesmen were mighty warriors, exclusively cavalry, seemingly connected to their horses by an almost telepathic understanding. Realizing that his forces could not hope to resist such an overwhelming foe, Hasan subsequently sought terms with the tribesmen. They were granted and the Nizaris continued to live in peace. This satisfying conclusion to the first contacts yet made between the Nizaris and the Mongols was, sadly for the former, a completely inappropriate portent of future relations between the two.

Hasan III reigned for just a decade. He died in 1221, supposedly from dysentery. There were however strong rumours at the time that he had been poisoned. Suspicion fell particularly on his wives, his sister and other close relatives. The mud stuck to such an extent that his vizier, who governed the Nizari territories in trust for his son and successor, the child Muhammad, had all those accused executed, some being burned alive. Certainly his death seemed premature, as he had not enjoyed a long reign. But it is perhaps fitting that his end is the subject of much debate, for his life certainly was.

The change in policy during his reign had been the most massive alteration of course during the entire history of the movement. The *qiyama* when it came was perhaps something of a surprise, but the declaration that the Imam had returned was a logical progression in the evolution of the doctrines of the movement, as the living Imam had been absent for so long. But the switch of direction initiated by Hasan was a total and complete reversal of all that had gone before. By his actions he had swung the Nizaris from one extreme of the Islamic spectrum hugely back towards the other. From being widely despised within Islam (certainly within the majority Sunni community) he had re-positioned the Nizaris back within the mainstream of religious orthodoxy. It was a political gamble of stunning proportions.

It is worth considering this change in policy in more depth. Despite the radicalism of it, there was no sign that any of the Nizaris, be it in Rudbar,

Quhistan or elsewhere resisted. Indeed, so secure did Hasan feel that he was able at one time to be absent on campaign for eighteen months without any apparent threat to his rule. That the Nizaris could cope so unequivocally with such swingeing policy changes speaks volumes for the status of the leader of the movement. At no time, be it during the period of *qiyama* initiated by Hasan II or the return to the Sunni fold led by Hasan III, was there any sign of widespread opposition on the part of the Nizaris. The authority of their leader appears to have been absolute. But possibly it was also obvious to many of the sect's rank and file that the policy of isolation introduced by Hasan's predecessor had failed. For one thing, neighbouring powers were not prepared to leave the Nizaris in peace. Nevertheless this change in direction must have also been psychologically difficult for many of them.

Many doubted the sincerity of Hasan's motivations for the change in policy. An Austrian historian, Joseph von Hammer, who wrote a history of the Nizaris in the early years of the nineteenth century, was blunt in his assessment, describing Hasan's conversion as 'nothing else than hypocrisy and deeply designed policy in order to re-establish the credit of the order'.[7] In his view, there was not one grain of authenticity in this change of heart, which was designed purely with the intention of achieving some legitimacy for Hasan and his movement, and was motivated purely by political self-interest. It is indeed quite possible that such was the case. The doctrine of caution, *taqiyya*, allowed members of the movement to dissimulate, that is hide their true beliefs, if it was in their interests, or the interests of the movement in a wider sense. A number of historians have argued that Hasan's actions represented the most spectacular manifestation of the doctrine ever attributable to the Nizaris.[8]

There was another doctrine that had long been associated with the movement, that of occultation. This was the name given to describe the situation in which the Imam was hidden from his followers, who thus waited patiently and expectantly for his return. But some historians have widened the scope of this particular concept to argue that in this instance it applied to the mission of the Nizaris more generally, arguing that the occultation in this case applied to the activities of the movement as a whole. In the absence of concrete evidence of course, both arguments – that is, that the concept of *taqiyya* applied to the movement during Hasan's reign, as did that of occultation – must remain speculative. Because of this, what really happened must remain essentially a matter of guesswork. Hasan's efforts to convince others that he really had changed his beliefs were certainly extreme, including burning some of the sect's sacred works, as well as cursing the memory of previous leaders of the *da'is*. Was this evidence of a truly dramatic conversion process or a spectacular ruse? We shall probably never know.

But it is worth noting that not all historians are as dismissive of Hasan's acceptance of Sunni Islam as Hammer. Hodgson, the twentieth century historian, for one argues that his loyalty to the caliph, his Sunni mother, his four Sunni wives and the fact that he mainly chose Sunnis in his circle of friends suggest the sincerity of his actions. Such assertions however must remain largely speculative.[9]

What is unarguable is that the policy was certainly successful, in that it did offer the Nizaris some hope of stability and security vis-à-vis their neighbours after decades on the periphery of the Islamic world. The caliph was certainly content to accept the movement back into the mainstream. It appeared that an air of respectability at last attended the Nizaris. Hasan's attempts to reach a form of rapprochement with his neighbours and to re-integrate the Nizaris back into the greater Islamic community bought the movement much needed respite. That the strategy ultimately failed was not the fault of Hasan's vision, but more because the change in policy arrived too late. A catastrophe loomed which would make this change of direction an irrelevance. The relative peace and tranquillity that attended Hasan's reign did not reflect what was to come. It was in every sense the calm before the storm. The tidal wave that was about to wash over the region would, when it was eventually spent, leave hardly a sign of the Nizaris in its wake.

TEN

Nemesis

Muhammad III was a child when he inherited the mantle of his father in 1221, and was far too young to rule in his own right. Hasan's vizier took control of the government at Alamut till Muhammad should be old enough to take over from him. For a time, it appeared that nothing would change. The old alliances with the caliph were continued and it appeared that the Nizaris would continue to comply with Sunni beliefs. But this was merely a superficial appearance: the reality was somewhat different. Beneath the surface, there were a number of undercurrents that, with a growing momentum, would eventually lead to the Nizaris abandoning their adherence to the Sunni cause and move them back towards more radical beliefs. Old habits die hard, and it is easy to believe that many Nizaris never really changed theirs, rather they just chose to adopt the appearance of abandoning them for a while while it was in their interests to do so. Certainly, a number of near-contemporaries thought so. Slowly, almost imperceptibly, increasing numbers of Nizaris began to ignore the requirements of the *sharīa* once more, and to adopt the more esoteric approach to Islam implicit in the long-established Isma'ili doctrine of the *batin*.

Juwayni, the Persian chronicler, was blunt in his apportionment of the blame for this change in direction. In his view, one need look no further than the young Imam, Muhammad III. As the boy grew into a youth, he began increasingly to assert his independence. Juwayni was scathing in his criticism of him and of his sect. He stated bluntly that the boy had received no education, and the real fault for what he saw to be his excesses was vested categorically in the Nizari system itself. He also, in a slightly bizarre passage, states that there were other reasons for Muhammad's actions:

'After this child [Muhammad] had reigned for some five or six years a physician whom they employed, acting contrary to instructions and advice and without the child's being ill or there being any other reason, opened a vein and took away an excessive quantity of blood. His brain was affected, apparitions appeared in front of him and in a short while he was overcome with the disease of melancholia'.[1]

Juwayni argued that the movement's beliefs were fundamentally flawed in that they accepted that the Imam must be, by his very nature, incapable of error and therefore the boy's misguided impulses were never corrected. Further, he claimed that there were many members of the movement who had never really abandoned their long-established beliefs when Hasan III had so radically altered direction. In Juwayni's opinion, they had never paid more than lip service to the new Nizari stance, and when the steadying influence of Hasan was no longer on the rudder, they quickly veered back to the course that they had followed so diligently before his reign.

There may well of course be some element of truth in this. It must indeed have been bewildering for the Nizaris to be faced with so violent a change in direction during the previous reign. To give up all the beliefs that they had suffered so much to protect in earlier reigns may have been hard for devout Nizaris to meekly accept. They had after all thought of the Sunnis as enemies for centuries. In time, a new concept emerged to explain the apparent deviation of Hasan's reign. The Isma'ilis had always recognized the concept of a Hidden Imam. But now, in an extension of the old doctrine of *taqiyya*, it was claimed that, even though Hasan was undoubtedly the true Imam, the true Nizari mission was concealed during his lifetime. This meant not that the truth had been abandoned but just, through necessity, hidden by Hasan during that time.

This concept, known as *satr*, was a clever development of previous Nizari beliefs but it is hard to avoid the conclusion that it hints at convenience. As an attempt to explain a very unusual sequence of events it is subtle but not wholly convincing. But it is altogether understandable that such an attempt might be made, as given this backwards and forwards movement in Nizari doctrine, matters must have been more than a little confusing for rank and file members of the movement.

Juwayni also asserts that, when Muhammad assumed power, he soon showed signs of being something of a megalomaniac. According to the historian, he proved oblivious to the advice of his councillors, and reacted angrily when any dared to contradict him. As a result, few men ventured to offer him any counsel, terrified that they would provoke an angry response from him. The chronicler also reports that during Muhammad's reign, his territories became ever more lawless. Robbery and assault were, it was claimed, commonplace across his domain: 'Theft, highway robbery and assault were daily occurrences in his Kingdom . . . and he thought he could excuse such conduct with false words and the bestowal of money. And when these things had passed all bounds his life, wives, children, home, kingdom and wealth were forfeited to that madness and insanity'.[2] It is once more important to note that Juwayni was diametrically opposed to Muhammad's form of Islam and as such is hardly a disinterested observer. But Muhammad's reign was eventually to end amidst a veritable deluge of blood, with a display of butchery that was egregious even by the standards of the time, so on this occasion we should perhaps beware before dismissing Juwayni's claims out of hand.

But there is an alternative aspect to Nizari life during this period, one that is rarely glimpsed through the thick clouds of mystery and intrigue that enshroud the history of the movement. In common with many other Muslim movements, the Nizaris valued learning highly. In particular, a number of marvellously stocked libraries were created throughout their territories, brimming with rare and beautiful works of literature. So magnificent were these centres of learning that men came from all over the Islamic world to take advantage of them. A significant proportion of them were it seems not even Isma'ilis. This trend appeared to reach something of a peak during Muhammad's reign and it was during it that one of the most renowned scholars of the time made his way to Alamut.

He was a man named Nasr al-Din al-Tusi. When he was still a youth, he entered into the service of the leader of the Quhistani Nizaris. During his time there, he wrote a substantial work on ethics. Subsequently, he moved to Alamut, a natural progression perhaps for an academic of Isma'ili leanings. Muhammad proved to be a staunch patron of his, as was his eventual successor. Al-Tusi wrote a number of works during his extended period at Alamut (which lasted for three decades) on a range of subjects, including philosophy and astronomy as well as religion. He is particularly important for his accounts of the Nizaris' theological development after the *qiyama*. He would still be at Alamut when it eventually passed into the hands of the Mongols.

However, he was nothing if not a survivor. When taken, he managed to persuade his Mongol captors that he was not really a Nizari at all. He had been kept at Alamut against his will and he was a 'Twelver' Shia rather than an Isma'ili. There seemed to be little evidence to support this claim, but al-Tusi managed to come out of this particular scrape rather well. The great Mongol conqueror, Hulagu, was so impressed by his talents and so convinced of his loyalty that he had a well-equipped observatory built for him, so that he could develop his skills further. He lived out his days serving Hulagu's successor and eventually died in Baghdad. Whether or not his claims to have been a captive of the Nizaris was true is conjectural. However, as a writer he made a great impression on a range of people, so much so that even down to modern times 'Twelver' Shiites continue to assert with passion that he was always of their persuasion.[3]

Al-Tusi helped in the further development of Nizari beliefs, particularly relating to the concept of the *satr*. But Muhammad's reign was also a very busy one politically. Their improved relations with the caliph in Baghdad and the disintegration of the Khwarazmian kingdom (for reasons which will shortly be examined) gave the Nizaris an opportunity to increase their influence. The Khwarazmians, in a desperate last attempt to hold on to some of their power in the face of relentless Mongol attacks, fought ferociously to retain their powerbase but ultimately in vain. In the confusion caused by their increasingly difficult position, the Nizaris were able to make some useful gains in Persia, particularly around the apparently impregnable citadel of Girdkuh. Nor was it just through force of arms that they furthered their cause. In or around 1222, a mission was sent by the sect to Rayy to seek new converts which was, unfortunately for the Nizari *da'is*, discovered. The missionaries were executed. A mission would also be launched to regions much further afield, including India. There had been Isma'ili enclaves in the country from Fatimid times but, during or around the thirteenth century, a Nizari community was established in the country.

The Nizaris had still not lost their flair for more dramatic gestures. The Sultan Jalal al-Din, Shah of the Khwarazmians, was still strong enough to force the Nizaris to keep their activities reasonably under control. In 1227, he forced them to enter into a truce. Not long before, a senior Khwarazmian official had been eliminated by Nizari *fida'is* (probably in revenge for Khwarazmian raids into Quhistan). Three of them fell upon him and stabbed him to death. They then went looking for Jalal al-Din's vizier, Sharaf al-Mulk, but, when they broke into his palace, they could not find him. Running out into the streets, they were set upon by the inhabitants of the city, who threw stones at them from the rooftops and killed them.

Curiously, while all this was going on, a Nizari ambassador was en route to see Jalal al-Din himself. When news of the assassination reached the envoy, he was naturally enough somewhat apprehensive of his reception. It was after all hardly an ideal time for him to approach the Sultan when, elsewhere in the country, the sect was killing some of his leading officials. He halted his journey and wrote to Jalal al-Din's vizier, asking for his advice. The vizier was terrified that he was a marked man – the group of assassins so recently killed had after all been looking for him – and went out of his way to stay in the ambassador's good books. He went so far as to offer to accompany the envoy to Jalal al-Din so that he might be more confident of a good reception.

The journey went without incident, indeed both men appeared to be getting on remarkably well, until everything turned around in an instant. On one particular evening, the party set up camp and the wine, it appears, started to flow a touch too freely. The Nizari ambassador was reputedly particularly the worse for wear, and began to boast to Sharaf al-Mulk that, even in his own bodyguard, there were Nizari assassins who would, at his command, kill the vizier there and then. Five men were then called into his presence, all of whom attested that they were Nizari *fida'is* who would not hesitate to eliminate the vizier if told to do so. Sharaf al-Mulk was terrified at this turn of events. Ripping off his shirt, he threw himself on their mercy, asking in terror what they wanted of him and swearing that he would never do anything to harm the movement.

In all probability, the whole thing had been brought about by an excess of alcohol. The ambassador presumably had had plenty of opportunity to eliminate Sharaf al-Mulk at other times, and did not need to wait until he was drunk to do so. In any event, the vizier was left unharmed. However, news of the incident reached Jalal al-Din, who was understandably livid, both at the Nizaris for their impudence and the vizier for his weakness.

Jalal al-Din determined to make an example of the *fida'is* that would serve as a warning to any others who were foolish enough to act in such a fashion. He sent word to Sharaf al-Mulk that the five Nizaris who had infiltrated his bodyguard were to be burned alive. The vizier was frantic; no doubt afraid that the Nizaris would take revenge on him if he were to carry out his orders, he begged his Sultan to exercise clemency. Jalal al-Din would not however countenance this and demanded that his instructions be carried out as he had directed. The continued weakness of the vizier merely served to harden his heart. Accordingly, a great pyre was erected close to the entrance of the vizier's tent and the five men were thrown into it. Before they perished, eye witnesses said that they accepted what they perceived to be their martyrdom with enthusiasm, believing that their place in Paradise was guaranteed by their sacrifice.

The vizier's concerns for his safety in the aftermath of this act were justified. Shortly afterwards, a delegation from Alamut arrived. They demanded that blood money of 10,000 dinars be paid for the lives of each of the five Nizaris killed. The news reportedly reduced the timid Sharaf al-Mulk to a nervous wreck. He treated the ambassadors with excessive generosity; no expense was spared in making them feel duly welcome. Gifts were showered upon them, and the annual tribute demanded by the Khwarazmians from the Nizaris was reduced, though not by the full amount demanded.[4]

The difficult relations between the Nizaris and the Khwarazmians were however overshadowed by other events. A holocaust was about to engulf Persia, which threatened the existence of the whole of the Islamic world. The origins of this tempest lay far to the east, in Mongolia and the surrounding areas.

In or around 1167, a boy was born, son of a tribal chief. He was a Mongol, the name given collectively to a group of people that were in fact formed of many different clans and tribes. He was a member of a tribe known as the Qiyat, who were a sub-clan of the Borjigin. Although his social position at birth was comfortable, it would quickly deteriorate. His father was murdered by a group of Tatar tribesmen (who were traditional enemies of his clan) who poisoned him while pretending to offer him hospitality. The son and his family quickly lost their position in the tribal hierarchy; they were shabbily treated and forced to seek their living in conditions of abject poverty in virtual exile. It was a slur that perhaps helped to shape the personality and future development of the boy who would grow up to be one of history's most formidable generals. His name was appropriate; he was called Temujin, which means 'man of iron'. But to the West he would be better known as Genghis Khan, the 'Universal Ruler'.

As a youth, the characteristics that were to carve his niche in history began to manifest themselves. He was tall and athletic; like most Mongols, he was an outstanding horseman. He also had an uncanny knack of dominating anyone that he came into contact with. He did this not through any histrionics but rather by the sheer force of his presence. Chroniclers especially noted his steely eyes, which seemed to magnetize an audience when he was present.

Despite his abject poverty, the leaders of several local tribes felt threatened by the youth. One day, they raided his homestead and he was taken away to their camp, where he was kept in a cage to await a lifetime of imprisonment or worse. But he managed to make good his escape, and proceeded to plot his revenge. By a succession of strategic alliances and his uncanny ability to ingratiate himself with men of far greater status than himself, he took over control of the Mongols once more and began to build up their strength to an amazing extent.

Eventually, he would have some very large forces at his disposal. As tribes were defeated, he sometimes added their military resources to his own (though as often, especially with tribes that were traditionally hostile to the Mongols, he would have most of the men executed). However, even when his power reached its zenith, he regularly went into battle at a substantial numerical disadvantage to his foes. But what he lacked in numbers, he made up for in discipline. His greatest strength was that he was a brilliant organizer. Each man had his appointed task, be it in battle or while the army was on the move. On campaign, there was never a moment's hesitation from any man because he was confused as to his role. Instructions were passed across the battlefield through a series of pre-determined signals.

His tactics were simple, but devastatingly effective. The Mongols were exclusively horsemen. They arrayed themselves across a wide front when they went into battle (a manoeuvre that they perfected by an annual hunt that the army were all required to take part in, which lasted for three months). The first attacks would be led by light cavalry, particularly through the use of horse archers. These men (whose tactics and skills closely reflected those of the Mongols' Turkish cousins) could fire with unerring accuracy even when their horses were running at a full gallop. Their task was to soften the enemy up; when they had done so, the way was then left clear for the Mongols' heavy cavalry (which was generally irresistible) to charge in and complete the task. Across the steppes of Asia, and into the heart of China itself, these tactics brought complete triumph for the Mongols. Genghis began to construct an empire the like of which the world had never seen before.

There was one enemy alone that offered a threat to the expansionist ambitions of Genghis. An alliance was formed between two great powers that threatened to halt any further growth of the Mongol empire. One half of it was composed of a vast tribal confederation known as the Naimans, who lived in the steppes of Central Asia to the west of the Mongols; the other half of the alliance was formed by the Khwarazmians. Together, the two formed a huge barrier to further progress as far as the Mongols were concerned. They could field a vast army which would also be well armed. It was a threat that Genghis could not, given his character, possibly ignore.

And so began a campaign unlike few others in history. Genghis had many qualities that many easily be admired; energy, resilience, organizational brilliance to name but three. But there was also another side to his character; he was possessed of quite extraordinary ruthlessness. He had already shown a ferocious streak in his dealings with some (but not all) of the tribes that opposed him.

But this did not adequately prepare the world for what was to come. The campaign that Genghis was about to launch on Central Asia and Persia was probably the most savage that the world had yet seen. It is doubtful whether the excesses of the Mongols were matched until the twentieth century. The tactics employed by the Mongols were simple and brutal; surrender without a fight and mercy might be anticipated, but if any resistance was forthcoming then, after the fall of the city or fortress that had been bold enough to resist (which almost inevitably followed any misguided attempt to rebuff the Mongols), nothing save annihilation could be expected.

It was in 1220 that the storm clouds first broke over Persia, and it was the stupidity of the Shah of the Khwarazmians that unleashed the hurricane. The Shah was a man named Muhammad (father of Jalal al-Din who later ordered the execution of the Nizari *fida'is* in Sharaf al-Mulk's entourage). In that year, a party of Mongol traders made their way into his lands. The governor of the town of Otrar, known as Ghayir-Khan ('the mighty Khan') was informed that they were spies. It is not clear whether this was true or not, but participation in the occasional act of espionage was almost expected of merchants in those days.

The reaction of the governor was draconian. The merchants, even the camel drivers with them, were killed and their goods were seized. Inevitably, the Mongols protested against this unwarranted action. A delegation was sent to ask Muhammad for restitution against his errant governor. To say that he turned a deaf ear is in fact the ultimate in understatement; the two guards accompanying the ambassador had their beards singed and they were sent back to the Mongols accompanied by the envoy's head which an executioner had detached from his body. There can have been few men in history who had made such a huge error of judgement. According to Juwayni, by his actions 'he [Ghayir-Khan] desolated and laid waste a whole world and rendered a whole creation without home, property or leaders. For every drop of their blood there flowed a whole Oxus; in retribution for every hair on their heads it seemed that a hundred thousand heads rolled in the dust at every crossroad . . .'.[5]

The Khwarazmians and their Naiman allies far outnumbered the Mongols but in the campaign that followed this counted for nothing. Muhammad's armies were consistently bested in battle and relentlessly pursued. The Mongol tactics proved irresistible. Some of the greatest cities in Central Asia, including the fabled Bokhara and the legendary Samarkand fell, though large numbers of the population survived. The citizens of Khurasan, which was attacked in 1221, were much less fortunate. People of the countryside round about fled to the cities for sanctuary but their hopes were vain. They merely added to the numbers slaughtered in the sack that followed once the cities had fallen.

Instant capitulation was the only way of avoiding wholesale, bloody massacre. Bamian, in the Hindu Kush, held out and, during the fighting that ensued, Mutugen, a favourite grandson of Genghis Khan, died. When the city subsequently fell, every inhabitant was slaughtered. Contemporary accounts speak of hundreds of thousands being slain and, although we should be cautious of taking their figures literally – chroniclers of the day were notoriously unreliable at statistical estimation – we should nevertheless assume that the bloodletting involved was on a huge scale.

The worst fate was reserved for Nishapur. During the assault on the city, one of Genghis' favourites, his son-in-law, Toghutsur, was killed. This infuriated him and he resolved on a terrible revenge. The aftermath of the city's capture was gruesome. Under the supervision of Toghutsur's widow, every living thing in the city was killed. Separate pyramids were made for the men, women, children, dogs and cats that were put to the sword. The city was then razed to the ground. Not a stone was left standing – it was as if Nishapur had never existed. The ferocity of these attacks shocked many; even one of Genghis' sons chastised him for his excess. But the end result of the campaign as a whole was clear enough. The power of Muhammad was broken and, although he escaped he died a lonely, penniless, hungry man on a deserted island in the Caspian Sea.[6] He was so destitute by this time that his shroud was a torn shirt, which was virtually all that was left to him.

Genghis was eventually distracted by events elsewhere and he returned home to die in a war against rebellious vassals in China. As the Mongols temporarily lowered their guard in the region, it gave Jalal al-Din, Muhammad's son, the opportunity to reinstate a form of Khwarazmian rule in the rump of their former territories (it was during the short period that this state was in existence that he came into contact with the Nizaris). But the effect of these campaigns must have had an immense impact on the region. An inescapable lesson had been taught: resistance was useless and would inevitably lead to catastrophe. Nothing save subservience and unconditional capitulation would save anyone caught in the path of the Mongol whirlwind. This is an important fact to bear in mind when considering the Nizaris' stance towards the Mongols in the decades to come.

The Nizaris had continued to support the Mongols in their war against the Khwarazmians before the final resolution of that particular conflict. No doubt the Nizaris regarded this as a sensible move, as the Khwarazmians were common enemies of the two groups and it also helped to deter the Mongols from attacking them, as least for the time being. This of course did little to endear them to their Khwarazmian neighbours. Inevitably, there was much friction as a result.[7]

One especially violent incident occurred when a caravan of Nizaris was passing through Azerbaijan. Jalal al-Din was at the time stopping all traffic into the region on the pretence that he was looking for a Mongol envoy whom he claimed was surreptitiously making his way into his territories. The caravan was ransacked and most of those with it were killed. The Nizaris complained bitterly to the Khwarazmians at this act, and were successful to the extent that they recovered at least some of the goods that had been stolen. The Khwarazmians actions however demonstrated clearly the tensions that existed between the two powers; truces were frequently made between them but they were never very secure, and they were frequently breached. On another occasion, while making his way towards Alamut, Muhammad's vizier was seized by an ally of the Khwarazmians and put to death. Soon after, Jalal al-Din sent envoys to Alamut to complain that the tribute due from the Nizaris was long overdue. It was all evidence of a deteriorating relationship between the Nizaris and the Khwarazmians. These are only some of the incidents that are recorded; it is certain that there were many others of a similar nature that were not.

Jalal al-Din's respite from the Mongols was a brief one. The Mongols returned to lay their claim to the region once more. The brutal excesses of the last Mongol attacks were too fresh in the minds of everyone to offer any real hope of extended resistance. Jalal al-Din was forced to flee for his life. In an epic journey, he made his way to safety by outriding a vast force of Mongol pursuers into India. He later travelled a thousand miles back into Central Asia, where he was to be murdered by brigands.

The effect of these tumultuous events on the Middle East was immense. The Khwarazmians were a fierce people without too many scruples and they were quick to offer themselves as mercenaries to almost anyone who wished to hire them. Large numbers were employed further west against the Crusaders occupying Outremer.[8] They also sent shock waves rippling across the Muslim world. The levels of ferocity employed by the Mongols against these Muslim states was merely the precursor of other great outrages yet to come.

For a while it appeared as if the entire Islamic world was in danger, and it would take a combination of a series of fortuitous events and a Muslim leader of truly epic proportions to halt the advance of the Mongol tide. For the Nizaris, there were clear signs of danger. They had met the first advances of the Mongols into the region with a subservient and friendly response, which for the time being kept their state safe. However, given the rapacity of the Mongol hordes, they surely had little confidence that this state of affairs would be a permanent one. Indeed, there is evidence that the Nizaris were on occasion very welcoming to Sunni refugees from the chaos, with one visitor noting that the leader of the Isma'ilis in Quhistan 'used greatly to cherish poor strangers and travellers; and such Muslims of Khurasan as had come into proximity with him he was wont to take under his guardianship and protection'.[9]

The Nizaris may have hoped to buy their independence by their support for the Mongols but it only bought them a little time. When the power of the Khwarazmians was broken once and for all by the Mongols, it was virtually inevitable that the Nizaris would be attacked soon after. To understand why this was unavoidable, it is necessary to appreciate something of the mentality of the Mongols, and especially of their Khans.

According to Mongol legend, at the beginning of time the great God, a deity known as Mongke Tengri, had decreed that it was the destiny of the Mongol Khan to rule the world. This claim was virtually an article of faith for the Mongol Khans. They regarded it as their right to rule over all men. This meant that there was never any possibility of any other man or race treating with the Khan or his people as an equal. The only way of enhancing one's prospects of survival was absolute subservience towards the Mongols. Any party that was seen by the Mongols as a threat could only look forward to a terrible fate. Given the past history of the Nizaris, their ability to have an influence out of proportion to their size in the politics of the region and their well-known proclivities for eliminating troublesome adversaries, it was always probable that they would be high up the list of Mongol targets. Soon after the fall of Jelal al-Din, the son and heir of Genghis, Ogadai, had decided that he wished to conquer all Persia and add it to his already huge empire. As part of his ongoing process of conquest, he attacked and overran several Nizari possessions in the region.

Muhammad III, leader of the Nizaris since 1221, reigned in all for thirty-four years. As he grew older, it became increasingly apparent that the Mongol threat was threatening to engulf Persia and the surrounding areas. It promised to consume the entire eastern Islamic world. Muhammad was well aware of the threat. In 1246, when the Khan Guyuk was enthroned far to the east in Mongolia, the Nizaris sent a delegation to deliver a message to him at the festivities that accompanied his formal accession to the position. They were accompanied by other representatives of the Muslim community in Persia, and the communication that they were to deliver was a conciliatory one. They wished to resolve their historical differences with the Mongols. Their mission was a failure; the Khan abruptly rejected them. In no uncertain terms, he told the envoys to return to their masters with the clear and unambiguous message that they should expect no mercy from him.

Seeing that his friendly overtures had not been reciprocated, and having little confidence that the Khan of the Mongols was likely to change his stance, Muhammad decided that he had no choice but to adopt other means to counter their threat. The Nizaris opted to use all the weapons at their disposal to face up to the danger posed by the Mongol threat. In 1238, they despatched a delegation of ambassadors to seek an alliance, not with other local leaders but with the Kings of England and France far away in Western Europe. It was unlikely but not impossible that there would be any tangible reward for their efforts. Western Europe was increasingly aware of the Mongols and their terrible military machine. Not only Asia had been exposed to their advances; they were threatening to sweep into Europe.[10] As such, they might well see some merit in joining an alliance against this awful threat.

Despite all the evidence that the Mongols were seeking nothing less than complete domination of every nation that they came into contact with, the West was surprisingly ambivalent in its attitude towards them. They had heard – correctly as it happened – that the Mongols numbered many Christians among their numbers. But although this was partially true, it did not tell the whole story. There were a large number of Mongols who retained their ancient, shamanistic, nature-worshipping beliefs. Further, those who were Christians practised their religion in a way that few in the West would understand. They were in fact Nestorian Christians, a branch of the religion that had originated in Persia a few centuries before and was heavily influenced by the mystical, esoteric heritage of the region. Their practise of Christianity was therefore far removed from that of Western Europe. Neither did the West understand the paradigms of the Mongol khans, who would not countenance a partnership of equals with any Western monarch.

But the leaders of the West did not understand this or, if they did, they did not want to fully believe it. There were consistent rumours of a mysterious King in the East, a man called Prester John, who was a Christian and who would one day come to the aid of the West to finally defeat the powers of Islam. Partly because of this misguided hope, and also because the West did not as yet fully comprehend the full extent of the Mongol threat, the Nizaris' delegation, innovative as such an approach was, came to nothing.

The West had little comprehension of the reality of affairs in the East. Its leaders did not distinguish between one potential enemy and another. The Bishop of Winchester, Peter of Roches, greeted these overtures for co-operation with the attitude that the West should 'allow these dogs to devour one another, that they may be consumed and perish. When we come upon those of Christ's enemies who remain, we shall slaughter them and cleanse the face of the earth'.[11]

Eventually, the Nizaris were to become so afraid of the Mongols, and so disappointed in their search for allies against them, that they resorted to their old, time-honoured ways. Large numbers of *fida'is* were sent to infiltrate the court of Mongke (a successor several times removed of Ogadai), but although they did succeed in manipulating their way into his court, none could get close enough to eliminate him. In fact, their efforts had the opposite effect to that desired. The Mongols, who had learned from many of their newly-acquired Islamic subjects of the terrible ways of the Nizaris, were now more convinced than ever of the danger they posed.

Further, the implication of the Nizaris in an attack in which Jagatai, a son of Genghis Khan, was killed added to the Mongols' hostility towards them. From this point on, they resolved that nothing save the extermination of the Nizaris would suffice to protect Mongol interests. Of all the Nizaris' assassinations, this was perhaps the one that was to have the most profound, and the most awful, of long-term consequences.

It was however not the Mongols who would prove the end of Muhammad III. Not for the first time, the terminal danger came from a source far closer to home. Muhammad had a son named Rukn ad-Din Khurshah. When he was still young, Muhammad declared him his successor. However, as time passed it became clear that this young man had a mind of his own. He began to develop his own set of beliefs, and his own brand of political values, that were contrary to those espoused by his father.

To make matters worse, there were increasing concerns about Muhammad's suitability to remain as the movement's leader. Some even began to cast aspersions on his sanity, as his behaviour was increasingly characterized by outbursts of uncontrolled and seemingly irrational anger. Certainly, he was so incensed at what he perceived to be the insolence of his son that he sought to have Rukn ad-Din removed as his successor. He did not succeed. His advisers told him that this was against the creed of the Nizaris (although as this had proved so flexible in the past, it is hard to understand why this argument should have convinced Muhammad to refrain from pursuing his demands). Nevertheless it was apparent that relations between father and son were alarmingly strained.

A crisis point had been reached. Juwayni states that 'Ala-ad-Din [Muhammad] was always annoying Rukn ad-Din. In his insanity and melancholy madness he would constantly torment, and persecute, and punish him without cause. He always had to stay with the womenfolk in a room adjoining his father's and did not dare to come out in daytime'.[12]

By 1255, the Mongols were standing once more on the threshold of the Nizari territories. Rukn ad-Din believed that nothing save capitulation could protect the Nizaris. He argued that it was nonsensical to send assassins against the Mongols; all this would succeed in doing was to intensify their determination to annihilate them. This argument was certainly not without its merits and would probably have been acceptable to many of the Nizaris. It could be argued that pretending to accept

French troops attacking a citadel are met by Saracen defenders. From a chronicle of France . . . *from Priam, King of Troy to the crowning of Charles VI*, 1388. (*BL*)

A Frankish knight and a Saracen doing battle. Illustration *c*. 1300–1325. (*BL*)

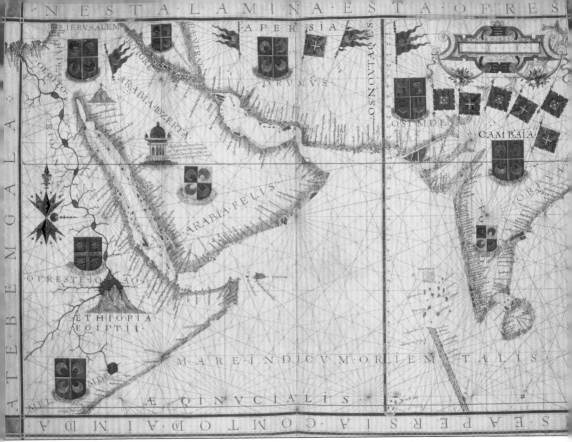

Map of the Middle East, 1573. A Portuguese map with coats of arms, showing what is now Iran, Saudi Arabia, Yemen, the Horn of Africa, Egypt and the River Nile. (*BL*)

King Louis IX lands at Tunis. The French are cut off by Saracens in a tower (*c.* 1325–50) (*BL*)

Opposite: The sacking of Isfahan by Mongol troops under Tamerlane, 1388 AD. 70,000 inhabitants were massacred following a failed revolt. A hill was made from the skulls of the dead. From *Timurnameh* by Abdullah Hatifi. (*BL*)

منصوم زوال السارع السَّت وَمُوحَرْ وحشَّضَ عنه وتَعَالَحَرَة عَزْ خَرِاسَه وَهَاكَلَه

Destruction by Al-Hakim of the Church of the Holy Sepulchre in Jerusalem, from the Al-Biruni Ms. (*Edinburgh University Library*)

Saracens attacking a Christian camp, *c.* 1325–50. The attack betrays evidence of treachery as the attackers are shielded by a delegation of unarmed emissaries. (*BL*)

a tou; les testes coper : se lost des xpïeñz
passoit iusques a tunes . et se il ni aloi
eut : il les deliuerroit tou; .

Comment melire jehan dare toute
her de france qui faisoit le guet da
tins sarrazins qui regioiet le baptesm

Deathbed of Godfrey de Bouillon, first
Frankish ruler of Jerusalem. The men
dressed in green and red may be Godfrey's
brothers: Eustache, and Baldwin, who
succeeded him as King. From a fifteenth
century French translation of a history of
the Crusades. (*BL*)

'The Archangel Gabriel': Persian
representation from *The Wonders of
Creation and the Oddities of Existence*,
c. 1400. (*BM*)

وَمِنهُمْ جَبرئيل

فَإِذا بِهِ أَمِينُ الوَحيِ وَخازِنُ القُدسِ وَقالَ لَهُ إِنَّهُ الرُوحُ الأَمينُ والرُوحُ القُدسُ
والناموسُ الأَكبَرُ وطاوُسُ المَلائِكَةِ جاءَ في القُرآنِ أَنَّهُ قالَ نَحنُ نَتَنَزَّلُ بِأَمرِ
رَبِّكَ لَهُ ما بَينَ أَيدينا وما خَلفَنا كَما اتَّصَلَ عَلى النَفَقاتِ جيثُ يَعقِدُ ولا يَزالُ الذينَ كَذَلِكَ
حَتّى ناتيهِمْ جِبريلُ فَإِذا جاءَهُمْ فَرَغَ عَن قُلوبِهِم فَقالوا يا جِبريلُ ماذا قالَ رَبُّكَ
فَيَقولونَ الحَقَّ نادى لِلحَقِّ الحَقُّ وجاءَ بِالعِلمِ أَنَّ النَبِيَّ صَلّى اللهُ عَلَيهِ وآلِهِ وسَلَّمَ
قالَ لِجِبريلَ إِنّي أُحِبُّ أَن أَراكَ عَلى صورَتِكَ فَقالَ إِنَّكَ لا تُطيقُ ذَلِكَ

'The battle of Ghengis Khan and Prester John': an imaginary scene, as Prester John was a mythical Christian ruler from the East. It is not explained why the Mongol soldiers are depicted as Arabs carrying Frankish swords. (*BL*)

The Qu'ran of Sultan Baibars. No pictorial representations of Baibars himself are known to exist although he left a substantial architectural legacy. (*BL*)

The capture of Acre, 1191, from *Chroniques de France ou de St Denis, c. 1325–50. (BL)*

Mongol cavalry doing battle with turbanned bowmen, late sixteenth century. From the *Shahnameh* by Ferdowsi. (*BL*)

Mongol rule while secretly retaining the age-old Nizari beliefs was just another example of *taqiyya*. There was certainly plenty of evidence that the fate of all those misguided enough to resist the Mongols (let alone assassinate one of their leaders) was a horrific one indeed. It was perhaps no coincidence that the worst excesses of the Mongols (and such a description is no small accolade given their history) had taken place in Khurasan, certainly close enough to the Nizari territories to register strongly in the consciousness of the movement and its supporters.

There was one major obstacle to this scheme: it was unlikely to reach fruition while Muhammad was still leader of the Nizaris. Rukn ad-Din therefore began to plot to remove him but, although many offered to support him, few would go so far as to support the elimination of his father, who occupied a revered and sacred position. Towards the end of 1255, Rukn ad-Din was taken ill. He took to his bed to recover. While his son was confined to his chamber, Muhammad went out to spend a night in the hut of a shepherd. He was a man who apparently enjoyed simple pleasures; he had a fondness for farming and he often did this. But on this particular night, his stay in the hut was to be somewhat more adventurous than usual. When he did not return, his attendants went to look for him. They found him lying dead in the hut. Death was clearly not from natural causes as his head lay next to his body.

Some saw this as no more than Muhammad's just desserts. He had acquired a reputation for excessive drinking among his enemies, though these claims may of course reflect nothing more than the prejudices of the latter. Such bias is evident enough in the writings of one chronicler who stated that: 'when the Angel of Death met his soul at the time set for its seizing, he complained of the calamitous day. The cupbearers of Hell came to meet him, to shatter the gladness of prosperity in his breast'.[13]

Rukn ad-Din naturally denied all responsibility for his father's murder but the timing of his illness seems altogether all to convenient an alibi for anyone to be confident that he really was not involved in this brutal act. He was, after all, the man who stood to gain from it more than any other, and it was inevitable that suspicion would fall upon him. Juwayni, while allowing that Rukn ad-Din cannot have personally carried out the act himself, nevertheless states reasonably enough that 'in view of the circumstances of the case it can be assumed that his father's death was not distasteful or unwelcome to him and that Hasan [the supposed murderer] did what he did with his consent'. However, in an unusually circumspect manner, he goes only so far as to say that the idea that 'Hasan had a prior arrangement with Rukn ad-Din and committed that act in consultation and agreement with him is possible', but no more than that.[14]

Perhaps conscious that the finger of suspicion inevitably pointed at him, Rukn ad-Din hastily launched a search for his father's killers. A number of people were suspected, but after only a week a definite accusation was laid. The target of this accusation was a courtier by the name of Hasan-i Mazandarani. He had been a favourite of the late Imam, and as such he had easier access to him than any other man. He was judged, found guilty and executed. His body was then thrown onto a pyre and cremated. As the flames took hold, two sons and a daughter who had also been accused of participating in the murder were thrown into the blaze. Rukn ad-Din had sent a powerful message at the start of his reign. The guilt of his victims must be in question and the incident certainly made a great impression. At the beginning of the twentieth century, Rukn ad-Din was described by an eminent historian as 'one of the most loathsome of characters in history'.[15] But his act did him or his movement little good. The policy he espoused would not save the Nizaris from destruction, it would instead precipitate it.

Rukn ad-Din quickly sought to amend the ways of his people in such a fashion that he hoped to reintegrate them into the mainstream of the Islamic world. By so doing, he also planned to avert draconian action on the part of the Mongols. He instructed his people to comply once more with the *sharia* and observe Islamic orthodoxy. He also ordered them to refrain from murder and political intrigue. But the cumulative effect of the stories of a number of newly-acquired subjects was too much for Mongke to ignore. Advised by them that the Nizaris were too great a danger to leave unchecked Mongke had decided that the movement must be crushed. Even as Rukn ad-Din took steps to pacify the Mongols, a great army was on its way towards Rudbar with the express intention of destroying the Nizaris. Despite Rukn ad-Din's early attempts to avoid a Mongol onslaught, the point of no return had already been passed; the fate of the Nizaris was already sealed.

The attack was led by one of the foremost Mongol generals of his day, Hulagu, who was effectively governor of Mongke's Persian territories, as well as other lands bordering the country. He had been ordered by Mongke to eliminate the Nizari threat. Hulagu had been somewhat desultory in his campaign so far, and there are hints that Mongke had expressed his displeasure at what appeared to be his apparent lack of urgency. The campaign had so far concentrated on Quhistan, but attention now turned towards Rudbar, the spiritual and physical heart of the Nizari world. The closest Mongol leader of note, Yasa'ur Noyon, was in the city of Hamadan, to the south of Rudbar. Rukn ad-Din sent an embassy to him, with the message that the Nizaris had changed their ways and had rejected the path of violence. As Juwayni put it, he was now 'ready to tread the path of submission'.[16]

Unfortunately for the Nizaris, Rukn ad-Din had misread the situation. Mongol policy was still shaped by the dicta of Genghis Khan, who had sought not submission but the extermination of those groups that he regarded as threats. And, although he was dead, this particular policy of his was not. Nevertheless, Mongke would clearly be more than satisfied if the Nizaris surrendered voluntarily rather than actively resisting. Some of the Nizari citadels were so well provisioned and intimidatingly sited that they were capable of resisting the Mongols for some time (as subsequent events would graphically prove). Seizing on Rukn ad-Din's overtures, Yasa'ur Noyon told the delegation that Rukn ad-Din should submit himself in person to Hulagu to demonstrate the sincerity of the reformation of the movement that he led.

Rukn ad-Din procrastinated, a sensible enough reaction given recent history. He chose not to go in person to Hulagu but instead sent a delegation led by his brother, Shahanshah. The Mongols reacted hastily to these initial approaches. Sensing weakness, they sent an army to attack the Nizari heartlands. However, the force despatched by Hulagu into Rudbar was resisted by the Nizaris and forced to retreat, although the Mongols destroyed many of the crops in the region in the process. Seeing that his actions had been premature, Hulagu changed tack. He sent word to Rukn ad-Din that he was pleased with the message that he had received through Shahanshah. The Imam had done nothing wrong himself; he was not implicated in the murderous ways of his predecessors and he could therefore expect to be well treated. However, he must do more to demonstrate that he was acting in good faith. As a start, he should dismantle all of the Nizari castles.

Rukn ad-Din again dissimulated. Perhaps aware that he was in danger of throwing away all his trump cards far too early in the game, he dismantled some of the lesser Nizari castles – 40 of which were lost – but removed only a small part of the defences of the great castles at Alamut, Maymundiz and Lamasar. To Hulagu's request that he present himself in person, he replied that he was not yet ready. He would need a year before he could do so, as he had to convince his people that he was acting in their best interests by doing so. He did however order some of his governors to surrender. His representatives in Quhistan did so, as did the commander of the great castle at Girdkuh (though significantly the castle itself was not handed over).

Hulagu was not satisfied by Rukn ad-Din's reasons for refusing to present himself in person. He demanded that he should come immediately; if this were not possible, then he should send his son instead. But when a boy of seven arrived before Hulagu, whom it was claimed was the son in question, Hulagu doubted his authenticity. Hulagu returned the child, saying that he was too young, and asked that Hulagu send another hostage instead. Probably fully aware that Rukn ad-Din was playing for time, Hulagu advanced at the head of his army into Rudbar itself. When Rukn ad-Din sent a delegation to meet him, the Mongols were just three days march from Alamut. Hulagu now issued Rukn ad-Din with an ultimatum. If the castle of Maymundiz were destroyed and Rukn ad-Din 'came to present himself in person to the King, he would . . . be received with kindness and honour; but that if he failed to consider the consequences of his actions, God alone knew [what would then befall him].'[17]

This was the moment of truth for Rukn ad-Din, the point of no return. He desperately sought to avoid making a firm decision one way or the other. His uncertainty was not helped by the divided opinions of his advisers. Some advocated resistance but others advised surrender. Prominent among the latter was the writer and astronomer Nasr al-Din al-Tusi, who told Rukn ad-Din that the stars were inauspicious for resistance. In the event, the Imam did not give himself up at once but instead attempted to prevaricate.

A large force advanced on Maymundiz. From all directions, Mongol armies converged on the castle. It must have presented a terrifying sight to the Nizaris. Juwayni describes, in a passage which is as vivid as any he wrote, how 'the valleys and mountains billowed with the great masses of men. The hills which had held their heads so high and with such strong hearts now lay trampled with broken necks under the hooves of horses and camels. And from the din of the braying of the camels and the noise of pipe and kettledrum the ears of the world were deafened, and from the neighing of the horses and flashing of the lances the hearts and eyes of the foe were blinded'.[18] A close siege was laid to Maymundiz. The Mongols denuded the area of its trees, so meticulously planted by the Nizaris as part of their master plan to provide bountiful sustenance for their castles, and turned them into catapults and mangonels with which they started to pound the great walls of the castle. However, Rukn al-Din's heart was not in the fight. After just four days, he gave himself up to Hulagu.

Politically, his surrender marked the end of the independent Nizari state in Persia. He was treated well at first by Hulagu. He was very interested in camels; Hulagu therefore presented a gift of 100 Bactrian camels to him. He developed an affection for a beautiful young Mongol girl; Hulagu presented her to Rukn al-Din as a wife. But the truth of all of this was that for the time being the Imam served a purpose. Once his usefulness had ended, then Rukn ad-Din would be living on borrowed time. For now, Hulagu used him by persuading him to order the surrender of all the remaining Nizari possessions in the region. Most places complied with this request, but among the few that refused the order were Lamasar and Alamut. The Mongols laid siege to both of them in 1256. The introduction of a Chinese catapult with an immense range at the latter proved decisive. Abandoning all hope, the garrison of Alamut sought terms. Rukn al-Din, who was present at the siege, interceded on their behalf and Hulagu agreed to let the garrison live.

The loss of Alamut was a devastating blow, given both its psychological importance to the Nizaris and its seemingly unconquerable situation. Centuries later, visitors to the region still could not bring themselves to believe that the castle had ever surrendered. The twentieth century traveller Freya Stark declared, when seeing the castle, that 'the central stronghold of Alamut might and should have held out. It stands in an impregnable valley . . .'.[19]

But she was wrong. The fight had gone from the Nizaris, who were faced with an overwhelmingly superior and grimly determined enemy. And on this occasion there was no Hasan-i Sabbah to encourage the garrison to redouble their efforts to repel the enemy: Rukn ad-Din was, it will be remembered, with the Mongols. In the absence of any leadership, it was understandable that the garrison surrendered.

When the Nizaris had removed themselves from Alamut, the Mongols walked in to take possession. They took whatever the Nizaris had left behind. Hulagu's vizier in Persia, Juwayni, visited the citadel. He was amazed at its strength, and the vast supply of stores available to the garrison. He was given permission by Hulagu to take what he wanted from the great library, and a number of works were thereby saved for posterity. But those that were considered heretical would not survive. When everything of use had been removed from Alamut, the place was torched. It was the funeral pyre of the Nizaris. The flames quickly took hold, consuming the fabric of Alamut and with it the soul of the movement that had once lived there. The life of the Nizaris as an effective political power in Persia was over. The heartbeat of the movement had been stilled with the loss of Alamut. It was a moment of devastating finality for the Nizaris.

It is easy to overlook the emotional effect of these awful events on the Nizaris. Alamut the mighty, the unconquerable, the 'place of good fortune', had fallen. For the Nizaris, it was the end of their world. The decimation of Alamut equated to the end of their dreams. But their enemies gloried in their triumph. Juwayni exulted, overjoyed that 'all the inmates of that seminary of iniquity and nest of Satan came down with all their goods and belongings.'[20] It was a moment of overwhelming disaster for the Nizaris. Juwayni's ecstasy rises to unprecedented heights when he gloats that:

'today, thanks to the glorious fortune of the World-Illuminating King, if an assassin still lingers in a corner he plies a woman's trade; wherever there is a *daï*, there is an announcer of death; and every *rafiq* [comrade] has become a thrall. The propagators of Isma'ilism have fallen victim to the swordsmen of Islam. Their *maulana* [a term often used by the Isma'ilis to address the Imam] . . . has become the serf of bastards. . . . Their governors have lost their power and their rulers their honour. The greatest of them have become as vile as dogs. Every commander of a fortress has been deemed fit for the gallows and every warden of a castle has forfeited his head and his mace'.[21]

With the fall of Alamut, there was little remaining Nizari territory in Persia for the Mongols to concern themselves with, although Lamasar did not fall to them immediately. It resisted for a year and was lost, not to force of arms but disease, which virtually wiped out the garrison. Girdkuh continued to resist stubbornly. Rukn al-Din sent word to the movement in Syria, telling them to surrender all their castles there to the Mongols (a demand that the Syrian Nizaris stubbornly turned a deaf ear to). This effectively ended the usefulness of Rukn al-Din as far as Hulagu was concerned. He was now something of an embarrassment, but Hulagu perhaps felt uncomfortable at eliminating him in cold blood after he had proved of such valuable service to his armies. It may therefore have been a relief when Rukn al-Din asked him if he could visit the Great Khan Mongke in person. The journey would take him away from Persia for many months, as it was a journey of thousands of miles to Mongolia across difficult and dangerous terrain.

Rukn al-Din's party accordingly set out. There was only a small delegation, accompanied by a Mongol escort. The Imam presumably wished to ingratiate himself still further with the Khan. On his success rested the survival of himself and his people. But his approaches came too late, for the future destiny of the Nizaris had already been decided.

The Mongols had set up a very efficient system for keeping their lines of communication open – something that was of incalculable value in such an extended empire. The well-trodden routes to Mongolia were amply stocked with staging posts, where fresh horses were kept in a state of constant readiness for official messengers to use. Even allowing for this, it was still a considerable journey for Rukn al-Din to make. He eventually arrived at Mongke's headquarters at Karakorum. However, when he sought an audience with the Khan he was brusquely rebuffed. Mongke turned on him angrily, asking him how he dared to present himself before him when both Lamasar and Girdkuh had not yet been surrendered to him. He berated him for wasting good post horses on such a futile mission. Then he abruptly dismissed him from his presence and told him to return home.

In those few moments everything must have become horrifically clear to the still young Imam. He had done everything asked of him. He had called off his assassins and given up most of his castles. He had meekly surrendered all that he had to the Mongols on the understanding that he would buy life for himself and his people in return. But the awful reality started to dawn that he had been completely duped by the Mongols. Now his people, whom he had instructed to desist from all resistance against the Mongol threat, were defenceless. It was ominously clear that there would be no gratitude displayed by the Khan, who appeared to have far more sinister aspirations in mind.

It was with a heavy heart that Rukn ad-Din started out on the long journey home, certainly afraid for his own safety and, if he had any decency about him, for his people also. His fears were well founded. In a remote area close to a rugged mountain range (perhaps similar in aspect to the mountain fastnesses in which Alamut, Girdkuh and Lamasar stood) his guard turned on him. They ran him through with their swords and left him dead where he fell. They must have been acting on the express orders of Mongke himself.

Rukn ad-Din's undignified end at least saved him from witnessing the fate of his people in Persia. Hulagu sent out orders that the Nizaris of Rudbar and Quhistan were to assemble for a census in the nearest town to their homes. Large numbers obeyed unquestioningly. When they arrived, the real reason for the order became clear. At a given signal, the Mongols present fell upon the Nizaris, who were defenceless and unprepared. Unknown to the Nizaris, orders had already been sent to Persia that 'Rukn ad-Din's sons and daughters, brothers and sisters and all of his seed and family should be laid on the fire of annihilation and none of their race be spared'. According to Juwayni, the edict emanated posthumously from Genghis Khan, who some years before had said that 'none of that people should be spared, not even the babes in the cradle'.[22] Regardless of age or sex, all those present were put to the sword. Babies were slaughtered next to old men and women. Of all the atrocities committed by the Mongols (and this is in itself a formidably long list) this was perhaps one of the most evil, as it was essentially a cowardly and cynical act.

The Nizaris had by and large done what the Mongols asked of them, and in return they were murdered in their thousands in cold blood. But their image had caught up with them. Tales of their violence had come home to roost. Their history had created a fear and a hatred deep in the Mongols' psyche that only the Nizaris' complete elimination could expunge. They were too dangerous a foe to be allowed to live.

A Frankish chronicler, William of Rubruck, had visited the court of Mongke a short time before Rukn al-Din's accession. William was surprised when he arrived at the elaborate security around the person of the Khan. He says that 'they began to enquire carefully where we were from, for what purpose we had come, and what was our occupation. This interrogation was being conducted because [Mongke] had been informed that four hundred Assassins, in various disguises, had made their way in with the aim of killing him'.

William goes on to explain that Mongke 'has sent one of [his] brothers into the territory of the Assassins, who are known to them as Mulihet, with orders for their complete extermination'.[23] In the light of this single-minded ambition, the only hope for the Nizaris was to resist, using the time honoured methods of retiring to their massive, generously provisioned citadels in the mountains. The most conclusive evidence for this comes from Girdkuh. The castle refused to surrender when ordered to, and it was to remain in Nizari hands for thirteen years after the fall of Alamut. A permanent Mongol encampment was erected next to it. The patience of the Mongol garrison of this camp was eventually rewarded. The Nizaris finally gave themselves up when they ran out of clothes to wear. As soon as they set foot outside Girdkuh, they were slaughtered like cattle.

But it is of course easy to assert that in retrospect the Nizaris should have resisted. Rukn ad-Din was a young man, with very limited experience as leader of the Nizaris. He was faced by an enemy that appeared to be irresistible. Far stronger groups than the Nizaris had been swept aside by the Mongols. Given the overwhelming superiority of the Mongols, submission to them was certainly a viable strategy to consider. Rukn ad-Din's greatest mistake though was not to know the mind of his enemy, who were set on the elimination of the movement that he led. He was not the first, nor the last, leader in history to make such an error of judgement.

The judgement of some historians has been especially severe regarding Rukn ad-Din. Curtin, in an attack of vitriolic proportions, calls him 'a piteous coward who had caused the death of his own father, killed the murderer of that father without trial lest he tell of his master's evil doing, and burned the children of the murderer with the corpse of their father lest they too might expose him. He gave away power without an effort to save it, and lost his own life with indignity'.[24] Although many elements of this may be true, it is nevertheless difficult to avoid the conclusion that, above all else, Rukn ad-Din was a man who was simply out of his depth, having been overwhelmed by powers greater than he could not possibly comprehend.

The holocaust launched by the Mongols against the Nizaris was neither their last nor their greatest act in Persia. For centuries, the caliph had survived in Baghdad, often it is true as nothing more than a figurehead, but still a powerful symbolic figure for all that. The Mongols determined that they would now also eliminate the caliphate from Persia. Impossible demands were sent to al-Mustasim, the caliph in Baghdad, which he refused to accept. The demands made left him with little choice. In 1258, a large Mongol army was sent to enforce Hulagu's demands. They were met by a sizeable army that had been despatched by the caliph to repulse them. But the Mongols lured them forward while they erected dams across strategically sited rivers in the region behind the advancing armies of their enemies. Then, when the moment was right, the dams were opened. The caliph's soldiers suddenly found that their line of retreat was cut off. They were caught like rats in a trap. The Mongols then unleashed an unstoppable attack on them, wiping them out. Baghdad was at the mercy of the Mongols.

A siege was laid around the city. It became apparent that this was unlikely to last for long. Seeing the writing on the wall, al-Mustasim surrendered himself to the Mongols. By so doing, he only forced himself to witness the terrible end of Baghdad, for centuries at the heart of the Islamic world. When the Mongols broke in, in February 1258, the resultant massacre was horrific. Every Muslim that was caught was killed or taken into slavery. Only the Christians praying in their churches were spared, as the Mongols respected the religion because some of their ruling family were Nestorians. On one street, a Mongol soldier found forty babies lying helplessly next to their slaughtered mothers. He killed them all there and then (he reckoned this as an act of mercy as they would otherwise starve to death).

After the sack, it was time for the caliph to die. Hulagu had withdrawn to a village some distance from Baghdad, possibly to escape the putrefying stench from thousands of decaying bodies that were already starting to pollute the atmosphere under the hot Iraqi sun. Al-Mustasim was brought before him. Hoping for mercy, he soon understood that there would be none. The Mongols always had an aversion to any of their soldiers killing a ruler in cold blood, even the ruler of an enemy.[25] Hulagu had thought of a way that this difficulty could be avoided. The caliph was stitched up in a felt bag, along with his eldest son. The bags were then ridden over by hundreds of horses. It could truly be said that none of the Mongol soldiery was individually directly responsible for the death of the caliph.

The shockwaves from the capture and destruction of Baghdad swept around the Muslim world, which realized that it was faced with nothing less than a fight for the survival of its religion and its culture. They would certainly have been felt strongly in Syria, which assumed (correctly) that its turn would come soon. The Nizaris in Syria must have been distraught at the loss of Alamut along with most of the Nizari heartland in Persia. Apart from the reign of Sinan, they had always looked to Alamut for their lead. Now they were on their own, with a fearfully uncertain future to look forward to. But they would survive, in a hugely emaciated form it is true, because they would effectively surrender to a greater power that would protect them against the Mongol threat. Islam was about to find a new champion, a ruthless and frightening figure but a mightily effective one for all that. His name was Baibars and, by offering subservience to him, the Nizaris in Syria would buy their lives and their continued existence.

ELEVEN

Syrian Sunset

Whereas in Persia the death of the Nizaris was a violent one, in Syria the effective end of the movement took a rather different form. As opposed to the dramatic and bloody extermination of the former group, the seeming demise of the Syrian movement was an altogether gentler one, almost as if it quietly slipped away in its sleep. It did not appear at one time that this would be the case; the Mongols had after all declared that they would treat Syria in the same way that they dealt with Persia, and there was little reason to suspect that they would not make good on their boast. But unforeseen events would intervene and, by a combination of accidents of history and the intervention of outside forces, the Syrian Nizaris would escape complete destruction at the hands of the Mongol hordes.[1]

Syria was not separated from Persia by a vast distance geographically but it was enough to make sure that the Nizaris in the west had a greater degree of protection than the Persian members of the movement, who were right in the path of the Mongol advance. At the same time, it meant that they had local politics of their own to concern them. They lived close to the Franks in their by-now much reduced Crusader enclave in Outremer and they also had the Ayyubid dynasty (the descendants of Saladin) to worry about (the dynasty had based itself in Damascus, although the other great cities in the area such as Aleppo continued to play an important role in the region).

During the lifetime of Sinan, in the previous century, the Syrian Nizaris had largely acted autonomously. However, although they were (partly forced by circumstances) to assert a degree of political independence, they accepted the spiritual supremacy of Alamut soon after the death of this great leader. Within a year of his death in approximately 1193, a new chief *da'i* had been installed. His name was Nasr al-Ajami, and he was a Persian appointed by Alamut. From then until the end of the Nizaris as an effective political force in Persia nearly a century later, it appears that the chief *da'is* installed at the head of the Syrian *da'wa* were almost exclusively appointees from Alamut. This suggests that the independence exercised by Sinan was perhaps not quite absolute; it is hard to reconcile the complete separation of Sinan's state from the Nizaris in Persia with the fact that within a year of his death Alamut had re-asserted its right to direct rule.

Perhaps this also reflected the fact that Sinan was an extraordinary personality. One writer noted that he 'died leaving his people with ample memories of his greatness, wisdom and heroism. A very capable successor was needed to fill his place, but it seems from the scanty materials recorded by historians on the post-Sinan period that the Isma'ilis did not again enjoy strong leadership like that of Sinan'.[2] In other words, Sinan was a unique character who dominated the Syrian Nizaris during his lifetime and whose death left a void that was simply too large to fill.

In the two decades following the death of Sinan, the Syrian Nizaris were involved in several political developments in the region. The first of these was a closer relationship with the Ayyubid dynasty in Damascus. Relations between the two had been reasonably amicable since the time that Sinan and Saladin had patched up their differences. However, this general spirit of co-operation was considerably enhanced by Hasan III. It may be remembered that he was the Imam who ordered that the teachings of the *sharia*, which had been completely ignored by the Nizaris for some time, should once more be strictly observed. His orders were sent to Syria, and they were it seems largely followed without resistance. Indeed, the Nizaris appear to have adopted the new teachings with enthusiasm, going so far as to erect new mosques in the region. This development was understandably greeted with enormous enthusiasm in Damascus. The Ayyubids were devout Sunnis, and the adoption of orthodox Islamic practices by the Nizaris was joyfully received. From that time on, there were few if any assassinations of leading Islamic figures by the Syrian Nizaris.

Relationships with the Franks of Outremer were altogether more complicated. At first, Sinan's successors attempted to build an understanding with the strange, light skinned Westerners who were occupying the coastal plain. After the death of Conrad of Montferrat, murdered by an Assassin's knife, the effective leadership of the state had been assumed by Henry of Champagne, who was related to both Richard I of England and Philip Augustus of France. He was never crowned (he fell out with some of the leading barons of the realm who refused to support his claim to the kingship as a result) but he effectively ran the country for a brief period until his premature death.[3] Early on in his short 'reign' he travelled north towards Antioch. There had been some unrest in the region (there was nothing particularly unusual in this; Antioch was remote from the rest of Outremer and its princes had long been known for their propensity to act independently of the King in Jerusalem). His journey took him close to the area where the Syrian Nizaris held most of their castles.

It was 1194, and the Nizaris had just lost Sinan, for so long their guide and inspiration. Perhaps feeling a little lost without his calming influence at the helm of Nizari affairs, his successor decided that he should try to build bridges with the Franks. Richard had by this stage returned to England (although he would spend an extended period in a number of prisons owned by his enemy, the Emperor Henry of Germany, before he eventually reached his kingdom once more). And Saladin, for so long the dominant influence in the politics of the Levant, had died shortly before. Already, it seemed quite clear that his successors were determined to fall out with each other in an undignified scramble to assume his role as leader of the Islamic states bordering the Mediterranean.[4] In short, the region was in a state of flux, there was likely to be a period of instability and the Nizaris needed friends.

Therefore, when they heard that Henry of Champagne was passing close to their lands, they determined to send out a delegation to meet him to offer him their friendship. Henry for his part was pleased to respond favourably to their overtures. After all, two decades earlier the Nizaris in Syria had approached the Franks for a formal alliance, and relations between the two groups had often been reasonably amicable. Admittedly, the latter years of Sinan's reign had been more difficult and the murder of Conrad of Montferrat had presumably fostered a good deal of resentment among his partisans in Outremer. But even this last heinous crime (as it was regarded in the West) maybe had its uses. It was after all a clear reminder to Henry of his own mortality, and it provided a very strong hint that the sect would be far better to have as friends rather than enemies. As a result, he responded positively when he was invited to the nearby castle of al-Kahf, where he had been promised sumptuous entertainment by the Nizaris.

What happened next is an integral part of the legend of the Assassins. The events of the next few days were so extraordinary that later historians would sometimes find them hard to credit. Matters began routinely enough. The new leader of the Nizaris offered his sincere apologies for the murder of Conrad of Montferrat. It is not difficult to believe that Henry forgave them this act readily enough. Richard I of England (who had been largely responsible for placing Henry in situ as the leader of the Franks in Outremer) had been no friend of Conrad of Montferrat. In fact, he had wanted a vassal of his, Guy of Lusignan, to take the crown. Therefore, Richard – Henry's patron – was probably quite glad to see the back of Conrad. And Henry of course had no reason to regret his death; after all, he only stood where he did now in the hierarchy of Outremer because of his murder.

Henry therefore accepted the apology with no sign of rancour. The political discussions duly being satisfactorily completed, it was now time for the entertainment to begin. The leader of the Nizaris was apparently quite keen to demonstrate to Henry that he enjoyed the absolute obedience of his followers. Whatever he ordered, they would do, even if it meant that they would lose their lives. He proceeded to show this in the most graphic way imaginable.

He summoned one of his *fidaïs* to him. When he presented himself, he was told to take himself to the top of a nearby tower. Once there, he was ordered to throw himself off. Without hesitation, he flung himself to his death on the jagged rocks around the base of the castle far below. Just in case Henry had failed to understand the significance of this act, the drama was re-enacted several times. Eventually, Henry begged his host to stop. The point had evidently been made clearly enough. Henry left soon after, presumably eternally grateful that he had managed to escape alive from these clearly demented fanatics. Another vivid chapter in the development of the Assassin legend had been written, which would seize the imaginations of a number of chroniclers. One of them, Arnold of Lübeck, an early thirteenth century German chronicler, was clearly influenced by the legend, writing that: 'many of them even, when standing on a high wall, will jump off at his [i.e. their leader's] nod or command, and, shattering their skulls, die a miserable death'.[5] Another legend had been born.[6]

This approach did not however herald the dawning of a bright new day as far as relations between the Nizaris and the Franks were concerned. The Franks were soon busy fighting each other; as a result, it was impossible for the Nizaris to support one party of Franks without being diametrically opposed to another. By this stage in Outremer's life, the Kings of Jerusalem relied more on the great military orders, especially the Templars and the Hospitallers, than they had ever done before. Manpower was a perennial problem for the Kingdom, and the poor net results achieved as a result of the massive efforts of the Third Crusade did little to encourage new recruits to make their way from Western Europe to the Holy Land. Therefore, the military commanders of the castles scattered around the country were usually knights from one of the military orders.

As their power grew, so did their influence. The commanders of garrisons all around the region came to dominate the lands surrounding their massive citadels, and often demanded tribute from the Muslim people that lived close at hand. The Nizaris were close to a number of Hospitaller possessions, such as the great castle of Krak des Chevaliers, and as a result they were forced to pay tribute to the Order. It soon appeared that this tribute was not only offered in monetary terms; the Hospitallers also seemed to be keen to obtain the practical help of the movement.

The Hospitallers were often at odds with other Franks. In 1213, they were involved in a bitter dispute with the Prince of Antioch, Bohemond IV. This was partly because Bohemond was an ally of the Templars, and by this stage the two leading Military Orders were so antagonistic towards each other that any friend of one was guaranteed to be an enemy of the other. Bohemond had a son, a youth (or perhaps by the standards of the time, a man) of eighteen years of age named Raymond. One day, Raymond attended the cathedral at Tortosa. He was unprepared when a band of Nizari assassins fell on him, and left him dying. A year later, the Patriarch of Jerusalem, Albert, was also killed by the Nizaris. Suspicious cynics cannot have failed to notice that both men were enemies of the Hospitallers, to whom the Nizaris were tributaries.

Bohemond was every bit a man of his time. Frankish warlords were not renowned for reacting to such aggression with equanimity. Driven by a natural desire for vengeance, he assembled his army together and besieged the Nizari fortress of Khawabi in 1214 or 1215. The Nizaris drove off the attack with the help of some local Muslim allies under the leadership of al-Malik al-Zahir of Aleppo, but the whole incident symbolised well enough the sometimes acrimonious relationships that the movement enjoyed with their Frankish neighbours. Such goings-on understandably added to the somewhat exaggerated view of demonic fanatics that the Franks held of their neighbours, the so called 'Assassins'.

Such perceptions clearly had their uses as far as the Nizaris were concerned. They made an impression on the West that encouraged many kings and princes of both Outremer and regions farther afield to attempt to buy the Nizaris' friendship, or at least their neutrality. One such man was Frederick II, the Emperor of Germany. Frederick was no ordinary man; he ranks as one of the most striking men of the thirteenth century, if not the entire Medieval period. He was extraordinarily knowledgeable, he spoke fluently in several languages and was aware of the beliefs of a number of religions apart from Christianity (a fairly uncommon attribute for the time). But he was also a cruel and ruthless man, and a politician that Machiavelli would have greatly admired.

Frederick resolved to lead an expedition to the East to recover Jerusalem, but his tactics would differ enormously from those of earlier expeditions. Rather than attempting to conquer the region through force of arms, he would form alliances with disaffected Muslims in the region (which was still in a state of virtual civil war some thirty years after the death of Saladin) and negotiate his way to success. The policy was remarkably successful, at least superficially. In 1227, he was crowned King of Jerusalem in the Church of the Holy Sepulchre. It was a somewhat empty ceremony though: there were few others present, as Frederick was excommunicate at the time (he had fallen out with the Pope shortly before he left for Outremer). At any event, he was certainly keen to stay on the right side of the Nizaris. A delegation was sent to them, carrying a generous bribe by which he hoped to buy a degree of security for his person. The gift was gratefully received and had the desired effect.

However, this situation was not without its problems for the Syrian Nizaris. Traditionally their loyalty was to the Hospitallers, and the Order was hostile towards the claims of Frederick. They demanded that the Nizaris should pay more tribute to them, as they were much displeased by the understanding that they had reached with Frederick. The Nizaris haughtily refused, claiming that, as they now themselves received tribute from Kings and Emperors, they were above the paying of tribute to the Hospitallers. The Nizaris had perhaps started to believe their own publicity a little too much.

Angered at the rebuff, the Hospitallers invaded the Nizari territories in Syria and only left again once they had grabbed a great deal of booty. This seems to have forced the Nizaris back into line. In fact, many in the West (who were remote from the region, and did not understand the realities of its politics) were alarmed by what they saw to be a formal alliance developing between the Hospitallers and the Nizaris.

By 1236, Pope Gregory IX was writing to the Master of the Order, admonishing him for the closeness of his relations with the Nizaris. There is little room for misinterpretation, as the letter is unequivocal in its condemnation of the understanding between the Hospitallers and the Nizaris. Gregory notes that: 'the . . . Master and brethen . . . support and protect them [the Nizaris] from Christian attacks, [in return for which the Nizaris] . . . have undertaken to pay them a certain sum of money every year. Therefore, we have sent you these orders in writing to desist from defending these same Assassins'.[7]

Gregory goes on to warn that the Hospitallers would incur the wrath of the Church if they insisted on continuing with the arrangement. This was no small matter; the Hospitallers, being a military order that owed its allegiance directly to the Pope, were under his direct orders. But Gregory's condemnation was naïve. The Hospitallers needed allies to be effective (there were simply too few Hospitallers to cope with all that was demanded of the Order, and they would be untenably overstretched if they were at war all the time) and the Nizaris, as tributaries, were very much the junior partner in the relationship.

Neither was it just the Hospitallers who adopted this strategy. The Nizaris were also forced to pay tribute to the Templars in order to survive, and they too would receive a Papal letter admonishing them for their stance, equally forceful in its warning that they should desist from prolonging the arrangement.

But such squalid deals were a routine, if rather unglamorous, part of everyday political life in the Middle East as this time. It was by no means unusual for groups such as the Nizaris to pay tribute to some, and demand it from others. At about the same time that the Emperor Frederick was paying tribute to the Nizaris, the movement in Syria were also to receive money from another source. A dynasty descended from the Seldjuks had set themselves up in Asia Minor. They had paid tribute to the Imam at Alamut for some years. The Syrian Nizaris, for reasons unknown, demanded that the money should be paid to them instead. The Seldjuks naturally enough wanted to make sure that the Persian Nizaris agreed with this change, and sent messengers to the headquarters of the movement at Alamut for confirmation that it was in order. Word was returned that the amendment was satisfactory and the money was accordingly sent to Syria in the future.

As the thirteenth century advanced, preparations were made in the West for another great Crusade. The first two expeditions launched in the century were damp squibs, or worse. The Fourth Crusade had not got anywhere near Outremer but decided to divert en route and sack Constantinople instead. The next great expedition launched had been even more of a disaster. Landing in Egypt in 1218, after months of siege warfare against the city of Damietta at the mouth of one of the branches in the Nile in the Delta region, the Crusade finally set off for the hinterland of the country. During the subsequent campaign, the Franks were totally outmanoeuvred by the Egyptians.

The Franks were finally surrounded and defeated. Only the surrender of Damietta – their one major gain from the Crusade – bought their freedom. The expedition of the Emperor Frederick of Germany had led to more success, despite his excommunicate status at the time that Jerusalem was handed over to him. However, the promise of better days ahead that his triumph suggested was to prove a false dawn. He did not stay in the region for long and, when he left, his influence would be largely a negative one. From far away in Europe, he attempted to interfere in the politics of Outremer, creating internal divisions that the weakened Crusader state could ill afford.

But the cataclysmic events taking place in Persia and the lands beyond as the Mongols inexorably advanced across Asia were to create a domino effect that would impact right the way across the Middle East. The first tangible sign of this came from the direction of the hordes of misplaced Khwarazmians arrived in the region searching for a new home in the wake of their huge defeat at the hands of the Mongols.

As we have seen, the Mongols' victory over the Khwarazmians led to a situation in which large bands of the latter roamed across the Middle East seeking employment. Eventually, they would become involved in the internal politics of Egypt and Outremer. This was to culminate in two catastrophic reverses for the Crusaders. In 1244, the Khwarazmians swept down on Jerusalem. To all intents and purposes, the city had largely been given up for lost by the Crusaders when they heard that the Khwarazmians were heading for it. Both the Templars and the Hospitallers in the city had evacuated it before the arrival of the ferocious warriors from Persia.

Jerusalem fell soon after, its walls simply too extensive to be adequately defended by the depleted garrison. Shortly afterwards, the combined forces of the Templars, the Hospitallers and the other Christian armies in Outremer were overwhelmingly defeated in battle against the Khwarazmians and the Egyptians, with whom they had entered into alliance. The standing army of Outremer was thus effectively wiped out. The end appeared to be near for the Crusader kingdom.

However, at this moment a new character was about to introduce himself into the drama, one who furthermore would become an integral part of the legend of the Assassins.

France was ruled at this time by a young King, Louis IX.[8] He was religious to the point of obsession. When Jerusalem fell to the Khwarazmians, Louis was dangerously ill. It looked for a while that his illness was so serious that he would never recover from it. But against the odds he survived. When he was restored to health, he told his nobles that he was determined to set out on a great Crusade. The objections against his proposed course of action were in vain (and there were many dissenters, as the frequent failures of the Crusading movement had disheartened Western Europe and enthusiasm for such expeditions was much diminished as a result). The Crusade duly set out.

Although Louis' preparations were meticulous, again the Crusade achieved little. It journeyed first to Egypt, which was perceived to be a weak spot in the defences of the Islamic world. But disaster followed close on the heels of a stunning initial victory (Damietta was abandoned to the

Crusaders virtually without a fight). The Crusaders were once more outmanoeuvred by their Egyptian foe, whose superior local knowledge proved decisive.

Virtually the entire army, including Louis, was captured. He was forced to ransom himself for a huge sum, but on his release he decided that he could not yet return to France. His honour had been besmirched by the inglorious fate of his Crusade and he resolved to recover something from his ignominious efforts by spending more time in Outremer. He therefore made his way to Acre, by now effectively the capital of Outremer following the irrevocable loss of Jerusalem.

It was while he was here that he received a delegation from the Nizaris. Fortunately for future historians, his dealings in Outremer were meticulously recorded by his friend, courtier and chronicler, Jean de Joinville. He describes the approach of the Nizaris in some detail. Initially, he says that they approached the King with a haughty and threatening attitude. The mission was led by a young man, whom de Joinville clearly feels had ideas above his station. His manner was abrupt and condescending. He told Louis that a number of princes – including the Emperor Frederick and the King of Hungary – paid tribute to the Nizaris in exchange for their lives. It would be advisable, he suggested, if Louis were to do the same.

If however he did not wish to himself pay tribute, then the Nizaris had an alternative suggestion to make. They were currently paying tribute to both the Hospitallers and the Templars, and the movement would be content if Louis were to cancel this obligation instead of paying protection money to them. Louis told the envoy that he could not give an answer at once but that he would do so the next day if he were good enough to present himself again then.

The envoy duly did so. It quickly dawned on him that he had badly misjudged the character of Louis. As the envoy was ushered into his presence, he saw that the Masters of both the Hospitallers and the Templars were flanking the king. Louis told him to repeat his demands once more. When the envoy did so, the Masters rounded on him, castigating him for his arrogance and temerity. He would be lucky, they suggested, to leave with his life after his patronizing and inappropriate demands to the King. They told him in the strongest possible terms that he should return to his master, and come back with a more suitable attitude.

Realizing that he had overstepped the mark, the envoy excused himself and hurried back to Syria. The next time he presented himself to Louis, his demeanour would be somewhat different. He came back laden with gifts and kind words. Among these gifts was one which might at first glance appear to be a little strange. It was the shirt worn by the master of the Syrian Nizaris. However, as the envoy explained, it was in fact the greatest gift that could be presented to the King. It had after all been worn by the master next to his skin – symbolically it was the closest of all possessions owned by him. It therefore represented something precious to the master.

All in all, this was a very different approach to that adopted on the occasion of the previous delegation. It was also more in tune with the needs of the Nizaris at that time. Although the Mongols had not as yet launched their genocidal assaults on the sect in Persia, they had been engaged in hostilities with them for some time. The extent of the great danger facing the Nizaris cannot have been lost on Syrian members of the movement. They therefore needed allies (a state of affairs well evidenced by the delegation that the sect had sent to the courts of France and England a few years previously). In this environment, they could not afford to make new enemies. They had already targeted the leaders of Western Europe as potential allies in the recent past, and a less aggressive approach than that previously adopted was therefore appropriate.

For his part, Louis also needed friends. He saw that it would be in his best interests to respond to these friendly overtures with a similarly positive gesture of his own. He sent a delegation of his own to the headquarters of the Syrian Nizaris at Masyaf. It was led by a cleric, Yves the Breton. He must have been a brave man; legends of the Assassins and their ferocity were already current in Europe and in his quieter moments the ambassador must have wondered whether or not he would ever return alive.

De Joinville, the chronicler of Louis' Crusade, was certainly well aware of the Nizaris' reputation for assassination and noted that 'if a man is killed while obeying his lord's orders his soul goes into a more pleasing body than before. That is why the Assassins are not in any way averse to being killed as and when their lord orders, because they believe that they will be happier after death than when they were alive'.[9]

But if Yves had known of the real history of the movement, he need not have worried. To those who came to them of their own will, and in peace, the Nizaris typically exhibited great hospitality. There was in truth little for him to fear given the fact that the Nizaris so badly needed allies. Yves made his way to the leader of the Syrian Nizaris carrying with him gifts from King Louis. In the event, Louis' envoy was fascinated with what he found. When he began to study the religious texts of the movement, he saw that their beliefs were very similar to those of the Christians in some respects. Among the unusual teachings that he came across was one that claimed that Saint Peter was the reincarnation of Abel (the brother of Cain and son of Adam and Eve), Noah and Abraham.

He was so enthused by the nature of some of his discoveries that he attempted to convert the leader of the Syrian Nizaris to Christianity, though with no success. This was unsurprising, as the Franks had misinterpreted the beliefs of the Nizaris. De Joinville showed his confusion when he said that Yves 'found that the Old Man of the Mountain was not a follower of Mahomet, but subscribed to the laws of Ali, who was Mahomet's uncle'[10] – a serious misinterpretation of Nizari beliefs.

In the event, there would be little in terms of tangible gain from his mission. Louis in fact was attempting to enjoy the best of all worlds. He had sent out feelers to the Mongols seeking an alliance with them. He had heard that they were Christians, and as a result he hoped that they could share common cause against the forces of orthodox Islam. As the Mongols were such hostile enemies of the Nizaris, it was never likely that Louis could enjoy a successful alliance with both groups when they were so diametrically opposed to each other. In the event, the approaches made by Louis towards the Mongols would achieve little. When his ambassadors reported back to him with details of what they had witnessed when they had reached the court of the Mongol Khan, Louis realized with increasing horror just how fierce a race they were and how, in return for alliance, they would expect nothing less than complete subservience from him.

Not long after, in 1256, came news of the defeat of the Nizaris in Persia and the subsequent murder of Rukn al-Din. The loss of the leadership previously offered by Alamut left a great vacuum in Syria. From this point on, there would be no Persian Imam to appoint the chief *daï* in Syria. Instead, he would be nominated by local men, and as a result the appointments were more open to controversy and debate than had previously been the case. This strained the unity of the movement. Long after the effective demise of the Nizaris as a political force in Syria, it would ultimately lead to a situation whereby there would be a further split among the Nizaris, with different groups following various of succession as far as the Imamate was concerned.

The more immediate problem though was that the loss of the Persian Nizari states and the destruction of the caliphate left the buffer zones of Persia and Iraq in Mongol hands. It was clear that it was only a matter of time before the Mongols swept into Syria itself. The assault duly came in 1260, once again led by Hulagu. It soon appeared to replicate previous Mongol campaigns, in that it seemed more like a triumphal procession than a military exercise. The Mongols were accompanied by local allies. When Hulagu entered Aleppo, at his side were Hethoum, the King of Armenia, and Bohemond VI of Antioch. Both men were undoubtedly elated at their part in the triumph but their people would live to regret the part that they played in the campaigns of the Mongols. Their involvement, understandably enough, was bitterly resented by the Muslims in the region and when the time for revenge came it would be delivered without pity. Damascus itself followed suit, when Hulagu's trusted general, Kitbuqa, led the Mongol hordes into the great city. Egypt appeared to lie wide open to the Mongols. The Nizaris themselves also suffered. Four castles, including Masyaf itself, were forced to capitulate. Nothing, it seemed, could stop the Mongol advance.

Then, just when a final, devastating Mongol victory seemed inevitable, fate played a dramatic and decisive hand. There was one event which, when it occurred, always left the Mongols vulnerable. The death of their Great Khan often resulted in an unseemly scramble for the succession. Such an event had possibly saved Eastern and Central Europe from Mongol domination fifteen years previously. Now it was to tip the balance in favour of the Islamic world at a truly critical moment. As the Mongol campaign progressed irresistibly through Syria – accompanied of course by the usual tales of atrocities – news came through that the year previously, in 1259, Mongke had died. This left Hulagu with little option but to return east. He had a strong claim to the succession but he was already behind the game as others were closer geographically to Mongolia than he was and had presumably already staked their claim in his absence.

He left the campaign in the hands of Kitbuqa, but took some of the army with him. This left a depleted force in Syria. Ironically, this depletion happened at the very moment that the Mongols were to be faced with their greatest challenge yet. Much had changed in Egypt since the fall of the weak Fatimid dynasty the best part of a century before. Since the establishment of an orthodox Sunni state in the country, a new military system had been introduced. The country now largely relied for its defence on a caste of warrior slaves. These men, known as Mamelukes, were bought from their families (often from regions far afield, such as the Caucasus) when they were young boys. But although in theory they were not free men, in practice they were far from normal slaves. They were treated well when they were purchased. Much effort was expended in training them in the arts of war. Their living conditions were good; what was the point, after all, in having a well trained but half-starved army? Rather then receiving the brutal and degrading treatment often reserved for slaves, the way they were treated was so good that often families happily sold their sons into service as it was regarded as a great honour.

The Mamelukes evolved into a formidable fighting force. They were regarded as fearsome warriors with good reason. All this of course had one huge downside for the ruling dynasty in Egypt, and that was that, as their military might grew, so inevitably did their political influence. They had already overthrown the ruling dynasty in Egypt a few years previously and were more than capable of doing so again. But allowing such considerations to come into the equation at this stage was a luxury that frankly the ruling caste in Egypt could not afford. That they must fight was not in doubt. When the Mongols sent ambassadors to Cairo demanding the surrender of Egypt, the Egyptians responded with a message that was unequivocal in its tone. The envoys were immediately sliced in half. It was a more powerful statement than any letter that the Sultan of Egypt, Qutuz, could have sent. Knowing that war was an inevitability now, he assembled his forces together and made his way into Palestine. At his back was a vast force of Mamelukes and other Egyptian troops. At his side was a general of genius, a giant of a man whose strength and ferocity were renowned (as also was his capacity for political intrigue). His name was Baibars.

The army moved into Palestine. In response, the Mongols came forward to meet them. They met at a place called Ain Jalut on 3 September 1260. The battle that followed is rarely mentioned in Western history books but deserves consideration as one of the most decisive in history. At a critical moment of the battle, Baibars fled from the field. The Mongols, ecstatic at their success, pursued him euphorically. They charged into a valley and were about to fall on their beaten foe when suddenly the hills around them were alive with the enemy. The rout had in fact been a brilliantly manufactured ruse. Baibars had led the Mongols right into the jaws of a trap. The superior numbers of the Egyptian army proved decisive and, as the sun set on the charnel house that was the field of Ain Jalut, it also set on the era of Mongol domination. Islam had triumphed in the battle for its soul; it had also won the war for its survival. Kitbuqa was taken before Qutuz. When the Sultan mocked him, the Mongol lord proudly replied that he was not intimidated by his insults as he knew that Qutuz would soon be overthrown. Incensed, Qutuz struck off his head with a sword. But the last words of Kitbuqa came home to roost. Shortly afterwards Qutuz was murdered. His throne was inherited by the man who would effectively drive the Franks out of Outremer and conquer all of Syria, Sultan Baibars.

Whether or not the Nizaris were involved at Ain Jalut is not known. However, there is clear evidence about whose side they would have been on if they had been involved in the battle. Adopting the political maxim that 'my enemy's enemy is my friend', it was inevitable that the Nizaris would side with the Egyptians. In 1258 – two years before Ain Jalut – a man called Radi al-Din had become the chief *da'i* of the Syrian Nizaris. Not long before he succeeded to that esteemed position, he had visited Egypt as an envoy for the Nizaris. In the immediate aftermath of the decisive Mongol defeat in 1260, the Nizaris were handed back the four castles that they had lost. The Egyptians were obviously keen to have the help, or at least the neutrality, of the Nizaris. But the alliance was an unequal one. The Egyptians could afford to be friendly towards the Nizaris. Their defeat in Persia had effectively left them as a spent force, one which could be largely ignored. The Egyptians now had bigger fish to fry.

But Baibars did not leave them completely to their own devices. In 1260, he gave many of the Nizari lands in Syria to one of his principal lieutenants, although this was for the moment more of a symbolic than a practical gesture. He certainly would have scented the current essential weakness of the sect. The general air of a loss of purpose that hung over the movement like a pall at this particular time would not have been helped by the death of Radi al-Din not long after the triumph of the Mamelukes at

Ain Jalut. His successor would be an eighty year-old man, Najm al-Din. Nothing bettered symbolised the essential insecurity of the Nizaris than the appointment of someone who, at least as far as his age was concerned, belonged far more to the past than the future. By now, anyway, their domain was drastically constricted.[11] The Syrian Nizaris were also divided in their attitude towards Baibars, which presumably did nothing to enhance its already diminished effectiveness. The custodians of some Nizari castles advocated a conciliatory attitude towards the new Sultan while others declared their willingness to fight to the death against him and his army.

The Nizaris were slow to recognize the threat to their independence which emanated from Baibars. This was surprising, as there were plenty of clues available to those prepared to look with an open mind, to warn them that in the long term he would not countenance their continued independence. However, it may reflect in part the fact that, following the fall of Alamut, the Syrian Nizaris increasingly began to show evidence of a sense of drift in their policies. They became increasingly localized in their operations and instead of one chief *da'i* to assume overall responsibility for the direction of the Nizaris in the region, several were appointed by local leaders, sometimes leading to disputes within the community.[12]

When a delegation from the Nizaris subsequently visited Baibars, he told their leader, Jamal al-Din, that Radi al-Din had died. He then appointed Jamal al-Din his successor. It was a clear usurpation of rights traditionally held by the Nizaris themselves, and as such it was an unmistakable sign that Baibars now viewed their independence as being at an end. It mattered not that Baibars was either misinformed or lying (Radi al-Din had not yet died when Baibars told the Nizari delegation of his demise). It was also of little consequence that the sect reacted with hostility towards the act (Jamal al-Din would be killed shortly after his return from the mission). The essential point was that Baibars had taken upon himself a duty that, by tradition and precedent, was not his. Nizari independence was in grave danger. But for the time being Baibars did not push the point. Preoccupied with greater threats elsewhere, he received a delegation from the Nizaris in 1262 (or possibly 1263) with cordiality if not warmth, reluctant at the moment to press home his claims with vigour.

But Baibars was merely biding his time. In 1265, he took another step which prejudiced the independent status of the Nizaris. The Nizaris had received gifts from the Franks for some time (the Crusaders were themselves keen to build as many alliances as possible to protect their own interests in the region, which were also under grave threat from Baibars and his all-conquering army). In addition, they traded regularly with other states, such as Yemen. Because of the expanding territories controlled by Baibars, many of the items traded passed through lands owned by him. He decided that from now on they could only pass through his lands if customs duties were paid on them. It was not a unique stance by any means, but by the judicious use (or non-use) of such duties, Medieval rulers often strengthened or threatened alliances. If they wished to ingratiate themselves with other powers, such men frequently reduced, or abandoned altogether, duties which disadvantaged those that they would be befriend. But the reverse was also true. The imposition of these tariffs by Baibars again sent a strong symbolic signal that he meant to exert more influence over the Nizaris.

His approach to the imposition of these duties offered several benefits to Baibars. There was of course a direct economic advantage. But Egypt was a rich country by the standards of the region. Its resources may have been strained by its long war against the Mongols, and they may also have been reduced because of the need to meet the demands of the assertive and demanding Mamelukes. However, the likelihood is that, if Baibars deemed it appropriate to retain the good wishes of the Nizaris, he would happily have foregone the extra revenue. There was almost certainly another and stronger motive. Baibars was a devout orthodox Sunni. He was well aware that many others in the region were of the same persuasion. The move to ostracize the Nizaris would certainly improve his standing in the eyes of many a heretical and errant Isma'ili sect. He had clearly shown in other ways that he wished to win their support when he had recognized the spiritual suzerainty of the Abbasid caliph (now resident in Cairo) soon after his accession. Any attempt to reduce the influence of the Nizaris was likely to increase his standing in the eyes of Sunni Muslims.

The noose was gradually tightening around the neck of the Nizaris. They were aware that they could ill afford to incur the wrath of Baibars. They therefore sent a delegation to him while he was besieging the Franks in the castle at Safed. His actions during this particular time suggest that he was not in the best of moods (which could swing alarmingly). He turned on the emissaries and demanded that they explain why they paid tribute still to the

Hospitallers, the avowed enemies of the Muslim world. The envoys were at a loss for an answer.

Baibars was a dangerous man to fall out with as his actions when he captured Safed unmistakably proved. He had tricked the garrison into surrendering by a promise of safe passage. In the event, after they gave themselves up they were given a choice of conversion to Islam or death. Almost without exception, the garrison – who refused to refute their faith – were beheaded. When a truce between the Mamelukes and the Franks was subsequently negotiated after the fall of Safed, one of its terms was that the Hospitallers would no longer demand tribute from the Nizaris. The latter sought to ingratiate themselves with Baibars after this deal was struck. Released from their requirement to pay the Hospitallers, the Nizaris calculated that they needed to improve their status with Baibars. They therefore presented the tribute they had previously offered to the Hospitallers as a gift to Baibars.

But if the Nizaris hoped that this would discourage the attentions of Baibars, they were mistaken. In 1270, the autonomy of the Syrian Nizaris would be lost once and for all. Amazingly, the ancient Najm al-Din was still alive and leading the movement in Syria. Perhaps because of his advancing years, he was about to make a drastic miscalculation. Baibars was still under threat from several quarters. Despite their retreat at Ain Jalut a decade before, the Mongols were back in the region, threatening the north of Syria. And King Louis IX of France was, it was rumoured, assembling another great Christian army to lead on another Crusade to the Holy Land. Baibars demanded that all the leading Muslim rulers in the region should pay homage to him as he passed through their lands. Alone, Najm al-Din refused to comply with this demand. It was an act of bravado perhaps but also one of immense foolhardiness. In response, Baibars told the Nizaris that Najm al-Din was now deposed. It was a symbolic gesture - Baibars had no authority to do this and he had no intention at this stage of enforcing this deposition by violent means – but it left Najm al-Din as a marked man.

His position would deteriorate still further shortly afterwards. He sent a delegation to Baibars asking that the tribute that the Nizaris paid to the Sultan should be reduced. Quite why he expected Baibars to comply with this so soon after he had been insulted by Najm al-Din is a question with no apparent logical answer. Certainly, it hints that he was losing touch with the reality of the political situation in the area. The Sultan's reaction was unequivocal. He told the leader of the emissaries, Sarim al-Din Mubarak, that Najm al-Din was deposed and he now appointed Sarim al-Din his successor. Sarim al-Din accepted the honour but the understanding reached between him and Baibars was to be short-lived. Baibars desired that the castle at Masyaf should be handed over to become part of his own personal landholdings rather than remaining as part of the emaciated Nizari territories. Although this was originally done, Sarim al-Din was upset at the loss of Masyaf to the sect. He tricked his way back into the castle and massacred the supporters of Baibars who had previously barred him from access to the castle.

It was an act of abject recklessness. A force was sent to eject Sarim al-Din from Masyaf. They captured him and sent him to Cairo. Shortly afterwards he died. It is unlikely, given his attitude towards Baibars, that he was not murdered. Najm al-Din still had enough of his wits about him to realize that total submission was the only realistic option available to him if he wished to live. He therefore apologised profusely to Baibars for his previous intransigence. His son Shams al-Din was sent to Cairo as a hostage for his future good behaviour. Soon after, Baibars received word of a plot that had been hatched to assassinate him. It was alleged that this had been jointly conceived between the Nizaris and Bohemond VI, the ruler of Antioch. Shams al-Din was among those implicated. He was arrested, and his prospects of living to old age appeared to be remote. But Najm al-Din pleaded for his son's freedom. Baibars agreed to his request but the conditions accompanying his release would be harsh. In return, Najm al-Din was to hand over all the remaining Nizari castles to the Mamelukes.

Najm al-Din handed himself over to Baibars and accompanied him to Cairo where he eventually died in 1274, a very old man indeed. Shams al-Din in contrast still did not appear to have assimilated the lesson that resisting the will of Baibars was a dangerous stance to take. When he was allowed to return to Syria to arrange for the handover of the castles there to Baibars, he instead fomented rebellion. It was a brave gesture and suggested that even now the fighting spirit of the Nizaris had not been completely subdued, but it was in truth one with no prospect of success. Soon, even Shams al-Din came to see this and gave himself up to Baibars. One castle held out at Kahf, but when that fell to Baibars in July 1273 it marked the end of the Nizaris as a major political force. The Nizari dream was, to all intents and purposes, over.

Baibars treated the conquered Nizaris humanely. This may have been something of a surprise; he was not a tolerant or merciful man, and the genocidal actions of the Mongols against them in Persia had left an awful precedent to follow. But the Sultan let them be, both because they were an irrelevance (their power was clearly spent forever) and also because he had a use for their traditional skills.[13] Several prominent victims from the West were targeted. In 1270, Philip of Montfort, a leading Crusader baron, was killed at Tyre. The year after the Count of Tripoli was threatened with a similar fate. Then, in 1272, one more drama was enacted, one which serves as a fitting and appropriate postcript to the history of the Syrian Nizaris as an effective force.

The West had launched one final Crusade. It was in truth a pallid, insipid affair when compared to the great expeditions of old. Christendom had lost interest in the Crusading movement, at least as far as Outremer was concerned. There were easier targets closer to home, and the rewards from the Crusades to the East of the previous century were pathetically small when compared to the effort involved. When this current Crusade arrived, it had only a thousand men or so in its ranks. But at its head was a young man of enormous ambition and immense promise. Eager to learn the skills of war, and fiercely devoted to his cause, Prince Edward of England appeared to be a potentially dangerous enemy who could create problems out of all proportion to the size of his tiny army. Baibars himself seems to have realized this. A truce was soon negotiated, the best perhaps that Edward could have hoped for in the circumstances.

However, Baibars was clearly nervous of the young man. Possibly he reckoned that he would return again in the future to cause far greater problems than he was able to at the moment. At any event, before Edward returned home an attempt would be made on his life. While he was in his tent, he was set upon by an assassin, a man well known to him as a trusted servant. Before he could fight him off, the attacker had stabbed him with a knife that was reputedly poisoned. Edward was a strong young man and managed to overpower and kill his assailant, but he was badly wounded. For a while, Edward's life hang in the balance. However, the expert care of his doctors (or the loving attention of his wife if the more romantic chroniclers are to be believed) saved him. He was slowly nursed back to health and eventually returned to England. Before he left, Baibars sent him a letter congratulating him on his escape but many saw this as an attempt to divert attention away from his part in the plot. Edward would never return to the East again but there was many a Scot who would curse the day that the assassins failed to finish Edward off. He would eventually become King Edward I of England, a mighty warrior whose sobriquet would be 'The Hammer of the Scots'.

The life of the Nizaris as an effective political power was drawing almost somnolently to a close. Baibars and his immediate successors suffered them to live on as an almost irrelevant force. Any dreams that the more optimistic Nizaris entertained of a dramatic reversal of fortunes would be in vain. The movement would survive, and their subsequent history, which lasts until the present day, deserves to be examined, if only to complete the story. But as a major player in the politics of the region, their days of influence were effectively over. Yet in all of this there was an irony. Although their history as a significant independent power was at an end, a massive impetus to the growth of their legend was about to arrive. As a result, the mysterious movement of the Nizaris, whose very way of life meant that they were always likely to be shrouded in obscurity, was about to slip beyond the world of reality and into the realm of fantasy.

TWELVE

From History to Legend

In 1298, a sea battle took place between a Venetian and a Genoese fleet. There was nothing particularly unusual in this – the two city-states were close, often acrimonious rivals, constantly at each other's throats. But this battle was, indirectly, to give massive impetus to the legend of the Assassins. It went badly for the Venetians and large numbers of them were captured. Among those taken prisoner was a middle-aged man, who was destined to spend the next year of his life in a dank Genoese cell. He resolved that he would not waste this time by wallowing in self-pity.

He was imprisoned with another man, a scribe by profession named Rusticello, and he determined that he would pass his time by dictating his life story to his companion. But this was no ordinary autobiography, it was more of a travelogue. Within its pages were described the events of one of the greatest adventures that any man has ever been involved in, a journey into the mysterious and exotic lands of the East, to the ends of the Earth itself. The story would become one of the most famous of history; the prisoner's name was Marco Polo.

Marco Polo told the scribe that he had left Venice in 1271, in the company of his father and uncle, who had already journeyed to the court of Kublai Khan (the successor of Mongke, the Khan who had previously ordered the destruction of the Nizaris). As a young man of 17 years of age, what lay before him must have seemed like a fabulous adventure but even in his moments of most vivid imagination he could not have conceived what he would actually experience.

Having made the sea crossing to Outremer (in itself a risky undertaking in the flimsy craft of the day) his party made their way eastwards from Acre in November 1271. Crossing the vast plains and mountain ranges of Central Asia, and then the withered wasteland of the Gobi Desert, it would take nearly four years of dangerous and exhausting travel before they arrived at the court of Kublai in May 1275. The young man quickly became a favourite of the Khan, who used him in a diplomatic capacity on a number of occasions. When eventually Marco Polo decided to return to Venice he had been away from the city for nearly 25 years, and had spent well over half of his life in the East.

In his journey eastwards, Marco Polo and his entourage passed through Persia. One day as they travelled in a pedestrian fashion through the searing heat of the midday sun, from out of the haze a jagged rock loomed on the horizon. As the party drew closer, they saw that the rock was awesomely situated, with its cliffs precipitately towering over the surrounding plains. At the summit of this towering rock stood a castle, seemingly invincible, unconquerable. Although we cannot be certain which castle it was that Marco Polo came across, it may well have been the rock of Girdkuh.

Travelling onwards through Persia, the party also passed through Quhistan. They came to a country that Marco Polo called '*mulehet*' or the 'land of the heretics'. As they progressed, they heard more tales of a strange sect that had not long before lived in Persia but had been overwhelmed by the Mongols only a few years previously. These stories inevitably took hold of the young mind of Marco Polo and made a huge impression. When he returned to the West many years later, he would have heard stories of the sect of the Assassins, for so long close (but little known) neighbours of the Crusaders in Outremer. He may even have heard tales of them before he departed. Synthesising his own experiences with these other stories, he was to create in his narrative the definitive legend of the Assassins, in which most (though not all) of the separate strands of the myths surrounding the sect were to find a place.

Marco Polo's account told how the mysterious sect that had come to his attention in Persia had a leader, a man named Alaodin, who inspired fanatical devotion among his followers. So intense was their loyalty that no ordinary motive could adequately explain it. There had to be some reason deeper than mundane attachment to justify the acts of this man's followers, who regularly sacrificed themselves in suicidal assassination missions from which they could not hope to return. Indeed, many of them seemed not to want to return.

At the centre of Marco Polo's explanation for this fanatical devotion was a wonderful garden, literally a paradise on earth, in which these Assassins spent some time before they left on their missions. The garden was set in a virtually impregnable valley, approached through a narrow pass between two immense mountains. The entrance was guarded by a huge castle and large numbers of guards, and the way to the garden, which was hidden away,[1] was anyway kept secret so that, except by accident, only the escorts who were to accompany those whose presence were required in the garden would know where it was.

The garden itself was described as 'the biggest and most beautiful garden that was ever seen'. Generously scattered throughout the valley were houses and palaces of indescribable beauty and opulence. They were gilded in azure and their walls were sumptuously draped with delicate silks of wonderful artistry. There were great numbers of amazing fountains around the palaces and conduits running off them, some carrying crystal-clear water, others milk, yet others wine. Some even carried honey.

And there were not only wonderful things to eat and drink provided in this garden. The most beautiful women in the world were also there in abundance. They were not only glorious to gaze upon, they were also chosen for their musical talents and their dancing skills. They danced enticingly around the fountains and sang melodies of sublime beauty. Their purpose for being in the garden was simple. The young *fida'is* of the Assassins were brought here. The women were to fulfil their every need or, as Marco Polo delicately put it, those men brought to the garden 'will have beautiful women to their hearts' content to do their bidding'. Everything in this garden was devoted to the pursuit of luxury and self-gratification. The leader of the Assassins, the 'Sheikh of the Mountain' as Marco Polo describes him, told those who were there that this place was, quite simply, Paradise.

The sheikh chose as his *fida'is* young men from the surrounding mountainous regions, aged from twelve to twenty. They were recruited to the ranks of his sect, and taught in the arts of assassination and intrigue. They were not, however, introduced at once to the otherworldly delights of the Garden of Paradise. That privilege was reserved only for a chosen few. These recruits were kept apart from the world, their days spent in honing their skills as Assassins.

Then, when he deemed the time to be right, he would bring those he had chosen to the garden, in a most interesting fashion: 'He would give them draughts that sent them to sleep on the spot. Then he had them taken and put in the garden, where they were wakened. When they awoke and found themselves in there and saw all the things I have told you of, they believed they really were in Paradise. And the ladies and damsels stayed with them all the time, singing and making music for their delight and administering to all their desires. So these youths had all they could wish for and asked nothing better than to remain there'.

Naturally enough, the indescribable delights of this place meant that the recruit would soon fall in love with it. He would only experience these pleasures for a short time however, just enough to receive a tantalizing taste of them. Understandably, the recruit would be eager for more. But this was all part of the Sheikh's plan. After just a few days in the garden, the recruit would once more be given a drink that was heavily laced with opiates. When he again fell into a deep sleep, he would be returned to the place from which he originally came. When the recruit awoke he was desperately disappointed to find that he was no longer in the garden, and also completely in the dark as to how he had firstly entered it, and then sub-sequently returned from it.

Soon after, the young man would be called into the presence of the sheikh, and the reason for this fantastic experience was revealed: 'When he asked them whence they came, they would answer that they came from Paradise, and that this was in truth the Paradise of which Mahomet had told their ancestors; and they would tell their listeners all they had found there. And the others who heard this and had not been there were filled with a great longing to go to this Paradise; they longed for death so that they might go there, and looked forward eagerly to the day of their going.'

Marco Polo asserts that the *fida'is* were sent out on missions to prove themselves by eliminating local enemies. Those who showed the greatest zeal and determination in the execution of their tasks could expect to be used on other, more difficult missions, the successful completion of which would redound greatly to their honour:

Then, in order to bring about the death of the lord or other man he desired, he would take some of these Assassins of his and send them wherever he might wish, telling them that he was minded to despatch them to Paradise: they were to go accordingly and kill such and such a man; if they died on their mission, they would go all the sooner. Those who received such a command obeyed it with a right good will, more readily than anything else they might have been called on to do. Away they went and did all that he commanded. Thus it happened that no one ever escaped when the Sheikh of the Mountain desired his death. And I can assure you that many kings and many lords paid tribute to him and cultivated his friendship for fear that he might bring about their death. This happened because at that time the nations were not united in their allegiance, but torn by conflicting loyalties and purposes.[2]

Most of the final ingredients of the Assassin legend were present in Marco Polo's tale: the training of young men since they were children for the purposes of making them into formidable killers; the use of drugs in the indoctrination process; the existence of Paradise in this latter-day Eden, the leadership of the sect by a strange and sinister being, 'The Sheikh'. But this story did not come about in isolation; it was a natural development from a number of early tales. And although it is now generally accepted that they were largely a Western invention, there is some evidence that earlier accusations levelled at the Nizaris (and its forebears) by fellow Muslims were to an extent reflected in the legend as told by Marco Polo.

The legends that developed concerning the Nizaris gestated in part because of the way the movement was perceived by other parts of the Muslim world. The elements that created this perception date back to the very beginning of the movement, when the Isma'ili division within Islam first became a reality. From the outset, the Nizaris' hold on life was tenuous indeed. They were therefore forced to lead a clandestine existence, lurking in the shadows, hidden from the view of mainstream Islam. Further, little was committed to writing; the Isma'ilis rarely appeared to be keen historiographers. In this environment, little was known about the movement, apart from the fact that they were inimically opposed to Sunni Muslims on political and doctrinal grounds. And what the opponents of the Isma'ilis did not know, their fevered imaginations made up.

Over time, a number of stories grew up around the Isma'ilis within the Islamic world. Collectively, they have been described by modern historians as 'the black legend'.³ Simplistically, these were a sequence of accusations against the Isma'ilis, which claimed that the movement aimed at nothing less than the destruction of Islam itself. Some extraordinary claims were made, including the assertion that the Isma'ilis were in fact Jewish interlopers who wished to discredit and demolish Islam. They arose because the Nizaris did not to have to look far for their enemies, even within the Muslim world. Not only were Sunni Muslims antagonistic towards them but many Shiites were deeply hostile towards them. Consequently, there is a significant collection of anti-Nizari literature from Islamic sources.⁴

But the hostile allegations against the Nizaris from Islamic sources were very different from the Western 'Assassin' legends that would later develop. Members of the movement were sometimes derogatorily labelled by their Islamic enemies as '*malahida*', that is to say 'heretics', though as will be noted below the derivation of the term 'Assassin' would come from another term of abuse, namely '*hashishiyya*'.⁵ The crucial effect of the 'black legend' was not in its specific details, most of which were different from the later Western legends, but in the climate of suspicion and intrigue that they helped to foster.

Islamic accusations about the Isma'ilis were however serious enough. A number of immoral acts were ascribed to the movement. The Qarmatis, who originally had their formative influences in the Isma'ili movement, were accused of promiscuity in that they shared their womenfolk throughout the community. Similar accusations would later be levelled at militant Nizari groups in Syria during the reign of Sinan. One account stated categorically that some of the Isma'ilis 'gave way to iniquity and debauchery and called themselves 'the Pure'. Men and women mingled in drinking sessions, no man abstained from his sister or daughter, the women wore men's clothes, and one of them declared that Sinan was his God.'⁷

The Isma'ilis were therefore connected even in the eyes of other Muslims with sexual licence. It is possible therefore that Christian observers who came into contact with Muslims in the region picked up snippets of these tales, and that this may have helped shape the carnal element of the more lurid stories concerning the Assassins and the Garden of Paradise.

Such assertions as this must remain largely speculative. After all, allegations of sexual depravity have frequently been levelled at many nonconformist groups throughout history (Christians were also not slow to charge those they regarded as heretical sects with such abhorrent behaviour). But there are areas where the link between the 'black legend' of Islam and the myth of the Assassins is more clear cut. This is most clearly shown by the name that the West was to give to the sect collectively, that is 'Assassins'. No one who was a member of it would have accepted the appellation, as they would generally have seen themselves as followers of Nizar, that is Nizaris. But early on in the life of the Nizaris, a name would be given to them by Muslim opponents, and in this lies the origin of the term 'Assassin', for in some quarters the sect were called '*hashishiyya*', which means 'hashish users'.

It is interesting to note that when the term first appears in written documents, no explanation is given of its meaning. There is therefore an implicit assumption that the reader will know of its meaning without further comment, as if it had already been in use for some time. The etymology of the word 'assassin' was traced back to this root by the nineteenth century historian of the schisms within Islam, Baron Antoine Isaac Silvestre de Sacy. In a presentation he made following a paper published in 1818, he linked the Nizaris (or the 'Assassins' as they were better known in the West) with several Syrian chronicles from the twelfth century. In one example, he discussed a chronicle by the Arab historian, Abu Shama, in a passage where he describes the unsuccessful attempt of the Nizaris on Saladin's life as follows: 'so on this occasion, God saved the life of the sultan from the daggers of *al-Hashishiyya*'.[8]

Until fairly recently, it was widely believed that the term was applied to the Nizaris exclusively by their Syrian opponents.[9] But as it transpired, modern research has identified that the term was applied both in Syria and Persia by the Zaydis.[10] Although it was not widely used, it did have a diverse geographical provenance as a term of abuse, being used most commonly in the thirteenth century.

Western chroniclers were aware of the name from fairly early on. William of Tyre wrote that 'both our people and the Saracens call them Assassini; we do not know the origin of the name'.[11] Before long, the term had passed into everyday parlance in Western Europe. For example, Dante – in his masterpiece *The Divine Comedy* – refers to a 'treacherous assassin'. At about the same time, another Italian, the Florentine Giovanni Villani, talks of the 'assassini' of the ruler of Lucca. Thus, within a couple of centuries of the noun coming into use in Syria (although it is of course possible – and perhaps implied by the non-explanation of the term in Syrian chronicles – that earlier records have not survived the ravages of time) it had become a new, previously unknown, noun in the West.

This is an interesting academic development that speaks volumes for the effect that the Nizaris had on the psyche of Western Europe and its literate inhabitants (who were admittedly in a fairly small minority of the general populace). But for centuries after the development, scholars struggled in vain to find the origin of the word. Some erroneously thought that the sect had been named after their supposed founder, who according to myth came from the city of Arsacia (the sect were called Arsacides by this etymologist) while others asserted that they were called 'Assassins' from the Arabic '*al-sisani*' (which means 'fortress dweller'). It was not until de Sacy's research that the origin of the word was clearly explained.

But if de Sacy helped to demonstrate the truth concerning the origin of the name of the sect, he was less helpful in other aspects of the legend of the Assassins. To him, the appellation 'hashish users' was one to be taken literally. He therefore quotes several sources which describe how the drug was prepared and used by those who partook of its dubious delights. This in part reflected the comprehension of de Sacy and indeed most educated people in the West at the time. There was little understanding of the mentality of the Assassins, and it was beyond the rational comprehension of many that they could so easily give up their lives in the cause that they were passionately affiliated to. Therefore other, more extreme explanations than mere religious devotion were required, hence the willingness to accept that the Nizaris were drug-crazed fanatics who had lost all control of their senses.

There was little tradition of such extremist groups of martyrs in the cultures of Christendom. Such actions seemed alien, both to later historians (those of the eighteenth and nineteenth centuries for example), and also probably among those Crusader inhabitants of Outremer who were contemporary with the Nizaris. Therefore, other more (supposedly) rational explanations were sought. There is a supreme irony in this. In modern times, there has been a greater awareness that so-called 'fundamentalist' or 'extremist' movements can psychologically create an environment in which individuals are prepared to sacrifice their lives in the cause that they believe in. The use of 'kamikaze' tactics in the Second World War, when Japanese pilots set out on suicide missions from which they would not return, was one example of how men were prepared to die for a supposedly divine cause (in this case their Emperor and his dynasty). And, in modern times, the tactic of using specially-trained bombers willing to sacrifice their own lives for a cause has had a powerful impact on modern consciousness. But no such memory existed in cultural paradigms in Western Europe in the Medieval past.

Western observers just could not understand what motivated the 'Assassins'. Some sought to justify their behaviour on the grounds that they sought material rewards for their actions. Thus, Brocardus, the fourteenth century chronicler, asserts that 'they sell themselves'[12] and Francesco da Buti, an Italian contemporary, can write by way of explanation that 'an Assassin is one who kills others for money'. Admittedly, da Buti may be talking of 'assassins' that he recognizes from contemporary Italian society, whose motivations may be very different than Islamic 'Assassins' from Syria, but it is revealing that the word had become synonymous with those seeking pecuniary advantage from their actions so soon after it entered the vocabulary of the West.

There are strong counter-arguments against the contention that the *fidaïs* of the movement were drug users. The practical arguments against the use of drugs are clear enough. The activities of the Nizaris' assassins were calculated. They required that the potential assassin should manipulate his way into the inner circle of the man that he had been ordered to kill. He was patiently to await a moment of opportunity to complete his appointed task. Only when the chances of success were good would he launch his attack. Timing was crucial, not so much for the purposes of escape (in many cases this would have been a hopeless ambition) but for the ultimate success of the project as achieved by the elimination of the target. This meant that the would-be assassin could be forced to wait for some time, watching with intense concentration for the correct moment to strike. This is the action of a methodical individual, in full control of his actions and emotions. It is definitely not the action of an individual who was high on drugs. It seems highly improbable therefore that the participants in such acts were drug users.

There were hints that a subtler explanation for the origin of the term '*hashishiyya*' existed. Obliquely, de Sacy himself referred to them when he quoted the Arab chronicler Maqrizi as saying that 'I know of a time when only people of the lowest class would eat it [that is hashish]; and even they were loath to hear themselves called by a name derived from the drug'. Maqrizi therefore insinuates that to be called a drug user was a social insult, implying that those who used stimulants such as hashish were members of the lowest caste imaginable. The reasons for this were as much practical as moral. Islam imposed certain rigid restrictions on the behaviour of Muslims. Adherence to the precepts of the religion required, for example, a rigid routine of prayer five times a day. The use of drugs would adversely affect the discipline of individuals, and their failure to comply with the requirements of the religion would seriously endanger their spiritual well being. Drug use was therefore not to be condoned or encouraged. The term '*hashishiyyin*' was, as one modern commentator vividly described it, synonymous to calling the Nizaris 'low-class rabble'.[13]

Despite the improbability of the Nizari assassins using hashish, the story was widely believed. It quickly became part of the folklore surrounding the 'Assassins' in the West, which could not otherwise comprehend the gladness with which Nizari *fidā'is* contemplated martyrdom. Allegations of drug use were therefore adopted enthusiastically in an attempt to explain the fanaticism of the Nizaris. Marco Polo enthusiastically uses the legend as an essential ingredient in his explanation of how the *fidā'is* were mysteriously spirited into the magical Garden of Paradise and, indeed, back out again.

There had been a number of mentions about the Nizaris in the literature of the West for some time before Marco Polo's account. By the time that Marco Polo wrote, the 'Assassin' legend was already firmly established. The first such known reference is that of Burchard of Strassburg. Burchard had been sent on a diplomatic mission to the Nizaris by Frederick Barbarossa, the Emperor of Germany. He calls the people that he met 'Heyssessini', showing that a derivative of the Islamic phrase sometimes used to describe the Nizaris was already in use fairly early on (Burchard's mission is believed to date to 1175). In the report that he sent back to his Emperor, he goes on to describe the movement in more detail. He first of all told the Emperor that the leader of the Assassins struck fear into both the Muslim lords living in the vicinity and also the barons of the Crusader kingdoms in the Levant. This fear he ascribes to the murderous activities of the group.

He describes how the Assassins lived in the mountains, in palaces of great beauty. These are surrounded by massive high walls and entry is only possible through a very small gate. Into these palaces, the leader of the sect ('the prince' as Burchard describes him) brings the sons of many of the local peasantry. They are educated within these palaces; as part of their training they are for example taught many different languages. This will help them to integrate themselves in the homes and entourages of would-be victims at some point in the future. Their education is thorough, and has one aim in mind, as Burchard makes clear:

> These young men are taught by their teachers from their earliest youth to their full manhood, that they must obey the lord of their land in all his words and commands; and that if they do so, he, who has power over all living gods, will give them the joys of Paradise. . . . When they are in the presence of the Prince, he asks them if they are willing to obey his commands, so that he may bestow Paradise upon them. Whereupon, as they have been instructed, and without any objection or doubt, they throw themselves at his feet and reply with fervour, that they will obey him in all things that he may command. Thereupon, the Prince gives each one of them a golden dagger and sends them out to kill whichever prince he has marked down.[14]

There are some significant elements in this description of the Assassin legend. Within it can be perceived some of the strands later to be found in Marco Polo's full-blown account of the sect. Clearly, Burchard implies that from an early age the would-be *fidaʾis* are indoctrinated to automatically follow the commands of their leader. As part of his account Burchard describes how the young boys recruited in this fashion are refused contact with the outside world. From now on, the leader of the sect will clearly be the centre of their universe.

The inference is clear; from this point in time, they will obey his commands to the letter, without hesitation or reserve. Modern historians point out that Burchard was not a local, but a visitor to the region. As such, they find his accounts fanciful and unlikely.[15] They also highlight the fact that no such accounts of the training of *fidaʾis* are to be found in the literature of the Nizaris. And as a conclusive argument that Burchard is guilty of gross exaggeration in his stories, they offer the fact that William of Tyre, while mentioning the Assassins in his text, does not describe any of the legends discussed above. This leads them to hypothesise that Burchard has picked up on some highly inaccurate local legends and postulated them as reality.

But these objections, although undoubtedly presenting difficulties, do not definitively represent insurmountable obstacles. Counter-arguments might be proposed to all these criticisms of Burchard's work. The Nizaris admittedly do not describe these training methods in their histories but this is not in itself conclusive. Few such histories have survived the passage of time. Neither does William of Tyre's failure to mention the training methods provide conclusive evidence that Burchard's account is largely a fabrication. William as a chronicler is generally not particularly interested in the Islamic world, and rarely discusses their ways of life in detail. The major exception to this rule was in a work that he wrote which exclusively describes the Islamic world around the Christian state of Outremer. This work – which is the most likely home for any extended mention of the Assassins – is unfortunately lost. Therefore, any contention that the legends may have been described in depth in here must, sadly, remain unproveable.

We must also consider the contention that young men were recruited to the ranks of the Nizaris specifically to be trained as assassins, and subsequently brainwashed to obey their leader's commands without question. Of course, the legend is probably exaggerated. But it is not without precedent that young men should be recruited to one cause or another, and lost to their families as a result. Later on in the Nizari age, Mamelukes would be recruited as young boys for training as soldiers. The example does not perfectly match that of the Nizaris – who were, after all, largely unique – but it does demonstrate that there are other situations in history when young men have been recruited, and have been given up by their families for the purposes of a particular cause.

Therefore, Burchard's account, at first sight improbable, is not totally an implausible one. The probability is that his narrative was more than likely based on legends, but that there were some elements of truth within these. History is liberally scattered with legendary details that are often regarded as mythical, only to find subsequently that they are, in some way, based on a foundation of historical fact. The question as far as the Nizaris' training methods is concerned – and it is largely an unanswerable one – is just how far that element of truth extends, and just how much of the content of stories such as these is myth.

Before leaving Burchard's account there is however one further element that must be considered. This is the promise of Paradise that is offered to the Assassins. In this early account may be seen the first shoots of the legend that would ultimately blossom in Marco Polo's story of the Garden of Paradise. There is one key element in this depiction of the story of the sect as told by Burchard. Ultimate authority over the *fida'is*, and more crucially the right or otherwise to enter into the delights of Paradise forever, is vested with the leader, the 'prince', of the Assassins. Therefore, he assumes powers not only of life or death but also of eternal delight or everlasting damnation over those with whom he comes into contact.

In other words, the leader becomes a God-like figure, a deity in his own right. Therefore, in this account we have not only the first gestation of the legend of the Garden of Paradise but also of the Old Man of the Mountain, the penumbral, almost ethereal figure, who possesses a power of life or death that is almost mystical, as if he – or, more pertinently, his followers – can almost unnoticed make their way into the good graces of those that they plan to kill.

Western chroniclers were quick to develop this image. Burchard was among the first to use the term 'The Old Man of the Mountain', although in a slightly different context from later chroniclers. As well as *Heyssessini*, he calls members of the sect 'segnors de montana', ascribing the name to the sect as a whole rather than the leader in isolation. William of Tyre assigns the title more specifically, describing the leader of the 'Assassini' as being chosen 'not by hereditary right but the prerogative of merit. This chief, when elected, they call the Old Man, disdaining a more dignified title' and goes on to note that they will do anything, 'even the most dangerous tasks', at his behest.[16]

There was however clearly a great deal of confusion in Western circles about the beliefs of the Nizaris, which must have helped significantly to distort perceptions of the movement. There was a general misunderstanding of the beliefs of the Muslims anyway; one of the most bizarre legends going around was that Muhammad himself was a rebellious Cardinal who had abandoned the Catholic Church and set up a Church of his own in Arabia.[17]

William of Tyre added to the misconceptions, noting that for many centuries members of the sect had obediently obeyed the commands of Islam, but in recent times they had started to disregard these, for example by eating pork and drinking wine. These accusations – mirrored by Burchard's account – interestingly provide strong evidence that something was known about the *qiyama*, the Resurrection, whereby the traditional teachings of Islam could be ignored. So far, then, it appears that there might be the germ of reality underlying these narratives.

But William then oversteps the mark. He asserts that the movement had come to own a number of Christian books, and were so impressed by the teaching that they found written there that the Old Man had sent envoys to the King of Jerusalem so that the sect might convert en masse. This is undoubtedly wishful thinking on the part of a man who was an Archbishop as well as a chronicler. Sinan, 'The Old Man' as he is termed by William, did indeed send envoys to Amalric I, King of Jerusalem, but only to discuss political alliance and an avoidance of the tribute currently being paid to the Knights Templar. The chronicler expected far too much from their mission – conversion to Christianity was never an option. It is possible – perhaps probable – that Sinan did know something of the Christian religion and it is certainly quite conceivable that he had an academic interest in it. However, knowledge of the beliefs of one's potential ally is a sensible tactic to use once he had decided that he wished to be on better terms with his neighbours. By understanding them better, he would increase his chances of allying himself with them.

Interestingly, William's accounts are quite similar to those of another writer, whose works probably slightly pre-date him. He was a Jewish Rabbi from Spain (which had a sizeable Jewish community at the time), travelling through the region. His name was Benjamin of Tudela, and he journeyed to the East in 1167. He mentioned a number of things which, in the space of a few short sentences, shows something of Western pre-conceptions about the Nizaris, how they were already becoming known as 'Assassins' in the West and the origin of the 'Old Man' nomenclature for their leader. Benjamin says that they: 'do not believe in the religion of Islam, but follow one of their own folk, whom they regard as their prophet, and all that he tells them to do they carry out, whether for life or death. They call him the Sheikh Al Hashishin, and he is known as their Elder'.[18]

Benjamin's analysis of the Nizaris' religious affiliations are particularly revealing. The fact that he can state so confidently that they have abandoned Islam shows how fundamentally he had failed to appreciate the reality of the schisms that had taken place within Islam itself. The *qiyama* had also taken place some three years before and even then it may be that this event, with its abandonment of the rules of the *shar'ia*, had already had an influence on the thinking of others, though given the short period of time that had then elapsed since this had taken place this cannot be too confident an assertion.

Generally speaking, William of Tyre's accounts added little to the Assassin legends. Indeed, on the whole they are far less extraordinary than those of Burchard. However, subsequently Western chroniclers would add other chapters to the legend (or, more accurately, add to those chapters already written). It is perhaps worth noting that these later writers wrote after the assassination of Conrad of Montferrat. This act made a great impression on the West, so much so that for a time the alleged involvement of Richard the Lionheart seriously damaged the image of the King.

It has been pointed out that the Assassins killed only a handful of Westerners – substantially fewer in fact than the number of Muslims that they murdered. But this tells only half the story. Some of the Christian lords that they killed were men of great standing. Conrad perhaps was the most significant Western victim. He was effectively the uncrowned King of Jerusalem. His death must have added greatly to the interest of the West in the Assassins and its knowledge, albeit very flawed, of the existence of the group. When later chroniclers wrote they therefore found a ready market for their narratives.

Certainly, when Arnold of Lübeck – a German historian – wrote a chronicle at the beginning of the thirteenth century he referred to the murder of Conrad. In addition, he wrote his own version of the 'Assassin' story, which probably owes much to Burchard, his fellow countryman and historian. His work is, in its own right, an important contributor to the development of the Assassin legend in the West as he not only copies Burchard's accounts but adds to them. He wrote about a number of aspects of the legend. He seems particularly fascinated by the role of the Old Man of the Mountain and, after admitting that some of the stories seem ridiculous, he goes on to relate them with gusto.

He states that the Old Man's followers 'believe in no God but himself'. Again, we see the Old Man as a virtually deified figure, a divine being in his own right. But according to Arnold this is not through his undeniable merits but through the use of witchcraft by which his followers are enchanted. The Old Man tells his followers that the delights of Paradise are so great that they become besotted with them, and will happily seek death to receive them earlier. 'They therefore think nothing of throwing themselves from high walls at the merest nod of command from the Old Man, smashing their skulls to pulp on the rocks far below. But the most blessed of men in his distorted creed are those who kill his enemies and themselves die as a result.'

Clearly however the reward of Paradise is not enough. Arnold tells his readers that the Old Man ensures the obedience of his Assassins in the following way: 'He [The 'Old Man'] hands them [his assassins] knives which are, so to speak, consecrated to this affair, and then intoxicates them with such a potion that they are plunged into ecstasy and oblivion, displays to them by his magic certain fantastic dreams, full of pleasures and delights, or rather of trumpery, and promises them eternal possession of these things in reward for such deeds'.[19] There are a number of important elements in Arnold's narrative which develop the Assassin legend. The Old Man is painted as a sinister and manipulative figure, whose word is law. His every command is obeyed as if he is himself God. The promise of Paradise is offered to all those who devote themselves to his cause (especially those indeed who die for it). But it is not enough, so he also has to brainwash his followers through the use of drugs. Thus, all those chosen to commit his acts of murder do so in a state when they are literally out of their minds. All of this is not terribly different that the final telling of the legend as outlined by Marco Polo, although there is no mention in Arnold's account of the Garden of Paradise so exotically and vividly described by the later Venetian adventurer.

However, there is one respect in which Arnold goes beyond the narrative of Marco Polo; the reference that he makes to the death-leap legends.[20] This is one particular strand of the legend that modern historians struggle to rationalize. Clearly, they ascribe to the view of Arnold himself that the thought of men throwing themselves like lemmings to their deaths on the rocks far below for no good purpose is frankly 'ridiculous'. For example,

Farhad Daftary – one of the leading historians of the Nizaris in modern times – rejects the story that Henry of Champagne witnessed such an event out of hand. He states categorically that 'such death-leap demonstrations did not take place in the presence of Henry of Champagne or any other European dignitary',[21] while Bernard Lewis calls it a 'somewhat questionable story'.[22]

But this particular story is not merely a product of exaggerated Western imaginings. The story turns up not only in Western accounts but also in local sources (although of course the former might well have developed because of the existence of the latter). Ibn Jubayr, a Muslim who wrote a contemporary travel journal, mentions the story in his writings, implying that it was a common occurrence in the time of Sinan, while other Muslim writers mention it (though sometimes stating that such acts took place in the time of Hasan-i Sabbah).[23] There is therefore a tradition of such events taking place and it is probable that Western chroniclers became aware of local legends and expanded on them.

Certainly, they embedded themselves in Western consciousness. A nineteenth century book of poems about an Assassin leader named 'Alaodin' outlines in its preface the story as it was then understood: 'When Henry, son-in-law of the King of Jerusalem [sic] was passing through Syria, boasting of the power he possessed, the sheik of the Assassins came to meet him. "Are your subjects", said he to the Count, "as ready in their submission as mine?" And without waiting for reply, he made a sign with his hand, when ten young men in white, who were standing on an adjacent tower, instantly threw themselves down'.[24]

While Arnold's narrative, written as it was at a distance, added another important chapter to the development of the legend of the Assassins in the West, the next impetus was to be given from a source much more local to the Nizaris. James of Vitry was both an important chronicler and a leading figure in Outremer, being Bishop of Acre from 1216 to 1228. He wrote more luridly of the Assassins than William of Tyre did, although he reiterated much of what William's account said. But he also added an important new element that in many ways foreshadows Marco Polo's version of events.

Of the legends already current at the time, he picks up particularly the story of the recruitment of young initiates into the sect. He again states that they are educated to speak a number of languages and that they are, when ready, sent to the courts of leading men of both the Christians and the 'Saracens', armed with daggers, ready to eliminate the enemies of their leader, 'The Old Man'. James says that he offered them eternal participation in the rewards of Paradise, especially if they should die carrying out his commands by destroying his adversaries. This is a reiteration of what other chroniclers had said: this particular part of the 'Assassin' legend had clearly begun to establish itself as a permanent feature.

James adds that, to ensure that the young men are truly loyal to him, the Old Man also gives many precious gifts to their parents. Nothing it seems is overlooked in his attempts to win the true devotion of his followers. Generally, however, his account is written in a less sensationalistic fashion than that of either Burchard of Strassburg or Arnold of Lübeck. But he does introduce an interesting new perspective when he mentions the secret training places of the Assassins, evocatively described as the 'secret and delightful places'. It is a hint, nothing more than that, but it does perhaps give the first glimpse, albeit in a distorted form, of Marco Polo's great flowering of the legend of the Garden of Paradise nearly a century later.

Interestingly, he is equally as confused as William when considering the Nizaris' relationship with Islam and Christianity. He states categorically that they:

> began with all diligence to read and examine the law of the Christians and the Gospels of Christ, admiring the virtue of the miracles, and the sanctity of the doctrine. From a comparison with these [the Old Man] began to abominate the frivolous and irrational doctrine of Mahomet, and at length when [the Old Man] knew the truth, he studied to recall his subjects by degrees from the rites of the cursed law. Wherefore he exhorted and commanded them that they should drink wine in moderation and eat the flesh of swine. At length, after many discourses and serious admonitions of their teacher, they all with one consent agreed to renounce the perfidy of Mahomet, and, by receiving the grace of baptism, to become Christians.[26]

It can therefore be seen that a number of Western chroniclers wrote about the 'Assassins'. All of them introduced, or emphasized anew, various aspects of the legend. Cumulatively, they built up the myth surrounding the Nizaris, each of them adding a brick or two to the evolving fabric of the structure of the legend. As a result, when Marco Polo wrote, he built on traditions and legends that were already known in the West.

There was of course also much in the very nature of the Nizaris that encouraged such myths. From their birth, the Isma'ilis had been forced to operate clandestinely by the great enmity that their existence generated among their enemies within Islam. They had been forced to hide their true identity to survive. Their leaders moved about the Islamic world in the utmost secrecy, hiding themselves from the great men of the regions through which they passed, for they knew that their life expectancy would be short indeed if they were at any time discovered. Even other Muslims regarded them as dangerous eccentrics, and if this were so among their Islamic neighbours then it was perhaps inevitable that they were regarded with terrified suspicion among those who understood so little about the sect in the West. Even the doctrine of *taqiyya* – which allowed members of the sect to change their purported beliefs with bewildering frequency – added to the mystique of the Assassins, as the West named them. The doctrine added to the perceived duplicity of the movement in the eyes of many.

The misconceptions of the West were not helped by the scant interest that Christian Europe generally showed in the teachings of Islam. To most contemporary Western commentators, the doctrines of Islam were the doctrines of Anti-Christ; no further analysis was required. Further distinctions generally were of little moment to such men. There was little examination of the teachings of movements such as the Nizaris within Western literature. Such matters were generally passed over. And on the odd occasion that such things were considered, the end result of any study of their beliefs was often erroneous.[27] In such fertile soil, it was easy for Western misconceptions to foster the growth of the legends surrounding the Nizaris.

But occasionally there were glimpses of the truth. For example, Western writers normally associated the Assassins with Syria alone. However, a few wrote of connections with Persia, suggesting that they knew something, however vaguely, of the wider field of influence enjoyed by the sect.

Benjamin of Tudela for one says that in the north of Persia there are 'a people who do not profess the Mohameddan religion, but live on high mountains, and worship the Old Man of the land of the Hashishin'.[28]

225

And Benjamin is of course not completely accurate but at least has it partly right when he says that the 'Assassins' (he calls them 'Assassini') who now live in Syria have their origin 'in the very remote parts of the east, near the city of Bagdad and the parts of the province of Persia'. William of Rubruck, writing a few decades later, wrote of his journey to see the Mongol Khan at Karakorum when he passed through Persia that 'to the east [lie] the mountains of the Mulihet (that is, the Assassins)'.[29] The origins of the Nizaris, geographically at least, were not completely misunderstood, although the quote from Benjamin of Tudela shows once more that the West were confused as to their religious affiliations.

There were other germs of truth in the Western legend. Marco Polo clearly exaggerated enormously when he wrote his tale of the Garden of Paradise, but he had perhaps heard something of the lengths to which the Nizaris went to provide adequate provisions to the remote regions that were their heartland. The Nizaris were indeed renowned for the attention they paid to cultivating every available area; they went to great lengths for example to irrigate such lands thoroughly. That such efforts were made for sound strategic and defensive reasons was lost on most commentators; the maintenance of such wonderful 'gardens' for the pursuit of pleasure made altogether a far more acceptable explanation of the enormous efforts expended in cultivating the countryside effectively.

Similarly, although the explanations to deify the leader of the sect went too far, the so-called 'Old Man of the Mountains' was clearly a seminal figure within the movement. That he inspired absolute devotion among his followers was a truism that was hard to argue against. It was he, after all, who directed the efforts of the Assassins against those whom he wished to see eliminated. When he said the word, his followers happily offered up their lives for him.

This was so widely recognized, even in the West, that the concept even entered the language of the troubadours, with one romantic poet of the time writing to his amour that 'I am your Assassin, who hopes to win paradise through doing your commands'.[30] The romanticism attending Western perceptions of the Assassins is clear in this fanciful comparison between a would-be lover and his lady, and the *fida'is* and their leader.

That the *fida'is* also believed that they were guaranteed Paradise as a result is in itself not an unreasonable hypothesis. Such supposed spiritual rewards are hardly unique among the religions of the world. On this foundation of truth, fanciful legends were constructed, growing more extreme as time passed. The flaw again is in the interpretation of events. The *fidā'is* did not obey the 'Old Man's' commands because they believed him to be a deity but because they thought that their actions would further the cause of their religion as a whole. The 'Old Man' was not God, although he was undoubtedly a holy man. He was rather the physical figurehead of the sect on earth.

It is important to note that the concept of Paradise, or its connection with a wondrous garden where the needs of the devout Muslim are amply catered for, is a core part of Islamic theology. There are a number of references to such a place in the Qur'an. For example, we can read that 'these are they that draw nigh to Allah, in the gardens of bliss. On thrones decorated, reclining on them, facing one another. Round about them shall go youths never altering in age, with goblets and ewers and a cup of pure drink; they shall not be affected with a headache thereby, nor shall they get exhausted; and fruits such as they choose, and the flesh of fowl such as they desire. And pure, beautiful ones, the like of the hidden pearls; a reward for what they used to do.'[31]

Similarly, there are a number of references in the Qur'an to 'gardens beneath which rivers flow' which is the reward for those who labour in the name of Allah, a garden 'the extensiveness of which is as the heavens and earth'.[32] There are even beautiful women, known as 'Hur' or 'Companions in Paradise', 'pure ones confined to the pavilions. . . . Man has not touched them before',[33] handmaidens, virgins to wait upon those who have served Allah well. There was therefore a theological basis for the Gardens and even for the beautiful women who lived there. It was therefore easy enough to see how the legends of the miraculous Garden came about, although the stories were a much embellished version of what can be found in the Qur'an.

For all the incomplete knowledge that the West had of the Nizaris, it is an irony of the first magnitude that, as the Medieval period advanced, knowledge of Muslim affairs became worse instead of better. While the Crusaders still occupied Outremer, there were a few clerics who had a knowledge, however flawed it might have been, of Muslim affairs. Generally, these men were students of Muslim affairs only so that they could criticise Islam and show how superior Christianity was as a religion. But when the Crusaders were humiliatingly ejected from Outremer at the close of the thirteenth century, Christianity was forced onto the back foot. At first, some clerics attempted to urge that a new Crusade should be launched against Islam but this time the aim should be to convert the enemy, not to conquer him.

But as the period drew to a close, even this interest was lost. Europe became increasingly self-centred, with a number of internal upheavals as one power after another sought to become the dominant force in the region. And when the rulers of such powers thought of the Islamic world, it was usually with terror as the Ottoman Turks threatened to strike right at the heart of Europe. In this environment, all semblance of interest in Islam was lost, so much so that it has been estimated that by the close of the fifteenth century only twenty men in the whole of Europe could speak in the Arabic tongue whereas just a couple of centuries before a number of posts had been set up to teach Arabic in some of Europe's greatest universities.[34]

This loss of what little knowledge there was in the West as far as Islam was concerned did nothing to increase the region's objectivity with regard to the Nizaris. Less than half a century after Marco Polo's account, another Western visitor to China, a friar by the name of Odoric of Pordenone, passed through Persia on his way to the Orient. He quoted Marco Polo's version of the Assassin tale almost verbatim. His version of the 'Assassin' legend states that:

The Old Man, when he has a mind to avenge himself or to slay any king or baron, commands him that is governor of the said paradise, to bring thereunto some of the acquaintance of the said king or baron, permitting him a while to take his pleasure therein, and then to give him a certain potion being of force to cast him in such a slumber as to make him quite void of all sense, and so being in a profound sleep to convey him out of his paradise: who being awaked and seeing himself thrust out of the paradise would become so sorrowful that he could not in the world devise what to do, or whither to turn him. Then he would go unto the foresaid Old Man, beseeching him that he might be admitted again into his paradise: who saith unto him, You cannot be admitted thither, unless you will slay such and such a man for my sake, and if you will give the attempt only, whether you kill him or not, I will place you again in paradise, that there you may remain always; then would the party without fail put the same in execution, endeavouring to murder all those against whom the said Old Man had conceived any hatred. And therefore all the kings of the East stood in awe of the said Old Man, and gave unto him great tribute.[35]

He concludes his account by saying that the last 'Old Man' had been overthrown by the Mongols (he calls them the Tartars in his narrative).[36] They had taken from him custody of his paradise, in return for which he had sent large numbers of assassins to destroy the Mongol Khan. As a result, the Old Man had died a violent death.

But after Odoric accounts of the Nizaris began to peter out. Interest in the movement declined. Studies of the Nizaris were to become less and less frequent as the years passed, and the movement's relevance to the modern world diminished. There was however something of a renaissance in the seventeenth century when the true origin and meaning of the Isma'ili schism within Islam was at last examined in the West. A French writer, Denis Lebey de Batilly, published an account of the movement in 1603 in Lyons, for example. His interest in them had been sparked by what was a serious upturn in the number of assassinations that were taking place in contemporary Western Europe. This not unnaturally led to a good deal of interest in groups such as the Assassins which had used assassination as an instrument of policy on previous occasions. However, Batilly added nothing new to Western understanding of the Nizaris, as he based his account on Christian chroniclers who, as we have seen, had failed to understand a number of important facts about the Nizaris.

A more helpful attempt came towards the end of the same century when, in 1697, Bartholomé d'Herbelot stated for the first time in the West some important features of the earlier development of the Islamic world. He understood for example that the Isma'ilis had their origins from among the Shiites, and that the latter were in turn formed when a great schism occurred within Islam. He also mentioned the importance of the Imam to the movement, and realized that they claimed to inherit authority via the line of Ali, the son-in-law of Muhammad.

Despite this, there was still a great deal of confusion surrounding the Nizaris. The origin of the name 'Assassin' was a subject of much speculation during the eighteenth century, most of it well wide of the mark. It was not until the pioneering work of Baron Silvestre de Sacy that the true origin of the term was identified. But although de Sacy was only one of several nineteenth century historians who undertook a great deal of work on the place of the Nizaris in history (another was the Austrian diplomat, Joseph von Hammer), Western attitudes were still largely uncritical towards the accounts that Crusader chroniclers had written about the sect. To these later historians, the Nizaris were still the Assassins of legend, drugged and brain-washed fanatics who threw their lives away with reckless abandon. Nowhere is this better illustrated than in Hammer's vitriolic attack on the Assassins, where he states categorically that they were:

'. . . a union of impostors and dupes which, under the mask of a more austere creed and severer morals, undermined all religion and morality; that order of murderers, beneath whose daggers the lords of nations fell. . . .'[37]

By this time, the 'Assassins' were seen through a haze, composed of both romanticism and terror. A nineteenth century poet described an attempt on the life of a would-be victim he names Selim in the following manner:

An unarmed youth advanced, and strove
To place a blow in Selim's breast.
Scarce shunn'd he the unbidden guest,
But quickly from its scabbard drew
His temper'd scymetar [sic], and clove
The villain to the earth; his eye
Had scarcely turned from him he slew,
When frantic rush'd another by
His comrade's fate to meet. Again,
Not daunted by his brethren's fate.
Whose still warm corses [sic] press'd the plain,
A third in view appear'd. Too late –
For now, though brief the deadly strife.
Th' attendant guards their chief surround –

Th' Assassin's arms are quickly bound,
And tortures soon their force apply
To wring the secret from his breast,
By whose command, at whose behest,
The murderous three were sent . . .

The torture did little good; the 'Assassin' was clearly euphoric at the thought of the delights of Paradise that were soon to be his:

Not from his lips escaped a word.
Save to express his soul-felt joy.
That he had won the bright reward
That crown'd his dangerous employ –
That, when his short lived pains were o'er,
His soul would dwell on that blest shore,
Where luscious fruits, and cooling streams,
And rich perfumes, and cloudless beams,
Surround for aye the happy bow'rs
Where black-eyed damsels charm the hours.[38]

It remained for twentieth century historians to put the Nizaris into some kind of perspective and remove this coating of melodramatic sentimentality. But once they did so, there was enough evidence remaining at least to hint at the reality. Sufficient nuggets of truth can be recovered to speculate in an informed way. The Assassins, or the *fida'is* of the Nizaris as they should more properly be called, used assassination as a policy to further their ends (though they used many other tactics as well). They were undoubtedly devoted to their leader and they would have obeyed his commands unquestioningly. It is also unarguable that these assassins undertook their missions because they thought that they would gain spiritual rewards in return for their martyrdom. But there was no mystical garden to which they were spirited away for a magical indoctrination into the delights that awaited them if they fulfilled their tasks as ordered. Neither were they drugged with hashish so that they would obediently do what they were told. The compensation of a glorious awakening in Paradise was more than enough to inspire them.

It is little surprise that Western writers did not fully comprehend the motivations of the *fida'is* when even Islamic writers refused to recognize the sincerity of their dedication. A fourteenth century traveller, Ibn Battuta, could write that: 'if the Sultan wishes to send [an Assassin] to kill an enemy, he pays them for the price of his blood. If the murderer escapes after performing his task, then the money is his, if he is caught the children get it. They use poisoned knives to strike down their enemies'.[39] Thus, the devotees are reduced to the ranks of murderous mercenaries, seeking only monetary reward for their actions. That the Nizaris were paid for their help on occasion is probable, but it was neither the only nor the main motivation for the devotees' acts of assassination, which few of them survived or even hoped to survive, and were in their eyes acts of martyrdom.

There were then a large volume of legends around the Nizaris from the outset, some inspired by the 'black legend' that surrounded the Isma'ilis, sinister and strange tales penned by orthodox Sunni writers who had no time for their particular brand of Islam. The stories have a basis in fact in some respects but were wildly exaggerated. Nevertheless, this distortion of reality did indeed cloud the truth for centuries. It is only in fairly recent times that it has been possible to reconstruct the true history of the Nizaris. When the mythological overlay is removed, what remains is still a remarkable story. That the Nizaris were an amazing phenomenon was clear enough; but in truth their history is every bit as fascinating as their legend.

EPILOGUE

The Twilight Years

The capture of Alamut by the Mongols effectively ended the period when the Nizaris possessed an independent state of their own in the Middle East. It would however be incorrect to assume that this was the end of the Nizari movement completely. Contemporary Western chroniclers rarely refer to the sect in the present tense after the loss of Alamut but in fact it survived, although it was certainly a less influential force than it had been in its heyday. Nor were they alone in this flawed interpretation of events; Juwayni's writings strongly imply that the end of Alamut equated to the end of the Nizaris. But not only did they outlive the Mongol onslaught; the movement lived on into modern times. Nizari communities are still present in the world right up until the present day. Some Western histories end their accounts of the 'Assassins' with the fall of Alamut or merely gloss over the subsequent history of the movement with the briefest of reviews. But this does not do the movement justice; they were an independent entity in their own right and they survived beyond the Mongol invasions. A detailed history is far beyond the scope of this book but something, however brief, needs to be said of their later history.[1]

Much of the story of the Nizaris was a mystery to the West after the mass destruction perpetrated by the Mongols in the Middle East; indeed, it was little better understood before this event. The reasons for this are not hard to find. Not long after the Nizaris lost their heartlands, the Crusaders themselves were ejected from Outremer, and so most of the reason that the West had to show any interest in the movement was lost. To some Western commentators, the history of the Nizaris ends definitively with the Mongol invasions. Marco Polo categorically states that 'from that time to this there have been no more of these Sheikhs and no more Assassins; but with him came an end to all the power that had been wielded of old by the Sheikhs of the Mountain and all the evil they had done'.[2] But although the assassinations may have come to an end, the movement as a whole did not.

The Nizaris – understandably cautious in their bid for survival – reverted to the ways of *taqiyya*. Their subsequent concealment therefore hid them from the consciousness of even much of the Islamic world as a result. But more recent studies have clarified some at least of the subsequent tale of the movement. So that the Nizaris may be kept in some form of perspective, a short review of what happened to them after their ejection from Alamut would be an appropriate conclusion to their history.

In this respect, the works of the twentieth century Russian historian, Ivanow, are especially helpful. He is a seminal figure in any historical analysis of the sect because he devoted much of his life's work to developing an understanding of the Nizaris, a process that was considerably helped by the fact that he spend most of his life in the East.[3] Ivanow sub-divided the later years of the movement into three categories; they inevitably oversimplify the situation in the interests of convenience but they are a good enough starting point nevertheless.

The first of these periods covers a timescale of approximately two centuries. It is a period characterized by a great deal of obscurity concerning the Nizaris, an inevitable consequence of the fact that members of the movement felt that they had to go into hiding to survive. The second also lasted for approximately two centuries, and was a period when there was something of a revival in the fortunes of the movement. This was epitomized both by a renaissance in Nizari literature and an upsurge in the *da'wa* activities of Nizari missionaries. This period was named the Anjudan revival, after the village in Persia which was the epicentre of the resurgent movement. A feature of the Anjudan revival was the renewed drive to restore centralized co-ordination and control of the Nizaris. The final period brings us into the modern epoch. This was a time when the Agha Khans, the leaders of the movement in recent times, attempted to strengthen their status as head of the Nizaris as well as improving the lot of their followers.

Their later history is further complicated by the fact that a number of Nizari groups lived on in discrete geographical areas, often as autonomous entities to all intents and purposes. There are therefore in effect several subsequent histories of the movement, each relating to a specific geographical region, and only the briefest of overviews is possible here, merely enough to give a general impression of their later years. The Nizaris continued in both their traditional centres of power, that is to say in Persia and Syria. But they also established themselves in the region of the Oxus valley, far to the east into India. Indeed, some of their most significant later developments were to take place here.

The loss of Alamut and the other fortresses in Persia to the Nizaris must have been a devastating blow to members of the movement, particularly when it was followed so closely by the murder of Rukn al-Din shortly afterwards. But the Imam had left a successor, a young son by the name of Shams al-Din. The survival of this heir was of immense significance to the Nizaris, as the Imamate was essentially a hereditary institution, and any interruption to this sacred bloodline would have created significant doctrinal difficulties.

Shams al-Din was therefore spirited away by loyal supporters before he could fall into the hands of the Mongols. He was taken to Azerbaijan, where he was hidden. He effectively lived his life in the shadows, adopting the clandestine pretence that he was a tradesman. This ushered in an extended period of *taqiyya* for the sect as a whole. As a result, this period of their history is obscure in the extreme. However, the challenges facing the Nizaris did not present insuperable obstacles; they had been through difficult times before and survived. For them, the survival of the Imamate – albeit effectively in a hidden form – was the primary requisite. As long as their Imam lived, then so too did hope.

In fact, although the Mongols had indulged in acts which bordered on genocide, the Nizaris had not been destroyed quite as thoroughly as they might have wished, even in Persia where Mongol domination had for a time been more or less total. Small enclaves of Nizaris lived on, particularly in Rudbar and Quhistan. Partly due to their dispersal throughout Persia, and also because of their partial assimilation into mainstream Sunni Islam during the decades pre-dating the loss of their key fortresses in the country, the Mongols did not succeed in destroying the movement with the totality that they desired. And although they did not ever again recreate the sense of unity and common purpose that they had achieved before the Mongol invasions, the Nizaris were still on occasion more than capable of making a nuisance of themselves. But inevitably, given the loss of a controlling influence in the form of the Imam, and the destruction of the Alamut infrastructure, the movement became ever more localized and peripheral.

In or around 1276, they launched a raid with the help of the Khwarazmians (themselves largely a spent power in the region by this stage). Perhaps the Mongols were caught off guard; they had certainly spent some time in strengthening the captured Nizari castles in Persia after they had captured them but these actions did not seem to particularly help them. The Nizaris and their allies attacked Alamut itself and, perhaps surprisingly, succeeded in taking it once more. The gain proved to be short-term; within a year the Mongols had sent a force to recapture the castle, a venture that they were duly successful in. But the very fact that it had fallen in the first place suggests that the Nizaris were not quite as weak following the Mongol invasion as has sometimes been assumed.

To keep this event in some kind of perspective, it should be stressed that this outstanding achievement on the part of the Nizaris did not herald in a momentous new dawn. There would no great Nizari revival following the recapture of Alamut, no Messianic period of reconquest. Shams al-Din would live a long life (he eventually died in Azerbaijan in 1310, or thereabouts) but he would never be able to live it in the open. His existence was spent in obscurity, as he was never strong enough to reveal himself openly to the world at large.

What we do know however is that at some time in this shadowy period in Nizari history, the movement would suffer from a succession dispute. Reliving the precedent set by the earlier Isma'ili experience when the Imam had effectively gone into hiding, the identity of the true Imam once again became a source of dispute within the movement. It appears that these difficulties occurred shortly after the death of Shams al-Din. His eldest son, Mu'min Shah, and his youngest, Qasim Shah, both claimed to be his successor.[4] The dispute would not effectively end until the eighteenth century, when the line of the former died out, leaving the supporters of Qasim Shah as the victorious party in this particular argument. The fact that such a disagreement could happen, and that its effects were so long lasting would not have been a surprise to earlier Isma'ilis who had witnessed such schisms.

Generally speaking, this obscure period in Nizari history passes virtually unnoticed in most Islamic chronicles of the time. It was as if contemporary historians genuinely believed that the movement had perished with the Mongol invasion. The effect was most marked in Syria. At one time, the Nizaris had been very well known, thanks to the personality of Sinan and the prominence of the Assassin legends which flowed forth from the region. But after their assimilation by Baibars, the Nizaris virtually disappeared in accounts of the area's subsequent history. There are occasional references, such as mention of their continued existence in Ottoman territories during the later Middle Ages, but these refer to the Nizaris in a way that suggests that their existence was a very low-key one. This hints that the earlier flames of passion that characterized the movement had long been extinguished. The use of assassination as a political tool – the method that did so much to create the Assassin legend – was, it seems, completely abandoned. Not until the first part of the nineteenth century would the Nizaris be rediscovered in Syria, and then they would be unrecognizable from the Assassins of old.

In Persia itself there would be subtle changes in the temperament of the country beginning during the thirteenth century that would enable at least a partial restoration of Nizari fortunes. This had always been one of the more dissident areas of the Islamic world, with its long history of connections with a number of dissentient movements. It was of course the traditional heartland of the Nizaris but it had in addition been home to various other Shiite movements. Dissatisfaction with the status quo festered in the country. There was much social unrest, increasingly manifesting itself via Mahdist tendencies. In this climate, the country moved inexorably toward the Shiite branch of Islam. And this environment fostered the conditions which enabled the Nizaris to make at least a partial comeback. They had long been associated with radicalism and social unrest, and were a natural beneficiary of the trends that were present then in Persia.

The Anjudan revival, the second period in post-Alamut Nizari history according to Ivanow, probably started in the latter part of the fifteenth century. It is believed that the first Imam to be closely connected to the Nizaris during this period of their history was Mustansir bi'llah II, who came from the Qasim Shahi branch of the Nizaris. The village of Anjudan was situated in central Persia, close to the base of a low but rocky range of hills. It is important to keep the revival in perspective, as well as the importance of the village. In modern times, it has generally had a population in the region of 1,000 people and, although what evidence we have suggests it was much larger in the Medieval period, it was never a major conurbation. The mausoleum of Mustansir, who died in 1480, still stands as evidence that he was regarded as an important man, albeit very much in a localized sense.

The major feature of this period was that the Nizaris once more felt enough to re-engage in *da'wa* activity. They were not yet so confident that they could abandon the policy of *taqiyya* and so on the surface most of the movement's members maintained an outwardly orthodox Islamic appearance. But the Anjudan revival did not miraculously materialize as if from thin air. Conditions in Persia had been congenial to such an event for several centuries, and this particular resurgence came merely as the final impetus to a generally favourable trend towards such an event that had been in existence for some time.

Not only did the growth of Shiism in the country help but a breakdown in centralization also benefited the Nizaris.[5] A loss of overall central direction in Persia gave movements like theirs the opportunity to assert a degree of autonomy once more. The choice of Anjudan as the centre for the Nizaris was, it seems, not entirely a coincidental one. The village was central to Persia, well away from the main centres of Sunni orthodoxy in the region. It was also close to cities which were traditionally in the Shiite sphere of influence.

The *da'wa* launched at this time had a twofold aim. It first of all aimed its efforts at re-asserting the position of the Nizaris in areas that had traditionally formed part of their heartlands. But it soon became something far more ambitious than this. Attempts were made to assert the hegemony of the leadership over areas further afield, such as the Nizari communities in central Asia and India that by now existed. Inevitably, these areas had become virtually autonomous in the period following the Mongol invasions when the centralized control of the movement from Alamut had been lost.

It may safely be assumed that the local leaders who had stepped into the vacuum created by this meltdown did not give up their positions of influence easily. The *daʿis* despatched by the Imams based in Anjudan must have had to manipulate their way into positions of influence in a subtle and politically adept way. A number of such *daʿis* were sent. Mustansir II despatched some, for example to Afghanistan, but he was always careful to keep them on a fairly tight rein and it appears that they were summoned back to Anjudan to report on progress on a fairly regular basis.

More practical measures had to be taken too. The loss of so much territory and influence after the Mongol period inevitably showed itself in the loss of many of the dues traditionally collected by the Nizaris. Finances were therefore stretched, and it appears that Mustansir II also spent a good deal of energy in regaining some of the dues that had been lost to the Nizaris. He could only do this by emphasizing anew the importance of the position of the Imam to affiliates of the movement; and a number of sermons were written down, which exhorted the faithful always to bear in mind how crucial a figure the Imam was. Some versions of these sermons eventually arrived in India.

The revival also manifested itself in other ways. The Nizaris do not own an extensive literary heritage. The work of one writer, Khayrkhwah, nevertheless gives valuable historical evidence that demonstrates how these moves towards renewed centralization had achieved at least partial success in areas such as Afghanistan as well as India. He relates that he travelled himself to Anjudan and while there he noted with interest how carefully the Imam checked that all the dues owed to him had been sent. But he also hints at other pressures influencing the direction of the Nizaris; how for example there appeared to be rivalry among some of the more ambitious members of the movement who were upset that Khayrkhwah had been given a position that they themselves felt they merited more.

The adoption of Shiism as the major religion in Persia appears to have increased the optimism of the Nizaris. As a result, they began to abandon *taqiyya*, at least to a partial extent. But this new-found confidence was misplaced. The rulers of Persia had a very clear view of the type of Shiism that they wished to see adopted, in which more extreme and radical branches (such as the Nizaris) most definitely did not feature. The ruling caste in fact began to persecute such unconventional elements quite ruthlessly.

Among their victims were the Nizaris. One Imam in particular, Murad, aroused the enmity of the ruling caste. Murad had developed quite a wide following (records show that his supporters in India for example sent him a large amount of money). Alarmed at his influence and the threat that it seemed to pose, the Shiite Shah, Tahmasp, sent a large force to Anjudan to suppress the movement there in 1573. This army attacked Anjudan with vigour, ruthlessly suppressing the Nizaris that they found there. But the real objective of their foray was absent; Murad was elsewhere.

However, he did not escape the clutches of the Persian army for long. He was captured soon after and imprisoned. But the old Nizari talent for influencing key people in positions of authority was clearly not dead. One of Murad's jailers fell under his influence and connived in his escape. The Shiite authorities reacted too late to recapture him. In a remarkably smooth operation that says much for the organization of the Nizaris, Murad was passed from one Nizari town to another. He eventually arrived at Qandahar in Afghanistan. Even there however he was not safe. He was captured by some of the Shah's guards who were patrolling in the region (which was still part of the Persian Empire). This time there would be no dramatic escape bid and he was executed soon after.

But old habits died hard within the Islamic world. Persia and the surrounding area had always been riven by internal dynastic disputes. The Shiite dynasty that had assumed power in Persia soon began to unravel as one family member argued with another (at one stage in the reign of Ismail II (1576-77) Sunnism was reintroduced as the state religion, though this had little permanent effect). This internal dissension arrived at an ideal time for the Nizaris, who won a reprieve from persecution as a result. Anjudan once more became the centre of the movement, though on this occasion the Nizari Imams were noticeably careful to keep a low profile politically so that they did not unnecessarily antagonize their neighbours again.

Before long, this policy was so successful that the Nizaris were granted exemption from various taxes (an edict to this effect dates from 1627). There was a hint that a time-honoured Nizari trick had once more been adopted; the exemption implies that the sect were regarded as 'Twelver' Shiites (this being the official state religion at the time) suggesting that they had again adopted a policy of *taqiyya* in the interests of survival. By the end of the seventeenth century, the Anjudan revival was well established.

It was not only in Persia that important developments were taking place. In India and the surrounding regions the influence of the Nizaris was also having an effect. The origins of the movement in the area are very obscure. However, we do know that by the early years of the fourteenth century a Nizari called Shams al-Din played an important role in the country. But he was by no means the first prominent Nizari in the country. He was the twentieth local leader of the Indian Nizaris (such men were given the title of 'pir' in India). He and his successors began to attract a following of their own, and seem to have enjoyed from fairly early on a degree of local autonomy. The community that he set up still survives to this day in the Punjab (they acknowledge the Agha Khan as their spiritual leader). In the ongoing process of conversion that took place, a number of Hindus opted to become Nizaris. For a time they paid at least nominal allegiance to the Imam in Persia and dues were sent to him.

At the start of the sixteenth century, there was yet another schism, this time affecting the movement in India. A man named Imam Shah had tried without success to take over a branch of the Nizaris in Sind known as the Khojas. Frustrated in this design, he took himself off to Gujarat. Here he proved himself to be an orator of some merit. A large number of Hindus were converted to Nizari Isma'ilism through his efforts, including the Sultan of the region if legend is to be believed (legend also claims that the Sultan married his daughter to Imam Shah's son).

On Imam Shah's death his baton was taken up by this son, who was called Nar Muhammad. Clearly, his father's preaching had created something of a personalized following, for when Nar Muhammad declared that the dues previously despatched to Anjudan should no longer be sent but should be kept by him, most Nizaris supported him in his stance. His views were not approved by all of the Nizari community in Gujarat however, a number of whom objected. The movement in the region therefore effectively divided between those who supported Nar Muhammad and those who did not. Soon after, those that sided with him refuted their links with Nizari Isma'ilism completely.

The schismatic effect of these developments in India typified much of the later Nizari period. A number of different Nizari communities sprang up in parts of western and central Asia as well as the Indian sub-continent. To any but the expert and informed eye such divisions are bewilderingly difficult to understand. Detailed expositions of them certainly lie far beyond the scope of books such as this. But the key point of note is that the

Nizaris did not stay static. As indeed they had done from their very beginnings, the movement evolved, swaying first this way and then the other in an attempt to retain a precarious balance in the delicate political equilibrium of the regions where they were based. To this extent at least, later Nizari developments very much mirror those of the early days of the movement.

In modern times, during the third period identified by Ivanow, the Imamate of the Nizaris has latterly been occupied by the Agha Khans. The first of these was the son of an Imam named Shah Khalil Allah III who was murdered in a brawl in Persia in 1817. The violence directed at him resulted from the resentment at the growing influence of the Nizaris on the part of some 'Twelver' Shiites. Khalil Allah III was replaced by his son, who became Agha Khan I (the honorific title subsequently became hereditary and has been passed on down the generations ever since. The title was bestowed on Agha Khan I by the then shah of Persia).

Agha Khan I initially proved a great ally to the ruling Persian dynasty in Teheran, putting down a rebellion in one of the Persian regions. But he waited fruitlessly for subsequent gratitude for his support from Teheran. It is possible that the authorities were envious of his popularity, as a number of Nizari recruits were attracted to the cause during this period. Whatever the motivation, in 1837 – just two years after he had successfully put down the revolt – he was dismissed from the positions that had been given to him by the authorities in Tehran and recalled.

However, he refused to meekly accept this rebuff and instead installed himself in one of the strong fortresses he had captured during his recent campaign in the city of Bam. The siege that followed probably in reality only ever had one likely ending, as the Persian forces arraigned against Agha Khan I vastly outgunned those at his disposal. Nevertheless, it was fourteen months before he was forced to capitulate. He was taken as a prisoner to Teheran but, surprisingly perhaps, he was not executed.

After eight months of imprisonment he was set free on condition that he went into internal exile at his home and involved himself in politics no longer. Rumours soon began to circulate that, far from being prepared to meekly live out his days in docile domesticity, and he was instead assembling a force with which to resume his resistance to the ruling Persian dynasty. Agha Khan I prevaricated when challenged on the point, and requested permission to travel to Mecca on the annual pilgrimage, the *hajj*. Permission was granted but, when he set out, he made his way instead towards the city of Yazd in central Persia.

The Persian authorities were now completely convinced that he was up to no good and forces were despatched to intercept him. However, Agha Khan I had rather the better of several skirmishes that took place. He eventually arrived at Shahr-i Babak in the south of Persia where he assisted in the successful attempts of the local populace to evict some unpopular Afghans who had taken possession of the citadel there. He continued to evade efforts to put an end to his intransigence for some time, significantly helped by the use of several British cannon that had somehow come into his possession. However, all his efforts would eventually prove futile. Once more, the huge material superiority of the Nizaris' opponents would intervene. After trying to outmanoeuvre a vast army sent against him, he was finally trapped at Rigan to the east. The battle that followed was a grotesque mismatch, its outcome a bloody inevitability. His small force was smashed to pieces.

Agha Khan I survived the battle but it was the end of his career in Persia. Only death awaited if he remained in the country; he therefore opted for flight. Arabia or India were the two most likely options for him but as the first meant travelling across the breadth of Persia, he headed east instead. As he left the country, he would not have been aware that he would be the last Nizari Imam to be based in Persia. He arrived first of all in Afghanistan in 1841. Here, the flair for flexibility that had always been the hallmark of the sect reasserted itself once more. There was a potential ally currently involved in a war in Afghanistan. The British were involved in a fierce and bitter colonial fray in the country. Six hundred years after the delegation of the so-called 'Assassins' had sought help from France and England against the Mongol invasion of central Asia, the Nizaris were about to be involved in an alliance with the West.

Agha Khan I subsequently reached an understanding with the British. He proved a loyal ally, helping them in the retreat from Qandahar in 1842, and in subsequent campaigns in Sind. From there, he moved on to Bombay to see for himself the state of the Nizari communities in India. The Nizaris in India had been loyal supporters of the movement for some time. They had even been noticed by a Frenchman, Rousseau, who had journeyed to Persia in 1811 and noted that: 'there are Isma'ilis as far away as India, and they can be seen regularly coming to Kehk from the banks of the Ganges and the Indus, to receive the blessings of their Imam'.[6]

Even here he was not immune from the attentions of the Persian authorities. They sought his extradition but the British refused to comply, instead offering to move Agha Khan I to Calcutta where he would be too far away to exercise any direct influence over Persian affairs. He moved there in 1848, but he never lost the desire to return to Persia, even though the many Indian Nizaris welcomed his arrival in the country. He tried unsuccessfully to win the affection of the new Persian shah, Nasir al-Din, by sending him a succession of presents. He clearly believed that the Shah had a deep interest in zoological matters, as an elephant and a giraffe sent in 1852 were followed 16 years later by three more elephants and a rhinoceros.

His attempts to rebuild bridges with Persia did not result in his return to the land of his birth, the land for which he clearly held a special affection. He was the first Imam to set foot in India but, deprived of the opportunity to return to Persia, he re-established the Nizari imamate here and effectively ushered in the modern era of the movement. He would become a respected and honoured member of the community, eventually being titled 'His Highness' by the British and being visited by the Prince of Wales (later to be King Edward VII) when he visited India.

We also have the benefit of much more detail about his domestic affairs than we have of the earlier Assassin era imams. Therefore, we know that Agha Khan I had seven wives. We also know that he maintained a superb stables at his home in Bombay (where he returned, remaining in Calcutta for a short period only), and that he was a regular and enthusiastic spectator and owner at the Bombay racecourse. He thus established an interest in horseracing for which the Agha Khans remain famous to this day. He lived a long, eventful and ultimately successful and fulfilled life (though his failure to return to Persia was presumably always something that gave him a great sense of personal loss). When he died in 1881, he was succeeded by his son, who was declared Agha Khan II. He showed himself to be an enthusiastic patron of charitable causes for the benefit of Muslims in India but his reign was to be tragically brief. After a hunting expedition in 1885, he contracted pneumonia and died shortly afterwards.

His successor, Agha Khan III, was Imam for some seventy-two years. He was only a child when he inherited the position and it was some years before he actively took up the reins of power. When he came of age, he visited Europe (where he would eventually settle), being fêted by Queen Victoria at Windsor Castle and becoming a good friend of the Prince of Wales. When the latter became King Edward VII, Agha Khan III was invited to his coronation, being honoured in the honours list that was announced to celebrate the occasion. Subsequently, he was a staunch supporter of the British in the First World War. In 1917, in an interesting example of historical role reversal, an unsuccessful attempt was made on his life by German agents. When the Second World War broke out he again urged his followers to support the British. But during his long reign, he also devoted much of his time to bettering the lot of his followers, especially in India. Only once though did he return to his ancestral homeland, visiting Persia in 1951, where he received a rapturous reception from members of the Nizari community there.

With some of the dues that were paid to him, Agha Khan III set up charitable funds and trading organisations to support Nizaris all over the world (among the beneficiaries of these were the significant Nizari community that had grown up in East Africa). But these secular acts should not detract from the fact that the Imam was still a spiritual leader. He adopted policies that accentuated the differences between the 'Twelver' Shiites and the Nizaris, and emphasized the *batini* meanings of the Koran to his followers, re-asserting an age-old tradition of the movement that may have been somewhat lost during the centuries when the Nizaris had been forced to practice *taqiyya*. This sometimes manifested itself in ways which, to the West, might appear surprisingly progressive. He was delighted for example to find that when he visited Persia many of the movement's female members had abandoned the veil which characterized much of the Muslim world.

After a reign of 72 years, Agha Khan III died in Switzerland in 1957. In perfect keeping with the romanticism that attends the movement (or at least its 'Assassin' ancestors), he was buried in a tomb erected in a place of stunning beauty at Aswan in Egypt. He rests on the edge of the Egyptian desert on the western bank of the Nile, the ancient Egyptian land of the dead, on a hill which looks down serenely on the slowly-flowing waters of the Nile below. His place was not taken by his eldest son but by a grandson, Karim, who became Agha Khan IV. He continued with the policies of his grandfather which sought to look after the interests of the Isma'ili community and modernize the movement. He also shows a keen interest in promoting a wider understanding of Islam and set up the Institute of Isma'ili Studies in London in 1977.

The Nizaris now have several million adherents spread around the globe. As well as their traditional communities in Persia, Syria, India, Pakistan, Afghanistan and other regions of Central Asia, numbers of them are to be found in East Africa. The modern trend towards more global mobility means that there are a number of Nizaris further afield in Europe (for example, there is a large community in London) and also in North America. While retaining much of their culture and traditions (although some communities have become 'Twelver' Shiites), they have also managed to assimilate themselves into contemporary civilization worldwide.

The wealth of knowledge that we have of the recent Agha Khans should not blind us to the fact that the post-Alamut history of the Nizaris is often obscure. During this period, many of the localized Nizari communities developed a significant degree of autonomy and centralized control, at times became very eroded indeed. But by any standard it is remarkable that a movement whose members once struck terror into the emperors and kings of the West, largely through the legends that obstinately held sway over the Western psyche, should in modern times be led by men who would mingle with the rulers of Western Europe as equals. In this perhaps lies, for now, the movement's final epitaph, a wonderfully apt example of the Nizaris' ability to adapt and survive. The old ways, the ways of assassination and seclusion in remote and impregnable mountain fastnesses, have been abandoned. They are gone of necessity, their usefulness exhausted. New ways have been developed which rely far more on accommodation, methods which have successfully ensured the survival of the movement into the modern world.

But although the post-Alamut period is generally an obscure one, even in the nineteenth century something remained of the memory of where the Nizaris had originated from. One final story of the Nizaris should be told, partly for its curiosity value but also because it serves as a reminder that even in times far removed from our own a vestige of the truth about the Nizaris was available for any who chose to look for it.

It came in a remarkable court case played out in the humid interior of a courtroom in Bombay in 1866. The precursor of the case was a violent, bloody and murderous dispute concerning members of a group known as the Khojas, part of the Nizari movement that then found itself under the jurisdiction of the British Raj. In 1850, in India, four men were attacked and killed in broad daylight. Nineteen men were tried for their part in the act, four of whom were subsequently hanged. The origins of this event went back to 1827, when some of the Khojas had opted to stop paying dues to the Agha Khan, who was then still in Persia. The Agha Khan sent a delegation to the region to bring the dissidents back into line and most in fact did so. But some persisted in their refusal, and obstinately refused to change their stance. The passions that this refusal generated ultimately revealed themselves in the outbreak of violence in 1850.

When the Agha Khan was forced to flee Persia to India, he had sought to assert his rights over all of the Khoja community once more. However, some of the Khojas who opposed him decided to appeal to the British legal system to uphold their right to exist free of his overlordship. They argued that the community had no connection to the Agha Khan and were therefore free to exist independently of his control. The court case that followed became something of a *cause célèbre* in Bombay. Most of the leading lawyers in the city took part in the debate that followed. A range of witnesses were called, including the Agha Khan himself. Barely a stone was left unturned as the court considered the history of the Khojas, their traditions and their origins. The case went on for 25 days before Chief Justice Sir Joseph Arnould announced his findings.

These findings proved, in part, surprisingly accurate. The community, said the Chief Justice, were part of the wider Khoja community in India. They were a group who were 'Hindu in origin, who had converted to and had throughout abided in the faith of the Shia Imamee Isma'ilis; which has been and is bound by ties of spiritual allegiance to the hereditary Imams of the Isma'ilis'. The right of the Agha Khan to claim spiritual authority over the community was therefore upheld. Thus, in a British court, the antecedents of the Agha Khan, and his relationship with the hereditary Imams of Alamut, were proved. In a strange end to a strange story, the Victorian legal system held that there was a proven link between the contemporary Nizari community in India and their so-called 'Assassin' forefathers. As a postscript to the curious history of the Nizaris and their relationship to the West, nothing could be more bizarre. But it is a fittingly unusual conclusion to a fascinating and unique story.

Notes

Prologue

1 See de Joinville, 280.
2 From Brocardus in *Directorium ad passegium faciendum* in *Documents armeniens*, ii, Paris, 1906, 496–7.
3 *Memoirs of an Arab-Syrian Gentleman*, 154.
4 See Daftary: *The Assassin Legends*, 3–4.
5 Ibid.
6 Although the Isma'ilis – the part of Shiite Islam from which the Nizaris originated – wrote extensive theological works, they were generally less prolific in writing accounts of their history. The Nizaris themselves were even less productive in this sense than other Shiite Muslims judging by the volume of records that have survived.
7 For biographical details of the three, see Daftary: *The Isma'ilis – Their history and doctrines*, 327–330.
8 See Hodgson, 156.
9 Daftary: *The Isma'ilis – Their history and doctrines*, 328. However, although he was definitely anti-Isma'ili, historians are not unanimous on their views as to how pro-Mongol he was. J.A. Boyle (Section III in the 'Translator's Introduction' to his translation of Juwayni) argues that as a Sunni he was horrified by the Mongols' excesses towards his own people and that this can on occasion be discerned in his writing, although other historians are not in universal agreement with this interpretation.
10 Juwayni, 725.
11 Mirza, 16.
12 *A History of the Crusades*, volume 2, 323.
13 Daftary: *The Assassin Legends*, 94.

Notes

Chapter One

1 For further references to the events discussed in this chapter see Saunders, chapters 1–5 and *The Cambridge Illustrated History of the Middle Ages*, Volume 1, Chapter 5. See also Daftary: *The Ismaïlis – Their history and doctrines*, Chapter 2 and *A short history of the Ismaïlis*, Chapter 2.

2 The story is to be found in the Bible, in Genesis Chapter 21.

3 This statement is known as the '*shahada*' or 'statement of witness'.

4 'Islam' became the word used generically to describe the Muslim world. It means literally 'submission (to God)'.

5 The name caliph was first given to Abu Bakr when he succeeded Muhammad. He was given the title '*Khalifat rasul Allah*', which means 'successor to the messenger of God'.

6 Muhammad regularized an already-existing system of polygamy by allowing no more than four wives to a man as a maximum.

7 Anti-Shiite propagandists claimed that this was because of his reputation for drunkenness, while others claimed that his father refused to accept his extreme views. See for example Juwayni, 642–3.

8 In the interests of simplicity, the above is a highly summarised account of the fragmentation that occurred within early Shiism. In the event, a complex network of sub-groups with a variety of views evolved. For further detail, see for example Daftary: *A short history of the Ismaïlis*, 26–36.

Chapter Two

1 Further reference to the following events may be found in Saunders, Chapters 6–10 and *The Cambridge Illustrated History of the Middle Ages*, Volume 1, Chapter 6 and Volume 2, Chapter 4. Refer also to Daftary, *The Ismaïlis – their history and doctrines*, Chapters 3–4 and *A Short History of the Ismaïlis*, Chapters 2 and 3.

2 It would be the presence of these tribesmen alone which would lead to the long-lived nature of the Abbasid dynasty. However, by the tenth century their power was effectively broken, and from that time on they were little more than puppets in the hands of stronger powers.

3 Sunnism developed gradually, as indeed did Shiism. By the middle of the eighth century, however, sharp theological distinctions could already be drawn between these two very different strands of Islam. The term Sunni is derived from the 'people of the Sunna', Sunna being translatable as 'the actions and sayings of the Prophet'. See Daftary, *The Assassin Legends*, 9.

4 References from article on 'Islam' in *Britannica Macropaedia*, 15th edition. It is interesting to note, when considering this concept of the infallibility of the majority that Juwayni, when rejecting the teachings of Hasan-i Sabbah, says that 'it is clear that he has done nothing towards refuting the belief of the majority'. See Juwayni, 672.

5 See page 168, below.

6 Daftary notes that although the concept of the '*batin*' was known to earlier Shiites, it was to find its most developed expression under the aegis of the Isma'ilis; see *A short history of the Isma'ilis*, 51.

7 For a detailed examination of the surviving records relating to the Isma'ilis, see *A short history of the Isma'ilis*, Chapter 1.

8 In the works of an anonymous writer of around 850 there is an account of a voyage to the Far East in which it is popularly supposed lie the origins of the famous tales of Sinbad the Sailor.

9 Interestingly, the first surviving written reference which refutes the claims of the Isma'ilis is from a 'Twelver' Shiite rather than a Sunni source. It was written by al-Fadl ibn Shadha, a 'Twelver' Shiite who died in 873. See Daftary, *The Assassin Legends*, 18.

10 See Saunders, 132.

11 The name developed because the Imams of the dynasty claimed their descent from Muhammad through his daughter, Fatima, who was both cousin and wife to Ali, the fourth caliph after the death of Muhammad. She was revered by her adherents, who claimed of her that she was 'the incarnation of everything divine in the nature of women'.

12 See for example Daftary, *The Isma'ilis – Their history and doctrines*, 164–5.

13 The Zoroastrians were members of an ancient Persian religion, which survives into modern times, who were renowned as fire-worshippers.

14 Lewis, *The Assassins*, 29.

15 With characteristic forthrightness, Juwayni describes him as being 'as light-headed and insane as his father had been mild and gentle; his tyranny and cruelty towards the people of Egypt was boundless'. Juwayni, 654.

16 It is important to note that, on the subject of the Crucifixion, Muslims and Christians held very different views. To the Muslims, the story of the Crucifixion was pure invention. A substitute had been crucified in place of Christ. On the Day of Judgement, Christ would return to earth and punish those who had led evil lives.

17 See Venture, quoted in de Sacy's 'Memoir' of 1818; translated in *The Assassin Legends*, 173–4. The Druze survive into modern times, being particularly prominent in Lebanon.

Chapter Three

1 What is known of his upbringing comes primarily from a fragment of his biography that survived down the centuries, through the periods of deliberate suppression and destruction of so many documents connected with the Isma'ilis. This is found in a work called '*Sargudhasht-i Sayyidna*', saved by the Persian Juwayni from the flames that consumed the great fortress of Alamut when it was obliterated by the Mongols in 1256. The original manuscript does not survive but it appears to have been much used by Juwayni, Rashid al-Din and Kashani. See Lewis, *The Assassins*, 146–7. Juwaini refers directly to the fact that he used this manuscript (666).

2 Juwayni, 667.

3 For the story of Hasan-i Sabbah and Nizam al-Mulk in their youth, see the article by E.G. Browne in the *Journal of the Royal Asiatic Society* (1899), 409–16.

4 For Hasan's journey to Egypt and the time spent there, see Juwayni, 668–9.

5 From *The Valleys of the Assassins* by Freya Stark, (a 20th Century traveller to Persia who wrote an account of her journey) London, 1934, 216.

6 Juwayni, 719.

7 Juwayni, 670.

8 The fertile landscape that he created may have helped to inspire Marco Polo's later legends of a paradise-like garden; see Chapter 12, below.

9 Juwayni; 673–4.

10 Juwayni; 674–5; quoting an Isma'ili account of the victory.

11 Nizam al-Mulk, *The Book of Government*, translated H. Darke, London, 1978.

12 Rashid al-Din, 110.

13 The timing of Nizam al-Mulk's death was especially unfortunate, as according to Juwayni (678) it was followed only forty days later by the death of Malikshah. The death of two men who were so important in the Seldjuk hierarchy in such a short space of time can have done nothing to enhance stability in the region.

14 See page 15, above. Daftary – *A Short History of the Isma'ilis*, 129 – identifies several earlier Islamic groups who had employed similar tactics.

15 Hodgson, 83.

16 See Chapter 12, below.

Chapter Four

1 See Daftary, *The Isma'ilis – their history and doctrines*, 350.

2 Interestingly enough, there was a claim – which was to gain credence – that some years later when an earthquake struck the region, a spring was to gush forth from the ground at the spot where the dry well had been dug. See Juwayni, 679.

3 It is suggestive that these tales relate to an event which took place when Hasan-i Sabbah's sect was very young, that is in 1093. The image of the Assassin 'bogeymen' haunting the nightmares of their enemies was in fact not a new one; Isma'ilis were already known for their radical leanings – evidenced for example by the Qarmatis, who had Isma'ili origins – and the terrors created by the movement were not new ones but rather re-statements of old ones.

4 Some unsubstantiated reports claimed that ibn Attash in fact spent his last years at Alamut.

5 Ahmad was to lead a long and successful career in his role as the leader of the Isma'ilis in the area, proving himself a worthy successor to his father, ibn Attash. It was claimed that he alone was responsible for converting 30,000 people to the Isma'ili cause.

6 For sources of this account, see Lewis, *The Assassins*, 151, n23. Lewis notes that the 'main' Persian scholars, that is Juwayni, Rashid al-Din and Kashani paid little attention

to these events, which took place away from the headquarters of the Persian Nizaris at Alamut.

7 Lewis estimates that the date these events took place is either 1096 or 1102; see *The Assassins*, 44.
8 Juwayni, 703–4.
9 Edited from a Persian text by Muhammad Taqi Danishazhuh, *Revue de la Faculté des Lettres*, Université de Tabriz, xvii/3, 1344s., 1964, 329.
10 Ibn al-Athir, anno 494, x, 221/viii, 204, quoted in Lewis, *The Assassins*, 53.
11 Ibn al-Athir, anno 500, x, 299/viii, 242.
12 Ibn al-Qalanisi, 153.
13 Juwayni, 681.

Chapter Five

1 Juwayni also asserted that the custom had survived on into his own times.
2 Juwayni, 681–2.
3 See Rashid al-Din, 133,137 and Kashani, 153, 156.
4 See pages 169–70, below.
5 See Ibn Muyassar, *Annales d'Egypte*, 65–6.
6 See Bernard Lewis, *The Assassins*, 37.
7 Juwayni, 680. The chronicler also attests to the austerity of Hasan by briefly mentioning the fact that Hasan had previously expelled someone from Alamut merely for playing a flute. He allowed no musical instruments in the Alamut Valley.
8 Juwayni, 680.
9 A simple example of such hidden inner meanings was the Isma'ili argument that the story of Noah and his ark should not be taken literally, but was in fact an allegory used to describe the way that Noah kept the *da'wa* (mission) alive when, all around, the world was rejecting its authenticity. For further discussions of Isma'ili beliefs, see for example Mirza, Chapter 5.
10 Juwayni, 671–2.
11 See Chapter 6.
12 Rashid al-Din, 134.
13 Juwayni, 682–3.
14 From the records of the Ecumenical Patriarchate of Constantinople, quoted by Enno Franzius, *A History of the Order of Assassins*, New York (1969), 60.

Chapter Six

1 From the city, Muhammad had been transported to Heaven and granted a vision. Consequently, after Mecca and Medina, Jerusalem was, to Muslims, the most sacred of cities.

2 Ibn al-Qalanasi, 57–8.
3 Defremery in *Journal Asiatique*, 3 (1854).
4 Bohemond laid claim to Antioch when it was taken by the Crusaders, and became its first Crusader Prince.
5 Ibn al-Qalanasi, 74.
6 See for example Mirza, 9–10.
7 Ibn al-Qalanasi, 145–6.
8 Ibid., 147–8.
9 Kamal al-Din, *Zubda*, ii, 235, quoted in Lewis, *The Assassins*, 105.
10 Ibn al-Qabnasi, 179.
11 Ibid., 187–8.
12 Ibid., 191–5.
13 Ibid., 191–5.
14 *Memoirs of an Arab-Syrian Gentleman*, 146.
15 Babcock and Krey, 391.
16 *A History of the Crusades*, Volume 2, 325.
17 Babcock and Krey, 214–15. Some modern historians speculate that the assassination was the result of a border dispute – see Franzius, 106.

Chapter Seven

1 Ibn al-Athir, anno 520, x, 445/viii, 319.
2 Juwayni, 685.
3 Ibid., 685.
4 Juwayni notes that 'the world, they [the Isma'ilis] said, had never been without an Imam and never would be. And if a man was Imam, his father had been before him, and his father's father before him, and so on back to Adam, or, as some say, back to Eternity Past, for they believe in the eternal existence of the world. And in the same way an Imam's son would be Imam and his son's son, and so on until Eternity to come. And it was impossible for an Imam to die until his son who was to be Imam after him had been born or begotten'. Juwayni, 645.
5 This appeared to enjoy a degree of success. A number of converts were won for the Nizari cause. However, this seemingly promising situation was illusory; when Ala-al Din, ruler of the region of Ghur where the Nizaris had established themselves, died, his son, Sayf al-Din Muhammad, soon after had all the Nizari missionaries and their converts in the country put to death.
6 Juwayni, 687.
7 There is a certain vagueness about what this meant in practice. It appeared to put Hasan in the same position as the Fatimid caliphs of old, and equate him personally with the Imam. It was soon widely held by Nizaris that he was indeed the Imam. There has been a good deal of academic debate about whether Hasan was claiming direct physical

descent from the Imam or whether his relationship was more a spiritual one. Over time, Nizari tradition would as a general rule argue that the relationship with the last known Imam, Nizar, was in fact a physical one. See Daftary: *A short history of the Ismailis*, 138–43.

8 From Quhistani, *Haft bab*, translated by W. Iwanow, Bombay (1959), 41. For the story of Hasan's actions, see Juwayni, 688–90.

9 The abandonment of *shar`ia* would have been particularly shocking to more orthodox Muslims. Daftary (*The Ismailis – their history and doctrines*, 389) notes that both Rashid al-Din and Kashani claim that the Nizaris were designated '*mulahida*' or 'heretics' for their actions with regard to the Holy Law.

10 Hodgson, 156.

11 Ibid., 157. For a full analysis of the effect of the *qiyama* see Appendix I to *Order of the Assassins*, entitled 'The popular effect of the *qiyama*'.

12 Daftary, *The Ismailis – their history and doctrines*, 329.

13 Juwayni, 691.

14 See for example Daftary, *The Ismailis – their history and doctrine*, 390. Daftary also notes that the absence of records from a Nizari perspective is particularly emphasised with regards to the *qiyama*. By his actions Hasan became the *qa'im al-qiyama* – 'the lord of the resurrection' – an imam who held especially high status in the Nizari spiritual hierarchy.

15 Juwayni – who was admittedly no friend of Nizaris or the Shiites more generally – was to claim a century later that many Nizaris had left Quhistan and made their way to Khurasan rather than accept this fundamental change in religious teaching. Sadly, again there are few original Nizari sources surviving from this period, and any argument that asserts that the Nizaris were not largely in agreement with Hasan must remain, to an extent, speculative given the bias of the chronicler.

16 See Juwayni, 696. Again, reference to the fact that such severe punishment was enforced for those who refused to accept the new teachings is suggestive that there may have been some opposition to Hasan's pronouncements.

17 Ibid., 697. Juwayni claims that the brother-in-law involved was one of the last surviving Buyids.

18 Lewis, *Kamal al-Din's biography of Rashid al-Din Sinan*, 231–2.

19 Some sources suggest that Sinan was actually sent before Hasan came to power but the majority view inclines to accepting that he received his orders to go to Syria after Hasan's accession. See Daftary, *The Ismailis – their history and doctrines*, 689, n156.

Chapter Eight

1 See page 85, above.

2 One should perhaps treat this figure of seven years with a degree of scepticism. There were certain numbers – such as three, seven and forty – which were deemed to be of

especial mystical significance. The attribution of this seven year period might be one example of this particular characteristic of Nizari Isma'ilism.

3 See for example Lewis, *The Assassins*, 111 and Daftary, *The Ismailis – their history and doctrines*, 396.

4 See Lewis, *Kamal al-Din's biography of Rashid al-Din Sinan*, 230.

5 For a history of the Temple see *The New Knighthood* by Malcolm Barber, Cambridge, 1994. For the Hospitallers see *Hospitallers – The History of the Order of St John* by Jonathan Riley-Smith, London, 1999. A good account of the orders generally can be found in *The Monks of War: The Military Religious Orders*, by D. Seward, 2nd edition, London (1995).

6 Shirkuh was well known to the Nizaris; he had fought against them at Inab and was reputedly personally responsible for killing Raymond of Antioch during the battle.

7 This is the version quoted by Runciman, see *A History of the Crusades*, Volume 2, 410. Runciman quotes Abu Firas, edited Guyard, *Journal Asiatique*, 7th series, Volume ix, 1877.

8 See Lewis, *Kamal al-Din's biography of Rashid al-Din Sinan*, 12–13.

9 For a brief discussion of the reasons why the siege of Masyaf was abandoned, see Mirza, 34–6.

10 Abu Firas was a Syrian Nizari writer, who wrote the only Nizari biography of Sinan. For a detailed bibliography of sources relating to him, see Daftary, *The Ismailis – their history and doctrines*, 689, n154.

11 Lewis, *Kamil al-Din's biography of Rashid al-Din Sinan*, 231–2.

12 There is some debate about the exact date of the Sufat episode. An anonymous chronicle dates it to 1165 but Kamal al-Din dates it far later in 1176–7. The balance of scholarly opinion now tends strongly towards the latter date (see for example, Mirza, 31).

13 It is not clear whether the Nizaris were involved in the battle, though at least one later chronicler – the seventeenth century Patriarch and chronicler, al-Duwayhi – states that they not only formed part of Saladin's army but also that a number of important Frankish prisoners were taken to Nizari castles afterwards. See Mirza, 35 and 118, n49.

14 *Itinerarium regis Ricardi*, edited W. Stubbs, Rolls Series, London, 1864.

15 Richard and Saladin had agreed a truce before the English king's eventual departure from Outremer in 1192. Saladin insisted that this should extend to the territories of the Syrian Nizaris.

16 The accusation was made by a contemporary Muslim historian hostile to Saladin, who also claimed that Saladin wanted to have Richard killed. See *Kitab al-kamil fi'l ta'rikh*, edited C.J. Tornberg, Leiden 1951–76, Volume 12, 51.

17 From *Arab Historians of the Crusades*, 241. The account closely matches that of Imad al-Din, *ibid*. 239.

18 For a full list of sources see Runciman, Volume 3, 65 n1.

19 Babcock and Krey, 391.

20 Mirza for example notes that the inhabitants of Masyaf and Qadmus even today regard Sinan as an Imam, unlike the majority of the Syrian Isma'ilis. Mirza, 39.

Notes

Chapter Nine

1 See Rashid al-Din, 170–3, Kashani, 192–4 and Hodgson, 183.
2 Juwayni, 699.
3 He had already reputedly made approaches both to the Twelver Shiites and the Isma'ilis in an attempt to improve relationships between the two.
4 Juwayni, 704–7.
5 Ibid., 700–1.
6 The circumstantial evidence suggesting that the Nizaris were not responsible for this outrage is that, during the reign of Hasan, the policy of assassination was virtually abandoned by them. There is little logic in believing that Hasan was trying to disturb the stability of the Muslim world at the same time that he was trying to build bridges with it.
7 See Hammer, *History of the Assassins*, translated O.C. Wood (London, 1835), 154–5.
8 See Lewis, *The Assassins*, 82 and Daftary, *The Ismailis – their history and doctrines*, 406. Daftary, while not saying that Hasan himself saw his actions as an example of *taqiyya*, speculates that many of his followers saw them as that.
9 Hodgson, 222–5.

Chapter Ten

1 Juwayni, 705.
2 Ibid., 704–7.
3 For an analysis of al-Tusi's work, see Hodgson, 239–43. Daftary states categorically that 'it is safe to assume that al-Tusi willingly embraced Isma'ilism sometime during his association with the Nizaris'. See *A short history of the Ismailis*, 149.
4 Mohammed en-Nasawi, *Histoire du Sultan Djelal ed-Din Mankobirti*, edited O. Houdas, Paris (1891), 132–4; French translation, Paris (1895), 358–9.
5 Juwayni, 80.
6 For a brief account of these events, see Runciman, Volume 3, 237–54.
7 Mirza believes that the antagonism of the Khwarazmians was a crucial factor in driving the Nizaris and their ally, the caliph in Baghdad, into the arms of the Mongols. See *Syrian Ismailism*, 53.
8 Jerusalem had been recovered by the Crusaders early in the thirteenth century. It was lost by them for the final time to a large Khwarazmian mercenary force in 1244.
9 Minhaj-I Siraj Juzjani, *Tabaqat-I Nasiri*, edited Abdul Hai Habibi, 2nd edition, Kabul (1964), 182–3.
10 They would eventually descend like a whirlwind on the unsuspecting lands of eastern Europe, decimating Christian armies sent to repel them in both Poland and Hungary. They would ultimately stop when they reached the Adriatic coast, dangerously close to the Italian peninsula.

11 From the thirteenth century chronicler Matthew Paris, as quoted in *The Mission of William of Rubruck*, translated by Peter Jackson, London (1990), 15.

12 Juwayni, 707.

13 Hamd Allah, *Ta'rikh-i Guzide*, from E.J.W. Gibb Memorial, xiv, Part 1, Leiden (1910), 526.

14 Juwayni, 711.

15 See Curtin, *The Mongols*, 246.

16 Juwayni, 712–13.

17 Ibid., 716.

18 Ibid., 627.

19 *The Valleys of the Assassins*, London (1934), 200.

20 Juwayni, 636–7.

21 Ibid., 639–40.

22 Ibid., 723–4.

23 William of Rubruck, 222–3.

24 Curtin, ibid.

25 Genghis Khan routinely executed any man who hoped to ingratiate himself with the Mongols by betraying his lord. This was in his view the most cardinal of all sins and those men who committed it could not be trusted.

Chapter Eleven

1 For an account of the Mongols in Syria, see Runciman, Volume 3, 293–314 and for the rise of Baibars 315–48 in the same volume. See also Mirza, Chapters 3–4.

2 Mirza, 41.

3 His reign would be cut tragically short when he fell backwards through an open upper storey window and was killed.

4 In fact, there would – perhaps predictably – be a period of civil war which eventually resulted in the fragmentation of the Empire that Saladin had worked so hard to build.

5 *Chronicon* m. iv, 16, edited Wattenbach, 178–9, quoted in Lewis, *The Assassins*, 4.

6 For further discussion of the so-called 'death leap legends', see Chapter 12.

7 Letter quoted in E.J. King, *The Knights Hospitaller in the Holy Land*, London, 234–5.

8 Later developments of the Nizari legend would say that the sect had sent assassins to France to murder the king when he was still a youth. There is not a scrap of evidence to support this assertion, and no obvious motive why they would want to do so.

9 De Joinville, 277–80.

10 Ibid.

11 Mirza estimates that by now the Nizaris held eight castles in Syria; see *Syrian Ismailism*, 58. These are named by Daftary (*The Ismailis – their history and doctrines*, 431) as Masyaf, Qadmus, Kahf, Khawabi, Rusafa, Maniqa, Ullayqa and Qulaya.

12 Mirza, 55.

13 Mirza considers that 'It is nevertheless remarkable that he [Baibars] kept up the policy of trying to bring the Isma'ilis under his domination which were essentially peaceful, though often accompanied by threats'. See *Syrian Ismailism*, 63.

14 Prestwich in *Edward I*, London (1997 edition), 78, believes that this was not the attack of a Nizari *fid'ai*. However, given the tactics adopted I see no reason to demur from other historians (e.g. Runciman, Volume 3, 338) that the attacker was in fact a Nizari. If the instigator of the attempt on Edward's life was Baibars – and despite his denials at the time some commentators insist that it was – it would also be consistent with the Sultan's use of the Nizaris on other occasions.

Chapter Twelve

1 It is of interest that the twentieth century traveller Dame Freya Stark, noted when visiting Alamut that 'the entrance to the valley is so well hidden that Dr Eccles and his party [fellow travellers accompanying her on her expedition] who came before me did not notice it and had to wade upstream'. See *The Valleys of the Assassins*, 214.

2 Marco Polo, *The Travels*, 70–3.

3 See for example Daftary, *The Assassin Legends*, 5.

4 For a brief review, see Daftary, *The Assassin Legends*, 36–8.

5 They were also known as 'Isma'iliyya' or 'Nizariyya'. On occasion they were sometimes termed '*batiniyya*', in acknowledgement of their devotion to the esoteric meanings of the Qu'ran (Juwayni calls them '*batinis*'). The appellation of '*hashishiyya*' appeared early on in Nizari history; see for example page 24, above.

6 An allusion to the Sufat, see page 114, above.

7 See Kamal al-Din, *Zubala*, Ms Paris, Arabe 1666, fol. 193b.ff

8 A complete transcript of the Baron's speech is quoted in an English translation by Azizeh Azodi and edited by Farhad Daftary in the latter's book, *The Assassin Legends*.

9 See for example, Lewis, *The Assassins*, 12.

10 See Daftary, *The Ismailis – their history and doctrines*, 19 and 573, n55 and *A Short History of the Ismailis*, Edinburgh (1998), 12–13; Madelung *Arabic Texts Concerning the History of the Zaydi Imams of Tabaristan*, Beirut (1987), 146, 329 and *Religious Trends in Early Islamic Iran*, Albany, New York (1988), 103. I am very grateful for the advice of Dr Daftary on this point.

11 Babcock and Krey, 391.

12 Brocardus, 'Directorium ad passegium daciendum' in *Documents armeniens*, ii, Paris, 1906, 496–7.

13 Daftary, *The Assassin Legends*, 92.

14 Cited by Arnold of Lübeck in *Chronicon Slavorum*, vii, 8 edited Wattenbach, *Deutschlands Geschichtsquellen*, Stuttgart-Berlin, 1907, ii, 240, and quoted by Lewis in *The Assassins*, 3.

Notes

15 See for example Daftary in *The Assassin Legends*, 97–8.

16 Babcock and Krey, Volume 2, 391.

17 Walter of Compiegne, *Otia di Marchonete*, edited R.B.C. Huygens in *Sacris Erudiri*, 8 (1956), 286–328.

18 From *The Itinerary of Benjamin of Tudela*, edited and translated Marcus Adler, London, 1907, 16–17.

19 *Chronicon*, 178–9, quoted in Lewis, *The Assassins*, 4.

20 The first known Western account of the legend is found in the continuation to William of Tyre's narrative (William himself was long dead by the time that Henry of Champagne's visit took place): see for example *Chronique d'Ernoul*, edited L. de Maslaitre, Paris, 1887, 323–4.

21 See Daftary, *The Assassin Legends*, 106–7.

22 Lewis, *The Assassins*, 5.

23 See Daftary, *The Assassin Legends*, 106–7. He also mentions an interesting hypothesis put forward by Hellmuth that the legend in fact dates back several millennia, and was inspired by tales from the region going back to the time of Alexander the Great.

24 *Alaodin, Prince of the Assassins and other poems*, London (1838), viii.

25 Brocardus, 496–7.

26 From 'Historia Orientalis', in *Gesta Dei per Francos*, Volume 1 1062–3; English translation in *Secret Societies of the Middle Ages* (London, 1846), 117–19.

27 For a full analysis of Western views towards Islam, see Daftary, *The Assassin Legends*, Chapter 3.

28 Benjamin of Tudela, 53–4.

29 William of Rubruck, *The Mission of Friar William of Rubruck: His Journey to the Court of the Great Khan Mongke 1253–1255*, translated P. Jackson, London, 1990) 128. As Daftary asserts, 'Mulihet' is derived from '*malahida*', the derogatory designation of 'heretic' applied to the Isma'ilis by other Muslims who disagreed with their beliefs: see *The Assassin Legends*, 82.

30 F.M. Chambers, 'The troubadours and the Assassins' in *Modern Language Notes*, lxiv (1949), 249–51.

31 The Qur'an, Surah LVI, 11–24.

32 See the Qur'an, Surah III, 136 and 133 respectively.

33 The Qur'an, 72, 74. All references to the Qur'an are based on the translation by M.H. Shakir, (New York, 11th edition, 1999).

34 Daftary, *The Assassin Legends*, 61–2.

35 Odoric of Pordenone, *The Journal of Friar Odoric in The Travels of Sir John Mandeville* edited A.W. Pollard, London (1915), 356–7.

36 Although not historically correct, the use by the West of the term Tartars is understandable enough. The phrase comes from the word 'Tartarus', which was the classical word for 'Hell'. The connection that the Mongols had with demons from Hades was a clear enough one for Western readers to appreciate all too well.

37 J. von Hammer, 'Geschichte der Assassinen aus morgenlandischen Quellen'; translated in *The History of the Assassins*, O.C. Wood, London, 1835, 217–18.

38 *Alaodin and Other Poems*, 106–7.

39 Ibn Battuta: *Voyages*, edited (in French) by C. Defremery and B.R. Sanguinetti, Paris 1853 – English translation H.R. Gibb, *The Travels of Ibn Battuta*, i, Cambridge (1958), 106.

Epilogue

1 This chapter provides a very short account of the later years of the Nizaris. For fuller details see Daftary, *The Ismailis – their history and doctrines*, Chapter 7 and *A Short History of the Ismailis*, Chapter 6.

2 Marco Polo, *The Travels*, 73.

3 The contribution of Ivanow to our understanding of the Nizaris has been immense – Daftary calls him 'the founder of modern Nizari studies'; see *The Ismailis – their history and doctrines*, 443.

4 It should be emphasized that the timing of the schism is not definitive. Syrian tradition asserts that it was at this stage, while some Persian sources state that the schism took place after the imamate of Mu'min Shah. But the timing is of little more than academic importance; the key point of note is that a schism did occur, and that it affected Nizari unity for an extended period of time after it happened.

5 Persia would ultimately evolve into a Shiite country – which it still predominantly remains – eventually becoming so at the beginning of the sixteenth century.

6 *Annales des Voyages*, xiv (1818), 279.

Select Bibliography

Included in the list below are those works that I have found most useful in my research for this book. It is by no means a definitive list and the reader will find references in footnotes to other books that I have referred to in the course of writing this work. For a more comprehensive analysis the reader may like to refer to *The Ismailis – their history and doctrines* by Farhad Daftary which has a very detailed bibliography having the added benefit that it is virtually up to date.

The major Persian primary sources are by Juwayni, Rashid al-Din and Kashani. Juwayni's history was edited by Mirza Muhammad Qazvini and published as *Ta'rikh-i Jahan-gusha* in London (1912–37) in 3 volumes. It was translated into English by J.A. Boyle as *The History of the World Conqueror* in 2 volumes (Manchester, 1958, republished 1997). The history of the Nizaris is dealt with in the 2nd Volume. Rashid al-Din's work was published as *Jami' al-tawarikh* (edited by Muhammad Taqi Danishpazhuh and Muhammad Mudarrisi Zanjani, Tehran, 1960) while Kashani's work was published as *Tarikh-i Ismailiyya* in Tabriz, 1964. Given the accessibility of Juwayni's work in Boyle's English translation, it is the 1997 edition of this that has largely been used as the primary source in this book.

Other useful references can be found in *The History of Damascus* by Ibn al-Qalanasi, edited H.F. Emedroz and published in Beirut (1908) and partly translated by H.A.R. Gibb in *The Damascus Chronicle of the Crusades*, London, 1932. Other accounts of the Nizaris can be found in the memoirs of Usamah ibn-Munqidh, translated by Philip K. Hitti and published as

Memoirs of an Arab-Syrian Gentleman (Beirut, 1984). English translations of relevant passages of Ibn al-Athir and Ibn al-Qalausi can be found in *Arab Historians of the Crusades*, translated into Italian by Gabrieli, English translation, 1969.

There are a number of Western primary sources that refer to the Nizaris (or 'Assassins') in greater or lesser detail; particularly useful references may be found in the translation of de Joinville in *Joinville and Villehardouin, Chronicles of the Crusades*, translated by M.R.B. Shaw (London, 1963) and *Marco Polo – The Travels*, translated by Ronald Latham, London, 1958. William of Tyre's account of life in Outremer gives a fascinating insight into life in the Crusader kingdoms as well as Western perceptions of the Nizaris. It can be found in *Historia rerum in oartibus transmarinis gestarum*, edited J.P. Migne (Paris, 1903) and translated into English in *A History of Deeds Done Beyond the Sea* by E.A. Babcock and A.C. Krey, New York, 1943. But note that there are many other references to the Nizaris in Western chronicles, many of which are detailed in footnotes throughout this book. I have chosen to list them as footnotes in an attempt to avoid overloading the bibliography with sources, some of which have only passing references to the Nizaris.

There are a number of more modern works which give an insight into the Nizaris. The most influential on my research has been *The Ismailis – their history and doctrines*, by Farhad Daftary, Cambridge, 1990, reprinted 1995 edition) described by one critic as 'a landmark in Isma'ili historical studies'. Though he disapproves of the name 'Assassins', Dr Daftary's book is probably the definitive account of the development of the myths surrounding the movement. It can be found in *The Assassin Legends – Myths of the Ismailis*, London, 1994. Daftary has a number of works in print; readers may also find *Mediaeval Ismaili history and thought*, which was edited by him, a useful source of reference (Cambridge, 1996). *A Short History of the Ismailis* (Edinburgh, 1998) is also an invaluable brief introduction to the Isma'ilis.

Bernard Lewis has also written a great deal on the Nizaris. Although overtaken by more recent research in some details, *The Assassins*, London 1967 (reprinted 1999) is still an excellent account of the movement. Another important piece of work by Lewis is *Kamal al-Din's biography of Rashid al-Din Sinan*, published in Arabica, xiii (1966).

An influential account is to be found in *The Order of Assassins* by M.G.S. Hodgson (The Hague, 1955 reprinted New York, 1980). An analysis of the Nizaris may also be found in *The Assassins* by Edward Burman (Wellingborough, 1987).

A useful, short but informative analysis of the Syrian Nizaris can be found in *Syrian Ismailism* by Nasseh Ahmad Mirza (Richmond, Surrey, 1997).

For the Crusades, Sir Steven Runciman's *A History of the Crusades* (published in 3 volumes, Cambridge, 1951) has stood the test of time. K.M. Setton's edited *A History of the Crusades* (2nd edn. Madison, 1969–85, 1955) also has detailed references to the Nizaris.

A very readable account of Medieval Islamic history can be found in *A History of Medieval Islam* by J.J. Saunders, London (1972, reprinted 1996). Other references may be found in *The Cambridge Illustrated History of the Middle Ages*, edited by Robert Fossier in Volume 1 (Cambridge, 1989), especially Chapters 5 and 6 and Volume 2 (Cambridge, 1997), especially Chapters 4 and 10.

Professor Wilferd Madelung is a widely published scholar. Among the many books he has published, the reader may find two in particular useful for an analysis of early Islamic and Isma'ili history, namely *The Succession to Muhammad – a study of the early Caliphate* (Cambridge, 1996) and *The Advent of the Fatimids* (edited with Paul Walker, London, 2000).

Finally, *The Mongols – A History* by Jeremiah Curtin, Boston (1908, reprinted 1996) is now quite dated and has been overtaken by a good deal of modern research but has several chapters devoted to the Mongol attacks on the Nizaris and is still a detailed and entertaining account. For more recent works, I would recommend *The History of the Mongol Conquests* by J.J. Saunders (London, 1971) and *The Mongols* by D.O. Morgan (Oxford, 1986).

Index

Index

Index